Financial Markets, Banking, and Monetary Policy

Milton H. Marquis

Professor of Economics
Florida State University

Cover Design by Robert Burke
Photograph by Milton H. Marquis

Copyright © 2017 by Milton H. Marquis
ISBN 978-1-5342-0345-7
Glasstree Publishing

Contents

CONTENTS

CONTENTS

II Asset Pricing and Financial Markets 159

Part I

Overview of the Financial System

Chapter 1

Introduction

As the recent Financial Crisis of 2007-2008 and the Great Recession of 2007-2009 that followed have made clear in the starkest of terms, a smoothly functioning financial system is critical to the operations of a healthy economy. Just think quickly about this fact: All of us participate in the financial markets almost daily, whether this involves major decisions such as applying for a student loan or a home mortgage, or the more routine activities, such as making a car loan payment, or simply depositing a check in a bank or conducting an online transaction. These financial decisions taken by individuals collectively comprise the fabric of a highly interconnected, worldwide network of markets and institutions scattered throughout the globe.

Obviously, the financial system in modern, western economies is multifaceted and very complex. it is subject, perhaps more than any other sector of the economy, to the rapid technological changes that we've witnessed in information technology over the past 30 years. This technology can bring substantial benefits to consumers of financial services, but may also leave our financial system vulnerable to excessive risk-taking and imprudent financial practices that can threaten the stability of modern market-based economies.

The goal of this text is to provide the background needed to obtain a broad understanding of the financial institutions and the financial markets that collectively make up this dynamic financial system. As we progress through this material, it should become obvious that innovation is a hallmark of this important sector of the economy, and the financial system we see today will not be the financial system of tomorrow. As consumers of financial services, being a well-informed participant in the financial markets can be a lifelong challenge, but one that can bring substantial rewards.

Over the first few chapters we'll explore the broad scope of the financial system to try to get our arms around it, so to speak. With this overview, we can then begin to ask more detailed questions. For example:

- What are the principal financial assets available to investors?

- What determines interest rates and stock prices?

- What are the key financial institutions and what roles do they play in the economy?

- How do government policy and government regulation affect the financial markets?

1.1 The Role of Financial Markets in the Economy

Let's begin by considering why financial markets exist in the first place. We'll organize our thoughts around three separate groups in the economy: Households, firms, and government.

- Households essentially own the *factors of production* (capital and labor), but they are primarily *consuming units* in the economy, in that they demand the goods and services produced in the economy.

- Firms and governments, then, possess the means of production, but must rent the factors of production from the households. They are primarily *producing units* in the economy, in that they supply the economy's goods and services.

As depicted in Figure 1.1, these groups in the economy meet up in markets, which we can partition into three different sets: goods or product markets, factor markets, and financial markets. Households supply the factors of production to the firms and governments in

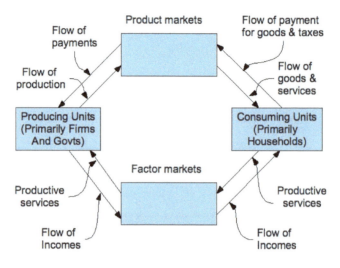

Figure 1.1 Flow of Income and Payments

the factor markets, which produce final goods and services that are then sold to households in the goods markets. To acquire the goods, funds flow from households to firms and governments, who use those funds to pay for the factors of production. Therefore, we have factors and goods flowing in one direction, and funds flowing in the other. The problem with this neat picture of the economy is timing. The firms must hire the factors of production before they can produce and sell their goods, but they must sell their produce before they can pay for the factors of production.

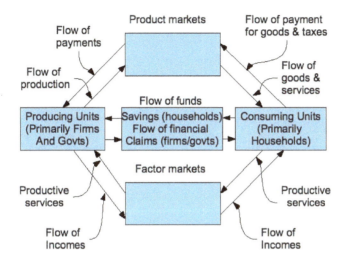

Figure 1.2: Flow of Income and Payments

Here is where the financial markets play a key role. For example, refer to Figure 1.2. Prior to production, a firm can write financial contracts, such as a debt contract, that it sells to the households. The firm thereby receives funds in exchange for claims against the revenues it expects to receive once its goods are produced and sold in the goods market. These funds can then be used to hire the capital and labor needed to initiate the production process. Once these goods are sold, it has the revenues to retire the bonds.

Now think about how a modern economy that relies on the financial markets for this type of operation is affected when the financial markets become dysfunctional! This happened during the Financial Crisis of 2007-2008, when many of the financial markets "froze up" and credit became extremely difficult to obtain, even for credit-worthy businesses. As a consequence, firms cut back on their planned investment and reduced employment. Obviously, in the absence of this crucial role that the financial markets play in the economy, overall economic activity can slow to a crawl, output for the economy can shrink, and unemployment rise.

Subsequent chapters are devoted to analyzing the sources and consequences of the financial crisis that precipitated the Great Recession and to examining the the regulatory reforms that have been put into place in the hope of avoiding a similar crisis in the future.

1.2 Savings in the U.S. Economy

While the basic picture that we have displayed in the previous section is accurate, where household savings is described as the source of funds to businesses and governments, actual household savings in modern industrialized economies also take place indirectly among businesses (which, of course, are owned by households).

For example, as shown in Table 1.1, in 2016, households personal savings in the United States totaled $824B, while the business sector set aside $552B out their total corporate earnings as undistributed profits. Governments' budgets can also add or subtract to the net savings in the economy. In 2016, the large budget deficits that have resulted in large measure from the attempt to fight the Great Recession, while falling sharply in recent years, was still $844 billion. This deficit substantially reduced the annual savings for the economy as a whole, which netted out to a still healthy $532 billion. We'll look at the allocation of net savings among various segments of the economy in more detail later.

Households Businesses Governments	$824 billion $552 billion -$844 billion
Aggregate Net Savings for the Economy	$532 billion

Table 1.1: Net Savings by Sector in 2016
Source: Federal Reserve

For now, note that savings plays an important role in the economy by providing the necessary funds for investment by households in their human capital, by firms in plant and equipment so that they can modernize and expand their productive capacity, and by governments for building infrastructure, where all of these items are important in establishing long-term economic growth that raises standards of living from one generation to the next.

1.3 Economic Functions Performed by the Financial System

Savings is only one of the many basic economic functions performed by the global system of financial institutions and markets. The complete list includes:

1. Savings and Wealth Function

2. Credit Function

3. Liquidity Function

4. Payments Function

5. Risk Protection Function

6. Macroeconomic Policy Function

Savings and Wealth Function

The *savings and wealth function* enables individuals to exchange current consumption for higher future consumption opportunities. Savings is a different concept than wealth.

Savings is an *economic flow variable* that is measured over some specific time interval. For example, an individual's personal savings may be taken as his or her monthly income minus the monthly expenses.

Wealth, on the other hand, is an *economic stock variable* that is measured at a point in time. For example, one important factor that determines an individual's wealth is his or her *total assets*. Typically, total assets represents the cumulative net savings of the individual plus the capital appreciation of those assets.

Credit Function

A second economic function performed by the financial markets that is the opposite of savings and wealth is the *credit function*. It enables an individual to increase consumption today by pledging future income that he or she anticipates receiving, thereby reducing consumption opportunities in the future. The total amount of indebtedness of an individual is also a stock variable referred to as *total liabilities*.

When determining the wealth of an individual, it is not sufficient to simply compute the value of the individual's total assets. From that measure, the total liabilities that the individual is obligated to pay must be subtracted. Therefore, an appropriate measure of an individual's wealth is give by his or her *net worth*, or the total value of all assets minus the total value of all liabilities.

It is possible to examine some data for the U.S. economy and obtain an approximate answer to the question: Just how wealthy is the average American?

Referring to Table 1.2, the total assets owned by households (and non-profit organizations) in the United States, including homes, bank accounts, etc. in 2016 amounted to $107.9 trillion. Their total liabilities, including mortgages, student loans, credit card debt, etc. amounted to $15.1 trillion. Therefore, in 2016 household net worth in the United States was $92.8 trillion. This was shared among 325 million Americans. So, the net worth per capita was $285 thousand or for a family of 3, the average net worth was $855 thousand. While this figure includes the very wealthy such as Bill Gates and Warren Buffett, and does not capture the extremely skewed nature of the wealth distribution, it still illustrates that the United States is indeed a very wealthy country.[1]

Liquidity Function

A third economic function performed by the financial system is the *liquidity function*. This function enables

---

[1]The Congressional Budget Office reported that in 2013, families in the top 10 percent of the wealth distribution owned 76 percent of the wealth, while those in bottom 50 percent owned only one percent. The remaining 23 percent was owned by the segment of the population in the 51 to 90 percentile range.

Aggregate value of Households' Total Assets	$107.9 trillion
Aggregate value of Households' Total Liabilities	$15.1 trillion
Household Net Worth	92.8 trillion
U.S. Population	325 million
Household Net Worth per Capita	$285 thousand
Household Net Worth for a Family of 3	$855 thousand

Table 1.2: U.S. Household (and Non-Profit Organizations) Aggregate Balance Sheet: 2016 Source: Federal Reserve & U.S. Department of Commerce

households to convert their wealth into current consumption at low cost. Different assets have different
degrees of liquidity and this property of the asset can
affect its value. For example, currency is said to have
perfect liquidity. You can immediately exchange this
form of wealth, for example, into a computer. Stocks
are less liquid. If you wished to transform a share of
IBM into a computer, you must first sell the stock to
acquire the cash that would then enable you to buy the
computer. Liquidating the stock thus involves some
cost. Therefore, it is generally true that the more liquid is the asset, the more highly it is valued.

There is a related concept that will be important
when comparing and contrasting various financial assets: *marketability*. An asset that is highly marketable
is one for which a buyer can be easily found. While a
highly liquid asset is also highly marketable, it is some-
thing more. A highly liquid asset can be converted into
cash on short notice without incurring large costs of
conversion. A highly marketable asset does not rule
out the possibility that, while a buyer can be easily
found, the cost of liquidating the asset into cash may
be high.[2]

---

[2]This distinction between liquidity and marketability that
survives today in the economics and finance literature grew out
of Keynes' (1930) original description of an asset with greater liquidity as one whose value is "more certainly realisable at short
notice without loss." In his 1962 presidential address to the Royal
Economic Society, the Nobel Economist John R. Hicks (1962) describes more fully the economist's notion of liquidity and mar-

Payments Function

A fourth economic function performed by the financial system is one that we often take for granted in the United States: the *payments function*. This function permits the transfer of ownership of assets. For example, it is the financial system that allows you to take possession of a computer by making the purchase with cash or credit card.

In countries were the payments system breaks down, commerce can come to a near halt. One example was when the former Soviet Union was breaking up. The currency was the Russian ruble, but no one had a sense about whether it would retain any value in the future. As a consequence, no one wanted to give up assets of real value or offer labor services for a paper currency that may turn out to be worthless. The classic problem in private exchange re-emerged: the *lack of a double coincidence of wants*, as many Russians reverted to barter.[3]

---

ketability, premised on: "the purposes for which liquid assets are held: to pay existing debts, in so far as they cannot be paid out of new receipts, and to meet necessary future expenditures in so far as they cannot be financed in the same way." Hence, more liquid assets do not require as high a rate of return to be willingly held.

[3]When government-provided currency is unavailable, an economy is likely to create a substitute. A classic paper by R.A. Radford, (1945), who was a prisoner-of-war during World War II, describes how cigarettes that prisoners periodically received in care packages began to circulate as currency among the pris-

There were tales, for example, of an airplane manufacturer that needed to obtain parts from its suppliers
who refused to be paid in rubles. The suppliers had
what the aircraft manufacturers wanted, but the latter
had nothing the suppliers would be willing to accept
in exchange. The manufacturer then converted part of
its production facilities into a stamping plant that produced kitchen utensils that were then bartered for the
machine tools it needed in the manufacturing process.
The kitchen utensils would then have to be used by the
suppliers to pay for the factors of production needed
to produce additional machine tools. Obviously, the
inefficiencies created by such a complicated barter arrangement were very detrimental to the economy as a
whole.

Risk Protection Function

A fifth function performed by the financial system is
risk protection. Whether you wish to insure against
theft, accident, natural disaster, or even death, there
is a market that allows you to shift the risk from your-
self to those willing to assume it. Americans spend
roughly one dollar of every \$9 earned on some form of

---

oners, where non-smokers as well as smokers would willing give
up goods of value to acquire them. It is an amazing story of
how the double coincidence of wants problem emerged and was
resolved in the stark realities of a P.O.W. Camp.

insurance.[4]

Macroeconomic Policy Function

Finally, the financial markets also play a key role in facilitating *macroeconomic policy*. The Treasury Department issues debt that is sold in the financial markets and levies taxes, with heavy reliance on the banking system to facilitate collection, in order the fund its public expenditures. Likewise, the Federal Reserve relies exclusively on the financial markets to implements its monetary policy. The government's involvement in the financial markets is covered extensively in future chapters.

1.4 Categories of Financial Markets

To complete this brief introductory overview of the financial markets and the roles that they play in the economy, it is useful to partition financial markets in several different ways. These various alternative parti-

---

[4]The Organization for Economic Development (OECD), whose 35 members include the world's most advanced economies as well as developing economies such as Mexico and Turkey, estimates in 2015 gross expenditures on all forms of insurance in the United States was 11.3 percent. By way of comparison, this figure is 4.4 percent for Canada, and 8.8 percent for the OECD as a whole.

tions will help illuminate why each individual market exists and why there are so many different kinds of markets.

First, a definition: A *financial market* is one where financial assets are: created, traded, and priced.

- One way of partitioning financial markets is by the maturity of the financial assets that comprise the market. Shorter-term assets with a year or less to maturity are often referred to as *monetary assets* while those with maturities that exceed one year are referred to as *capital market assets*. This distinction is not perfect, and we will come across exceptions when we begin to explore the wide range of financial assets in the economy. However, as we'll see, the maturity of the asset can affect the way in which it is priced and how its interest rate is determined.

- A second partition divides the markets between primary versus secondary markets. A *primary market* is one where the asset is initially introduced. For example, the primary market for U.S. Treasury securities, which is covered in detail in subsequent chapters, is the Treasury auction conducted by the Federal Reserve. A *secondary market* is one in which existing financial assets are traded. A good example is the New York Stock Exchange where equity shares of publicly traded firms are traded. The mechanism by which these trades take place and the resulting pricing of these stocks will be given a lot of emphasis later.

- A third useful partitioning of the financial markets is whether the market is said to be open or negotiated. An asset traded in an *open market* can be freely sold by the asset owner to any third party, regardless of who issued the asset. A *negotiated market*, on the other hand, is essentially a financial contract that is exclusively between two parties. For example, a small certificate of deposit, or CD, at a bank is effectively a deal between the depositor and the bank. If the depositor wants to cash out the CD, he or she will normally be required to pay the bank a penalty for early withdrawal in accordance with the terms of their financial contract.

- A final partition is between a spot market versus forward, futures, or options markets. The difference here is whether the transaction that is agreed in the financial contract involves the transference of ownership immediately, as for example when you purchase a share of stock (subject, of course, to a short delay for the transaction to be processed) in which case the asset is said to be sold in a *spot market*. By comparison, *forward, futures, and options markets* specify that claims are to be received (if at all) in the future. A good example of a very active forward market is the purchase of a foreign currency at a predetermined exchange rate, when the actual currency transaction will not actually take place until perhaps one month from today.

1.5   Summary

A smoothly functioning financial system is critical to a healthy modern economy. When the financial markets become dysfunctional and fail to perform as expected, the entire macroeconomy is at risk.

However, because of the numerous important economic functions that the financial markets perform, they are necessarily very complex. Their principal *modus operandi* is to process information, whether that information reflects the value of firm's stock or an assessment of risk and the likelihood of financial gain or loss. Consequently, innovation in information technology of the kind we've witnessed over the past 30 years has had a tremendous impact on these markets. In most ways, the markets have become ever more efficient and reliable and consumers of financial services have been the major beneficiaries.

The next chapter continues the overview of the financial system by examining categories of selected financial assets a little more closely. Then, we will get a perspective on the broad array of financial institutions that provide the financial services that we have come to rely on in our daily lives.

With this background, we will be ready in the following chapter to plunge headlong into the complex workings of the financial markets that ultimately led to the Great Recession of 2007-2009.

Key Terms

factors of production
consuming units
producing units
savings and wealth function
economic flow variables
economic stock variables
credit function
net worth
liquidity function
marketability
payments function
risk protection
macroeconomic policy
financial market
monetary assets
capital market assets
open market
negotiated market
spot market
forward, futures, and options markets

1.6 Review Questions

1. Identify which of the following statements is correct and which is false. If the statement is false, identify the error and correct the statement.

   a) The change in a household's wealth over a quarter is its income minus its expenses plus interest earned on its wealth held at the beginning of the period.

   b) The market value of a household's home is equal to the equity that the household has in the home and is therefore part of the household's net worth.

   c) The saving and wealth functions performed by the financial markets enable households to increase current consumption at the expense of future consumption.

2. Which of the following economic functions that financial markets perform would be best represented by the following properties of U.S. Treasury bills: (i) the fact they retain their value over time and (ii) their ability to be sold on short notice at their true market value?

   a) Liquidity and risk protection

   b) Wealth and liquidity

   c) Policy and wealth

d) Risk protection and policy

3. John Jacobs looks over his balance sheet from the beginning of the month. He observes that his assets include: (i) a market value of $120,000 for his home; (ii) $25,000 in corporate stock; (iii) a Treasury bill with a face value of $1,000 to be received at the end of the month, for which the current market value was $983; (iv) a bank deposit account of $6,000; and (vi) some miscellaneous items that he values at $35,000. His only outstanding liability is the mortgage on his house, which has a balance totaling $40,000. It is now the end of the month and he just received his $6,000 salary, along with the income from the maturing T-bill and interest on his bank deposits, which were paying an annualized interest rate of 2 percent (2/12 percent per month). His mortgage payment was $1,500, of which $500 would go toward the principal. His other expenses for the month came to $4,000. He had planned to make an additional house payment for the month, all of which would go to paying down the principal on the loan. However, his daughter is in college and wants to go to the Bahamas for spring break. The expense of her trip would be an additional $1,800.

a) Would he be able to make the additional house payment and fund his daughter's trip without reducing his account balance in the bank deposit account?

b) What would his net worth be if he funded his daughter's trip and made the additional mortgage payment?

c) What would his net worth be if he did not fund his daughter's trip and made the additional mortgage payment?

d) Would his net worth change if he decided to fund the trip, but did not make the additional mortgage payment? Explain.

4. Classify the market in which each of the following financial transactions takes place as: (a) money versus capital, (b) primary versus secondary, (c) open versus negotiated, or (d) spot versus futures or forward.

a) A contract to receive wheat three months from today.

b) The purchase of a share of IBM on the New York Stock Exchange.

c) A six-month CD purchased from your bank.

d) A newly issued three-month Treasury bill purchased at the government's weekly auction.

e) You open a bank savings account.

f) You write a check to purchase a computer.

5. At the end of the calendar year, a firm has total financial assets amounting to \$4.32 billion, while its total liabilities are \$3.58 billion. What is the firm's net financial wealth? If the firm saved \$50 million over the previous year, representing the amount by which its financial assets rose relative to its liabilities, and it had begun the year with \$3.72 billion in total financial assets, how much did it earn on its previously accumulated assets?

1.7 References

Hicks, John R. 1962. "Liquidity," *The Economic Journal*, vol. 72, no. 288. December: 787-802.

Keynes, John Maynard. 1930. *A Trestise on Money*. Harcourt Brace and Company: New York.

Organization for Economic Cooperation and Development (OECD) "OECD Data: Insurance Spending" can be found at: https://data.oecd.org/insurance/insurance-spending.htm

Radford, Richard A. 1945. "The Economic Organization of a P.O.W. Camp," *Economica*, vol. 12, no. 48, November: 189-201.

Trends in Family Wealth, 1989 to 2013 (Congressional Budget Office, August 2016), www.cbo.gov/publication/51846.

Chapter 2

Financial Assets

This chapter focuses on an important classification of financial assets – the details of which will carry us throughout much of the book. As we will see, there is a wide range of financial assets, each with its own characteristics as both a source of funds for the issuer and as an asset for the purchaser.

Obviously, investors have an extraordinary variety of financial assets between which they may choose to save and invest. On what criteria should investors' decisions be based? Returns on most investments come in the form of a stream of payments denominated in domestic currency, such as the U.S. dollar, that the investor expects to receive at future dates. The investor must assess the likelihood that the expected stream of payments will be received and understand how difficult and costly it would be to disinvest, should he or she choose to do so.

An important consideration for investing in ANY asset is inflation. As inflation increases, the purchasing power of the dollar falls and the value of that stream of returns declines. Therefore, households must be informed about what inflation they should expect in order to understand the value of the financial assets that they are purchasing. In future chapters, we'll take a closer look at how the Federal Reserve's monetary policy decisions affect inflation and therefore the value of nearly all financial assets that we have available to us as investors.

2.1   Investment Characteristics of Financial Assets

Every financial asset represents a stream of prospective income that an investor would expect to receive, if he or she chose to purchase the asset. However, in deciding how much an asset is worth, the asset's principal characteristics of: *risk, expected rate of return (or interest rate)* that incorporates the investor's expectation of future inflation, and *liquidity*, as described in the previous chapter must be jointly evaluated and compared with other assets in the marketplace.

Essentially, the greater the risk of not receiving the expected income stream from the asset, the higher will be the expected rate of return demanded by the investor. High risk means high expected rate of return. Liquidity, on the other hand, has the opposite effect on the expected rate of return. Investors will accept a lower rate of return if the asset is highly liquid.

Investment Characteristics of Financial Assets

Risk
Expected Rate of Return
Liquidity

↑ Risk (for a given level of Liquidity)
⇒ ↑ Expected Rate of Return

↑ Liquidity (for a given level of Risk)
⇒ ↓ Expected Rate of Return

Table 2.1: Investment Characteristics of Financial Assets

When formulating expectations of future returns on any asset, the potential buyer of that asset will have to take into account the possibility of private information that the seller of the asset may possess that can be exploited to the detriment of the buyer. The next section considers ways in which this private information can affect the valuation of financial assets.

# 2.2	Asymmetric Information and Agency Problems

There are two forms of *asymmetric information* where the seller of an asset possesses private information that can affect the value of the asset.[1] The seller may have superior knowledge of the quality of the asset at the time it is sold. In this case, his incentive is to withhold negative information that would lower the asset's value. Alternatively, if the actions of the seller *after* the asset is sold affect the returns on the asset, the seller may have an incentive to shirk his responsibilities for personal gain at the expense of the asset holder.

Adverse Selection

Suppose the buyer of an asset (for example, a lender in the bond market or an investor in the stock market or the purchaser of a capital asset, such as an automobile or a house) knows ahead of time that the seller of the asset has access to some private information that is relevant to asset's true value. How would this *ex ante*

---

[1]See the review by the Nobel committee of the contributions that Akerlov, Spence, and Stiglitz made toward an understanding of the importance of asymmetric information, for which they received the Nobel Prize for Economics: http://www.nobelprize.org/nobel_prizes/economic-sciences/laureates/2001/popular.html Also, recommended is George Akerlov's 2001 Nobel Prize Lecture: "Writing the "The Market for Lemons": A Personal and Interpretive Essay."

private information, that is, asymmetric information existing prior to the sale, affect the willingness of the buyer to acquire the asset?

The classic example is the used car dealer.[2] While the purchase of an automobile is not a financial contract, the basic principle applies more broadly: In this example, the used car dealer knows of any potential defects that the car may have. Obviously, he has an incentive to withhold this private information from the potential buyer. However, the buyer understands that such private information may exist, and this knowledge would likely cause him to perceive a higher probability that some unforeseen maintenance costs would be incurred in the future. To be able to absorb those potential costs, he would lower his valuation of the car and reduce his offer.

However, the car dealer may have been perfectly forthcoming about all aspects of the car's integrity. In this case, the offer will be less than the true value of the car. What incentive does this asymmetric information produce for the car dealer? He simply cannot sell high quality cars, since potential buyers have no way of verifying the quality. He has no choice but to offer only low quality cars and fulfill the potential buyer's expectations about the car's quality. In essence, he can only sell "lemons." This outcome is referred to as *adverse selection*.

Obviously, the buyer can take the car to an indepen-

---

[2]Akerlov (1970).

dent mechanic and get a true assessment of the car's quality, but this comes at a cost and may not be possible until the car is sold. To deal with this problem, many states have passed so-called "lemon laws" that allow buyers a limited amount of time to void the contract with the dealer.

This problem appears in many circumstances, particularly where high-pressure sales tactics are employed. States have once again passed consumer protection laws that allow for a "cooling off" period, during which the lender may decide on reflection against the purchase or investment and walk away from the agreement.

Moral Hazard

Suppose that an entrepreneur with an investment project wishes to borrow money from a lender or investor. He makes the case that his project is sound and will become profitable in the future. Further suppose that an independent evaluation of the project resulted in all relevant information being truthfully revealed prior to the loan having been made. That is, there is no *ex ante private information* as would be present in the case of adverse selection, as described in the previous example.

However, once this loan or investment is made, the entrepreneur has the funds and may misappropriate them to his own benefit. This misappropriation could take on many forms, such as diverting the funds into plush offices or shirking on his responsibilities to guide the project to a successful conclusion by channeling the funds to inefficient, but favored suppliers, or simply not properly overseeing the evolution of the project. These various activities could be hidden from the investor, and thereby represent *ex post private information*, that is, knowledge that the entrepreneur alone retains after the investment has been made. The existence of this private information could affect the viability of the project and thereby alter the returns that the investor could expect to receive.

2.3   Debt Contracts versus Equity Contracts

Moral hazard is especially important in the design of financial contracts. In the previous example, the investor would like to alter the contract in a manner that would prevent an unexpected loss on his or her investment associated with any actions taken by the entrepreneur after he has received the funds. Efforts to achieve this objective may rely on establishing provisions to monitor the *ex post* activities of the entrepreneur. This monitoring may take different forms, and is generally tailored to the nature of the individual financial asset.

Debt Contract

One way to deal with this moral hazard is to write a *debt contract* whose provisions include repayment of a fixed amount according to a predetermined schedule. One example is a small business loan from a commercial bank, where the entrepreneur makes monthly payments of a predetermined amount for a fixed number of years, after which time the loan is fully repaid. If the entrepreneur fails to make these payments, he can be forced into bankruptcy. The terms of the contract could then specify seizure of assets held by the entrepreneur that had been placed as collateral for the loan in order for the bank to recover some of the uncollectible debt.

There are a couple of important features of this debt contract that need to be stressed. First, as long as the entrepreneur meets his loan payments, there is no need to monitor his activities, hence the monitoring costs are minimal. Second, if the entrepreneur defaults on his payments, monitoring must take place. An audit of the entrepreneur's books must be conducted and an inventory of his assets would have to be taken. The purpose of this monitoring is to ensure that the the entrepreneur does not conceal any assets that were pledged as collateral against the loan and that no fraudulent activities were undertaken by the entrepreneur. Thus, in the event of default, the *ex post* private information is revealed by the bank's monitoring activities, but at a cost to the bank.

Banks will attempt to minimize the likelihood of incurring these costs, since they could be substantial for an individual loan. Even if the bank seizes a firm's assets, it must then sell them in markets in which they normally do not participate and thus have no expertise in order to recover whatever they can. As a consequence, banks will screen loan applicants to maximize the probability that the loans they grant will be repaid. As discussed more fully in Chapter 9, commercial banks fill an important economic niche by specializing in screening loan applicants and monitoring the loans they make using mostly depositors' funds.

Other debt contracts have similar features. One important example that will be covered in detail in subsequent chapters is the corporate bond. As described below, the corporation borrows money from the bondholder for a fixed period of time, determined by the maturity of the bond, and during which periodic payments are made to the bondholder. Bankruptcy is the consequence for the firm who defaults on those periodic payments. Screening of the bond issuers is accomplished to some extent by the bond rating agencies, about which much more will be said in the future.

Equity Contract

Now suppose that the financial contract that an individual investor (rather than a commercial bank) writes with the entrepreneur specifies that the stream of future payments to the investor is contingent upon the profits generated by the entrepreneur as a result of the funds turned over to the entrepreneur. Such an agreement is referred to as an *equity contract*. For example they may agree to split the profits 50-50, but with no recourse for the investor to declare the firm bankrupt and seize the firm's assets in the event that the reported profits of the firm are zero or negative.

The investor only knows what profits are reported by the entrepreneur. How the entrepreneur arrives at those reported profits is another form of *ex post* private information that the entrepreneur can exploit for personal benefit. His incentive is to "low ball" the reported profits such as diverting funds into activities for personal gain, such as corporate yachts, expensive office furniture, excessive salaries to favored employees, etc. or he may simply shirk his management responsibilities leading to a less profitable business due to inefficiencies and waste that could have been avoided.

This example illustrates an important difference between a debt contract and an *equity contract*. The latter requires frequent costly monitoring, as profits change over time, and the investor must have knowledge of the profits and whether the entrepreneur is seeking to hide them, if the investor is to obtain his fair share. Rooting out those activities by which management can reduce the returns on the investment to the investor can be a difficult process. An important example of an equity contract is corporate stock, which is discussed below and the pricing of which is described in detail in subsequent chapters.

2.4 Categorizing Financial Assets

There are four broad categories into which the economy's financial assets may be usefully divided: money, equities, debt securities, and derivatives. It is important to distinguish between these various groups of assets to better understand the role they play in the economy, and therefore to understand why they exist. We can take them up one at a time.

Monetary Assets

When we hear the word money, many different ideas come to mind. Some associate it with wealth, some with luxury goods, such as expensive automobiles or jewelry. Suppose you were tasked to be more specific about just: what is money? How would you approach the problem? We should note that this problem is precisely one that the Federal Reserve must confront.

A place to begin is a return to a principles of economics textbook question: what are the essential properties of a financial asset that we want to call *money*?

The traditional properties of money are:

- *Unit of Account* whereby the asset establishes a standard of value against which all goods and services can be compared. For example, the U.S. dollar in the United States allows all goods and services to be priced in dollars;

- *Store of Value* which allows the asset holder to carry his or her wealth forward through time; and

- *Medium of Exchange* that enables the asset to be used in the purchase of goods and services.

Begin with a narrow definition that *currency is money*. Note that *commodity money* serving as currency (such as gold coins) differs from *fiat money* (such as paper money), in that the latter has no intrinsic value; whereas, the former does. Ideally, a commodity money should be *homogeneous* (to be a good unit of account), *durable* (to be a good store of value), and *divisible* into small units (to be a good medium of exchange). These features enable money to solve the *lack of a double coincidence of wants* problem that can stifle trade in a purely barter economy.[3] Fiat money can be perfectly homogeneous and highly divisible, but generally needs backing in some form to be seen as a credible store of value such that individuals would be willing to it accept in exchange for a real commodity. This backing could come from gold or through the taxing power

---

[3]Radford's (1945) excellent description of the emergence of "cigarette currency" in a POW camp vividly demonstrates the importance of these features of a commodity money.

of a centralized government, which also has the authority to declare the fiat money as *legal tender* that must
be accepted as a medium of exchange.

How does it help to focus on those properties when
establishing a definition of the nation's money supply?
Here is a thought experiment. Suppose you were able
to look around the economy at all of the financial assets
out there and select those with these three properties,
what would you come up with?

As for *unit of account*, currency is the ONLY financial asset that satisfies that property. Therefore,
relying exclusively on this property would lead to a
very restrictive definition of money that is too limited
to be of much practical use as will be described. The
problem with using *store of value* to identify what we
want to call money is just the opposite: it is not restrictive enough. That is, ALL financial assets are stores
of value, although some are better stores of value than
others. This leaves *medium of exchange*. So, what assets in the economy have this property?

Monetary Aggregates: M1

When the Federal Reserve examined financial assets in
accordance with these various properties of money, it
created what are referred to as the *monetary aggregates*.

The narrowest definition of money as determined
by the Federal Reserve is the monetary aggregate labeled *M1*. M1 includes all of the financial assets in

Currency	1,433.4
Demand Deposits (DDAs)	1,384.6
Other Checkable Deposits (OCDs)	552.0
Traveler's Checks	2.1
M1	3,372.1

Table 2.1: Monetary Aggregate: M1
as of February, 2017
(in Seasonally Adjusted Billions of $)
Source: Federal Reserve

the economy that can serve as a medium of exchange. There are essentially four main assets that satisfy this property:

Currency that comes in the form of Federal Reserve Notes (or paper money), which are liabilities of the Federal Reserve, and coins, which are liabilities of the U.S. Treasury Dept. The total dollar value of U.S. currency in circulation (that is, in the hands of the public and outside of the banking system) as of February 2017 was nearly $1.4 trillion. Well over 90 percent of this total was Federal Reserve Notes.

Let's pause for a moment and ask ourselves the question: Does this seem like a large number?

Consider that there are about 325 million Ameri-

cans, so on a per capita basis, currency holdings amount
to more than $4,000 for every man, woman, and child
in the United States. For a family of three that would
amount to approximately $13,000! That is an aston-
ishing number. However, a study conducted by the
Federal Reserve has estimated that somewhere between
75-90 percent of U.S. currency is held overseas. Much
of that currency is in the vaults of central banks around
the world.

Checking accounts come in two forms: *Demand Deposit Accounts, or DDAs*, which are checking accounts
that do not pay interest, and *Other Checkable Deposits,
or OCDs*, that are interest-bearing. As shown in Table 2.1, as of February 2017, there was approximately
$1.9 trillion dollars in checking accounts, with approx-
imately 70 percent held in DDAs. The loss of interest
that depositors incur in DDAs versus OCDs is normally
offset by the lack of service charges for check processing
that accompany OCD accounts. Therefore, individuals
who write a large number of checks would benefit by
holding their deposits in DDAs. Also, with short-term
interest rates near zero today, the loss in interest income from holding DDAs versus OCDs is very modest
for most depositors.

Finally, a dwindling component of M1 is *Traveler's
Checks*, representing approximately $3 billion, bringing
the *Total Value of M1 Assets* to nearly $3.4 trillion.

The Money Supply and the Economy

As we stated, the Federal Reserve determines what constitutes the nation's money supply, and they monitor these monetary aggregates closely. Why do they care? There are two reasons.[4]

- First, movements in the money supply as measured by the monetary aggregates provide them with information on changes that are taken place within the financial system.

- Second, changes in the money supply in general tend to help forecast the economy, i.e., GDP and inflation.

$$\text{Money Supply} \uparrow \quad \Rightarrow \quad \text{GDP} \uparrow \quad \Rightarrow \quad \text{Inflation} \uparrow$$
$$\left(\text{lag 3-6 months}\right) \qquad \left(\text{lag 12-18 months}\right)$$

Figure 2.1: Transmission of an Increase in the Money Supply to the Macroeconomy

An increase in the money supply tends to be followed by an increase in GDP with a lag of about

---

[4]See https://www.federalreserve.gov/faqs/money_12845.htm for a discussion by the Federal Reserve of this rationale and how it has changed over time

3-6 months. This pickup in the economy is then followed with a lag of an additional 12-18 months by a rise in inflation.

Prior to 1980, this statistical relationship between the money supply, GDP, and inflation was fairly strong when the money supply was measured as M1. However, after 1980, there were radical changes in the payments system in the United States, as debit and credit cards, smart cards, and eventually internet transactions altered the way people used the media of exchange contained in M1 and its relationship with GDP began to weaken. To deal with this problem the Federal Reserve began to look more closely at a second measure of the money supply referred to as the monetary aggregate *M2*.

Monetary Aggregates: M2

M2 is a broader measure of the money supply than M1, in that it includes all of M1 and then adds to that the principal short-term savings assets of households.

As indicated in Table 2.2, the largest single component of these savings assets is *savings accounts* and *money market deposit accounts (or MMDAs)* at banks, savings and loans, and credit unions. This grouping amounts to just over $8.9 trillion.

A second major short-term savings asset for households is *small time deposits* (or *certificates of deposit (CDs)* with denomination smaller than $100,000). These

M1	3,372.1 billion
Savings Accounts & Money Market Deposit Accounts (MMDAs)	8,920.6 billion
Small Time Deposits (Certificates of Deposits < $100,000)	355.2 billion
Retail Money Market Mutual Funds (MMMFs) for accounts <$100,000	663.3 billion
Total Value of M2 Assets	13,311.2

Table 2.2: Monetary Aggregate M2 as of February,
2017
(in Seasonally Adjusted Billions of $)
Source: Federal Reserve

assets typically carry slightly higher interest rates to compensate the depositor for the loss of liquidity, or access to the funds, since small CD contracts typically require that a penalty be paid for early withdrawal.

Retail money market mutual funds (MMMFs with less than $100,000 per account) have also become an important short-term savings vehicle for households. While these funds are not federally insured, they do offer an advantage over savings accounts and MMDAs in that they generally pay a slightly higher interest rate. The higher rate reflects the fact that the deposits in MMMFs are invested in a portfolio of money market assets, some paying relatively high interest rates and these interest rates determine the returns to the depositors.

Taken together, these small time deposits and retail MMMFs comprise just over $1 trillion, bringing the total value of M2 assets to approximately $13.3 trillion.

The reliance on certain of these monetary assets to depository institutions, such as commercial banks, as a principal source of funds will be discussed in detail later in the text. Also, the increasingly important role of money market mutual funds in the allocation of funds outside the traditional banking system, in the collection of financial institutions that have collectively come to be called the *shadow banking system* will be described at various points throughout the text.[5]

Equities

The second major category of financial assets is *equities*. Equities represent ownership shares of publicly held firms. There are essentially two basic types of equities: *common stock* and *preferred stock*.

The vast majority of equities come in the form of common stock. Ownership of common stock entitles the stockholders to quarterly dividends as determined

---

[5]See Kodres (2013) for a description of the shadow banking system.

by the management. These dividends can vary from one quarter to the next, and in lean economic times, the dividends may be canceled altogether. The owners of common stock also have voting rights in the election of the *board of directors* of the firm who are charged with ensuring that management decisions are in the best interests of the shareholders. The intention of this form of corporate governance is to eliminate to the extent possible the moral hazard issues that arise in the ownership of common stock. Essentially, the board members are acting as agents on behalf of the shareholders and their decisions are subject to the same *agency problem* of *moral hazard*, in that the self-interests of the board members may deviate from those of the shareholders.

Moral hazard arises in virtually every financial contract where the party acquiring funds has more private information that can be exploited to the detriment of the lender or investor. This issue will resurface in subsequent chapters in various contexts, where market mechanisms as well as government regulations have been put in place to mitigate the *agency costs* associated with moral hazard.

The other principal type of equity is preferred stock. Unlike common stock, holders of preferred stock do not have any voting rights. However, the dividend that the stockholders are promised is fixed. The company cannot change the amount of the dividend once the preferred stock is issued. It does have the authority to temporarily suspend dividend payments, which is an extreme measure that would only be taken if the firm was losing money and was trying to conserve cash to avoid bankruptcy. Again, unlike common stock, any missed dividends are made up to the owners of preferred stock once the firm's sales pick up again. Moreover, these dividends will be made up prior to the resumption of dividend payments to common stockholders, who do not receive any compensation for the loss of dividends.

Let's pause for a minute and consider how the dividend policy affects the characteristics of the two forms of equities as possible investments. First compare the risk of not receiving the claims against the firm that you, as an equity investor, anticipate. Those claims consist entirely of future expected dividend payments. If the firm can modify those payments each quarter, as is the case for common stock, as opposed to payments that are fixed and not subject to change, as is the case for preferred stock, then common stock looks a lot riskier.

Suppose a firm suffers losses for a couple of quarters and decides that it must suspend its dividends to conserve its cash in order to avoid bankruptcy. Once the firm returns to profitability the preferred stockers will receive all of their missed payments, while the common stock holders receive none of theirs. Knowledge of this feature of the financial contracts once again suggests that common stock is a riskier asset than preferred stock.

Finally, dividend payments must be made to preferred stockholders before a firm can pay dividends to common stock shareholders. This provision in the financial contracts also increases the risk of investing in common stock relative to preferred stock.

What can we conclude when comparing common versus preferred stock as investments? Investors in common stock have a higher tolerance for risk, and require a higher expected rate of return on their investments than do investors in preferred stock, where the higher expected rate of return compensates them for taking this higher risk.

Debt Securities

The next major category of financial assets is *debt securities*, often referred to as *fixed income securities*. There are many types of debt securities, including both money and capital market assets. What the vast majority of debt securities tend to have in common is a finite maturity and they represent a set of fixed claims that never vary once the asset is issued. An important feature of debt securities is the inverse relationship between their price and the expected rate of return, or interest rate, demanded by new investors. We will explore this logic in detail later.

However, for now, consider for example a 10-yr Treasury bond. When this bond is initially issued, the government promises the buyer to pay a series of semi-annual coupon payments, and upon maturity, the investor receives the face (or *par*) value of the bond. Once the bond is issued, the dollar amounts of those promised coupon payments as well as the par value can never be changed. Since the buyer knows how much he or she is paying for that bond, a rate of return on the investment can be computed – as we will do later. Over time, the interest rate that "the market" demands in order to purchase that bond changes. However, the promised stream of payments does not change. Therefore, if the market increases the interest rate that it needs to make the investment, then it will have to pay less for the bond, since the stream of payments it receives is fixed.

We are thus led to a very important conclusion: *As interest rates rise, the price of the bond (and debt securities in general) must fall.*

Note that if the bond in our example is a corporate bond, then the risk of not receiving the promised coupon payments is reflected in the interest rate demanded by the market. When the risk rises, interest rates go up, and the bond price falls. However, in comparing the risk of investing in debt securities versus equities, unlike stockholders who may see their dividends cut, the owners of debt securities have recourse to take legal action against the issuer of the debt security who fails to pay the promised coupon payments. Essentially, failure to make these payments renders the firm bankrupt.

What effect does this bankruptcy provision have on the risk of the investment in debt securities? Of course, it lowers the risk, since a firm will do whatever it can to avoid bankruptcy, and will therefore be less likely to miss a coupon payment.

Therefore, in comparing the risk and expected returns on debt securities versus equities, this bankruptcy feature of debt securities drastically reduces the risk and therefore tends to reduce the expected rate of return on debt securities relative to equities.

Financial Derivatives

The final major category of financial assets is *financial derivatives*. A financial derivative, as the name implies, is a financial asset that normally derives its value from the market value of underlying assets or commodities.

Derivatives have been around for a long time. They began with simple futures contracts on agricultural products, such as wheat, corn, coffee, and soybeans. The farmer is able to sell, say, his wheat forward, i.e., during the planting season, he can lock in a price at which he can sell the wheat when it is eventually harvested. The investor who purchased the contract would incur the risk of falling wheat prices. That is, if the future *spot price* of the wheat falls below the agreed *futures price*, then the investor will have to buy the farmer's wheat at a price above the market price, and

would therefore suffer a loss when he he sold it in the
market. In contrast, if the wheat price were to rise
in the future, then the future spot price at which the
investor could sell the wheat would exceed the agreed
futures price at which he purchases the wheat, and the
investor would realize a profit. Such derivative products are very important in shifting risk from those who
do not wish to bear it to those who, for a price, are
willing take on that risk.

Over the past 50 years, there has been an explosion
of new derivative products. One area, in particular,
that has seen a tremendous increase in interest in the
markets is financial derivatives, where the underlying
asset on which the derivatives are based is a financial
contract. These financial derivatives played a very important role in bringing about the financial crisis that
ultimately led to the Great Recession of 2007-2009. We
will examine the role they played in detail in subsequent chapters.

2.5 Inflation and Asset Prices

An important consideration for the decision on whether
to purchase any financial asset is inflation. As indicated earlier, most financial contracts represent claims
to a stream of future payments, where those payments
are made in units of domestic currency, such as the U.S.
dollar. Because of inflation, the dollars you receive in
the future will be worth less than the dollars you use to

purchase the financial asset today. Therefore, it is essential to factor in your expectation of future inflation when you make the asset purchase.

For example, suppose you purchase a one-year Treasury bill with a guaranteed interest rate of 2 percent. If the inflation rate during the time from when you made the purchase until the T-bill matured was 3 percent, then the net real rate of return on your investment would be a minus 1 percent. You would effectively be paying the government to hold your money, not the other way around. Of course, had you simply stuck the currency in your mattress, then your real rate of return would have been a minus 3 percent. Some interest is better than no interest.

So, how do we measure inflation? In fact there are many such measures. An important one is the *Consumer Price Index or CPI* that is compiled by the US Department of Labor's Bureau of Labor Statistics. The CPI is intended to help measure changes in the price of a typical market basket of consumer goods. It is constructed from surveys taken by a large number of individuals who literally go to retail outlets, such as Publix, each month and write done the cost of a set of goods, such as a bar of Ivory soap and a box of Wheaties. These figures are compiled into an index, which is set to 100 in *base years* for each of the components. Most of the current base years are 1982-1984. Percent changes in the overall index are then taken as the CPI inflation rate. Therefore, the CPI inflation rate in percent is given by this formula, where the subscript represents time.

$$\text{CPI Inflation Rate}_t = \frac{\text{CPI}_t - \text{CPI}_{t-1}}{\text{CPI}_{t-1}} \times 100\% \quad (2.1)$$

Here is an example. The CPI index for February 2016 was 237.111 and for February, 2017 was 243.603. Plugging these numbers into equation 2.1 allows us to compute the annual inflation rate over the twelve month period prior to February 2016:

CPI Inflation Rate (February 2016 to February 2017)

$$= \frac{243.603 - 237.111}{237.111} \times 100\% = 2.74\% \quad (2.2)$$

In this case, the CPI Inflation rate was 2.74% over the past 12 months. Therefore, any financial asset that had a nominal interest rate or market rate of return during this period that was less than 2.74% would have yielded a negative real return to investors.

2.6 Summary

In this chapter, we have taken an initial look at the broad categories of financial assets that include money, equities, debt securities, and derivatives. We have also had a brief discussion of the important relationship between expected rate of return, risk, and liquidity that vary from one financial asset to another. Emphasis was given to inflation as a major factor affecting ALL investments. The importance of private information that is not shared by both parties to a financial contract gives rise to agency costs associated with moral hazard and adverse selection. This asymmetric information affects asset prices and has led to various market mechanisms and government regulations intended to mitigate its impact on the viability of important classes of financial assets. All of these issues will be explored in greater detail throughout the remainder of the text.

In the next chapter, we will shift our focus from individual assets to the financial institutions that provide the financial services and often supply the financial assets that are available to us as consumers and investors. These institutions have undergone significant evolution over the past the 50 years, due in large measure to the technological innovations affecting the telecommunications industry. As smart consumers of financial products, it is important to understand how those changes are affecting us, since seldom does a day go by when we do not – in one way or another – come in contact with the institutions that comprise the economy's financial system.

Key Terms

risk
expected rate of return
liquidity
asymmetric information
adverse selection
lemon laws
ex ante private information
debt contract
equity contract
moral hazard
ex post private information
monetary assets
medium of exchange
store of value
unit of account
monetary aggregates
commodity money
fiat money
lack of double coincidence of wants
legal tender
M1
currency
checking accounts
demand deposit accounts (DDAs)
other checkable deposits (OCDs)
traveler's checks
M2
savings accounts

money market deposit accounts (MMDAs)
small time deposits (certificates of deposits)
retail money market mutual funds (MMMFs)
shadow banking system
equities
common stock
preferred stock
board of directors
agency costs
debt securities
fixed income securities
financial derivatives
inflation rate
consumer price index (CPI)

2.7 Review Questions

1. Can the effect of the risk of investing in an asset be offset to some extent by the asset's liquidity when determining the rate of return demanded by an investor in the asset? Explain.

2. What is the basic difference between adverse selection and moral hazard?

3. Why do lemon laws exist?

4. Describe the role of a corporation's board of directors. Does this form of corporate governance completely eliminate the problem of moral hazard for stockholders? Explain.

5. What criteria does the Federal Reserve use in the construction of the monetary aggregates M1 and M2 in terms of the traditional properties of the monetary assets?

6. Why does the Federal Reserve bother to keep close track of the money supply numbers?

7. What is the advantage to investors of retail money market mutual funds over savings & MMDAs? Over CDs? What is the principal advantage to investors of CDs as a short-term savings vehicle?

8. What is the Federal Reserve's principal measure of the nation's money supply? Has this always been the case? Explain.

9. Explain the relative differences between common stock, preferred stock, and corporate bonds in terms of the risk and expected rates or return.

10. Explain the following statement: *A speculator who buys a derivatives contract for an agricultural product, such as coffee, is a risk-taker, while the issuer of the contract, who owns the agricultural product (coffee) wishes to avoid risk.*

11. Describe the consequences for the purchasing power of the dollar from the end of 1983 through the end of each of the following years, where the Consumer Price Index (CPI), which has a base-year value of 100 at the end of 1983, is listed. How much did the dollar depreciate between 1985 and 2016?

Year	CPI
1985	109.3
1990	133.8
1995	153.5
2000	174.0
2005	196.8
2010	219.8
2015	236.5
2016	241.4

2.8   References

Akerlov, George A. 2001. "Writing the "The Market for Lemons": A Personal and Interpretative Essay," Nobel Lecture available at: http://www.nobelprize.org /nobel_prizes/economic-sciences/laureates/2001/aker-lof-article.html

Akerlov, George A. 1970. "The Market for Lemons: Quality Uncertainty and the Market Mechanism," *Quarterly Journal of Economics*, 84(3): 488-500.

Kodres, Laura E. 2013. "What Is Shadow Banking?" *Finance and Development*, IMF: June.

Radford, Richard A. 1945. "The Economic Organization of a P.O.W. Camp," *Economica*, vol. 12, no. 48, November: 189-201.

http://www.nobelprize.org/nobel_prizes/economic-sciences/laureates/2001/popular.html

https://www.federalreserve.gov/faqs/money_12845.htm

Chapter 3

Financial Institutions

This chapter concludes the initial discussion of financial assets by examining how new financial assets that are just introduced into the economy affect the balance sheets of the issuers and of the purchasers. That is, how do they alter the assets and liabilities of each party to the transaction.

Of course, a large share of the financial market transactions that take place in the economy involve borrowing and lending, and at any point in time, nearly everyone is both a borrower and a lender. An important question to ask is whether, for example, an individual has borrowed more than he or she has lent over, say, the last month. That is, is that individual a *net lender* who supplies credit to the economy, or a *net borrower* who absorbs some of the total credit that is available in the economy?

After examining these issues vis-á-vis the respective balance sheets, a look at some data will help give perspective to two important aspects of the U.S. economy's financial markets. First, it will reveal which sectors of the economy are the big net borrowers and which are the big net lenders and how this pattern has changed over time. There may be some surprises there.

Finally, the data can reveal the relative size of the major groups of financial institutions, such as commercial banks and mutual funds, that provide financial services to consumers. This evidence will provide some guidance on just how important they are to the economy. This exercise necessarily involves dealing in big numbers – 100s of billions and even trillions of dollars, so to gain perspective, emphasis is placed on the relative size of these important financial institutions. This overview of the financial system will provide a backdrop for much of what's to come.

3.1   The Balance Sheets of Households and Firms

Consider how financial contracts originate and how this affects the buyers and sellers. It is easiest to think about the creation of a financial asset by considering the balance sheets of the parties to the contract, such as a household and a firm.

A typical balance sheet of firm can appear as shown in Table 3.1, with the assets divided between *financial assets*, such as bank deposits or government bonds,

Asset Side	Liability Side
Financial Assets (FA) – bank deposits – government bonds – other *Non-Financial Assets (NFA)* – buildings - equipment (computers, etc.) – inventories – other	*Liabilities (TL)* – bank loans – short-term debt – other *Capital Account (NW)* – capital paid in *[NW(STOCK)]* – cumulative retained earnings *[NW(RE)]*
Total Assets (TA)	*Total Liabilities (TL)* *+ Owner's Equity, (NW)*

Table 3.1: Firm's Balance Sheet

and *nonfinancial assets*, including the firm's structures, equipment, and inventories. On the liability side of the balance sheet, a firm will typically have a list of *borrowings*, such as bank loans and short-term debt along with other liabilities.

By subtracting *Total Liabilities* from *Total Assets*, you can determine *Owner's Equity*, or the total value of the firm. We divide owner's equity into two components: *Capital Paid In*, which is the value of the stock issued by the firm at the time that it was originally issued, or how much money was raised by issuing the stock; and *Cumulative Retained Earnings*, or the total amount of profits that the firm has chosen to not pay out in dividends to its shareholders, but rather to reinvest in the company.

Since Balance Sheets must balance, we have the following *accounting identity*:

$$FA + NFA = TL + NW(STOCK) + NW(RE) \qquad (3.1)$$

where the firm's financial and nonfinancial assets must sum to the total liabilities and its owner's equity.

Households have similar balance sheets. A typical balance sheet may appear as shown in Table 3.2. Its assets and liabilities differ somewhat from firms, with the largest single nonfinancial asset being housing, and the largest single liability the mortgage. Of course, households don't issue stock, but they do in general have a computable amount of *Net Worth*, which represents the household's cumulative savings, and is found by subtracting its total liabilities from its total assets. So, we have the household's accounting identity:

$$FA + NFA = TL + NW(HH) \qquad (3.2)$$

Asset Side	Liability Side
Financial Assets (FA) – bank deposits – corporate stock – mutual funds – other *Non-Financial Assets (NFA)* – housing – durable goods (autos, etc.) – other	*Liabilities (TL)* – bank loans – credit card debt –mortgages other *Net Worth [(NW (HH)]*
Total Assets (TA)	*Total Liabilities (TL) + Net Worth, (NW)*

Table 3.2: Household's Balance Sheet

Now consider what happens when we combine the balance sheets for all of the firms in the economy with those for all of the households. Ignoring government and the foreign sector, the sum of all of the assets in the economy must equal the sum of all of the liabilities in the economy plus the net worth of households and the net worth (or owner's equity) of firms.

However, it is also true that for every financial asset there exists an offsetting claim on another economic unit, e.g., a household or a firm. This implies that the following must also be true:

The sum of all financial assets equals the sum of all liabilities and value of all stock issued by firms.

Therefore, ignoring government and foreign sectors, from equations (3.1) and (3.2), we can add up across all sectors of the economy:

$$\sum_{all\ sectors} FA + \sum_{all\ sectors} NFA = \sum_{all\ sectors} TL$$

$$+ \sum_{all\ firms} NW(Stock) + \sum_{all\ firms} NW(RE)$$

$$+ \sum_{all\ households} NW(HH) \qquad (3.3)$$

However, for every financial asset, there exists a claim on another economic unit. Therefore, we have the following relationship:

$$\sum_{all\ sectors} FA = \sum_{all\ sectors} TL + \sum_{all\ firms} NW(Stock)$$

$$(3.4)$$

Now, if we subtract equation (3.4) from equation (3.3), we have an important result.

$$\sum_{all\ sectors} NFA = \sum_{all\ households} NW(HH) + \sum_{all\ firms} NW(RE)$$

$$(3.5)$$

<u>Conclusion</u>: Ignoring the government and foreign sectors of the economy: *The total value of the economy's non-financial assets equates to the economy's total net worth, which consists of the aggregate net worth of households and the aggregate retained earnings of firms.*

3.2   The Introduction of a New Financial Asset into the Economy

What happens when a new financial asset is created? T-accounts can be very helpful here. A T-account shows changes in balance sheets as a result of a transaction.

Example: A firm issues a $100,000 ($100K) bond to purchase a computer from Dell Computer. The bond is purchased by a household with cash. The cash is then used to buy the computer equipment, which has an inventory value to Dell of $90K. Take these transactions in two steps.

Step 1: The household buys the bond from the firm. On the asset side of its balance sheet the household sees a reduction in cash of $100K and an increase in bond holdings by that same amount.

Asset Side	Liability Side
Δ Cash = -$100K Δ Bonds = +$100K	

Table 3.3: Changes to the Household's Balance Sheet

Therefore, the household simply exchanged one financial asset for another with no net change in total financial assets. No other changes take place on its balance sheet and there was no increase in the household's net worth.

$$\Delta\text{FA} = \Delta\text{NFA} = \Delta\text{TA} = \Delta\text{TL} = \Delta NW(HH) = 0 \tag{3.6}$$

Now examine the firm's balance sheet. The firm has seen a $100K increase in its cash holdings, which is exactly offset by the additional liability resulting from the bond issue. Therefore, the firm's assets and liabilities both increased, but there was no change in the firm's net worth.

$$\Delta \text{FA} = \Delta \text{TL} = \$100K \qquad (3.7)$$

$$\Delta \text{NFA} = \Delta \text{NW(STOCK)} = \Delta \text{NW(RE)} = 0 \qquad (3.8)$$

Asset Side	Liability Side
Δ Cash = \$100K	Δ Bonds = +\$100K

Table 3.4: Changes to the Firm's Balance Sheet

What can be learned from this exercise?

Conclusion: *The creation of the new financial asset expanded the firm's balance sheet, but had no effect on the net worth in the economy nor has it created any new non-financial assets.*

Now examine the effects on balance sheets resulting from the purchase of the computer equipment from Dell.

Step 2: The firm uses the $100,000 in cash raised by the bond issue to buy computer equipment from Dell.

In this case, the firm exchanges a financial asset for a non-financial asset of the same value, with no change in its net worth.

$$\Delta FA = -\$100K, \quad \Delta NFA = +\$100K \qquad (3.9)$$

$$\Delta TL = \Delta NW(STOCK) = \Delta NW(RE) = 0 \quad (3.10)$$

Asset Side	Liability Side
Δ Cash = -$100K Δ Equipment +$100K	

Table 3.5: Changes to the Firm's Balance Sheet

However, for this transaction, Dell sees an increase in its financial assets, as its cash holdings rise by $100,000, while its non-financial assets decline by the $90,000 drop in its inventories. The result is that its total assets have risen by $10,000.

$$\Delta \text{FA} = +\$100K, \quad \Delta NFA = -\$90K, \quad \Delta \text{TA} = +\$10K \tag{3.11}$$

Since balance sheets must balance, there is an offsetting entry. Initially, the additional $10,000 shows up as an increase the firm's retained earnings, while leaving its liabilities and the capital paid in portion of its net worth unchanged.

$$\Delta \text{TL} = \Delta \text{NW(STOCK)} = 0, \quad \Delta \text{NW(RE)} = +\$10K \tag{3.12}$$

Asset Side	Liability Side
Δ Cash = $100K Δ Inventories -$90K	Δ NW (RE) = +$10K

Table 3.6: Changes in Dell's Balance Sheet

What can be concluded from the combination of the two transactions that resulted in the firm acquiring the computer equipment from Dell?

<u>Conclusion</u>: *For the economy as a whole, non-financial assets rose in value by $10K, that is, the $100K increase for the firm minus the $90K decrease for Dell, and this amount exactly coincided with the total increase in net worth, reflecting the profits for Dell, all of which was realized initially as retained earnings.*

3.3   Net Lenders and Net Borrowers

In economic terms, balance sheet items are *economic stock variables*, i.e., they exist at a point in time; whereas changes to balance sheet items are *economic flow variables*, since they have positive or negative values only when measured over some time interval.

These concepts are useful to identify who the *net borrowers* and *net lenders* in the economy are, since most all economic units are both borrowing and lending at the same time. The question is: are they lending more than they're borrowing or vice versa?

A simple equation (3.13) will help illuminate this concept.

$$R - E = \Delta FA - \Delta D \qquad (3.13)$$

where:

R = Current Income Receipts
E = Current Expenditures out of Current Income

R-E = Net Savings
ΔFA = Change in Financial Assets
ΔD = Change in Debt

Essentially it states that the *net savings* of an individual must equate to the net increase in the financial asset holdings plus the net decrease in debt.

On the left-hand side of the equation, net savings is given by the current income receipts minus the expenditures out of current income. On the right-hand side is the change in financial assets minus the change in debt.

Recognizing that equation (3.13) is simply a budget constraint that individuals always face, a couple of definitions can be used to identify net borrowers and net lenders.

Net Borrowers, or Deficit-Budget Units (DBUs)

A net borrower is often referred to as a *deficit-budget unit (DBU)* and is one for whom expenditures exceed receipts over some time period. What equation (3.13) states that for this deficit budget unit, the net accumulation of debt exceeds its net accumulation of financial assets.

$$E > R \Rightarrow \Delta D > \Delta FA \qquad (3.14)$$

A simple example illustrates the use of equation (3.13).

Example: An individual receives $3000 in income for the month, spends $4000, and also buys $2000 in bonds. What has happened to his debt?

Solve equation (3.13) for the change in debt and plug in the numbers:

$$\Delta D = E - R + \Delta FA = \$4000 - \$3000 + \$2000 = +\$3000 \tag{3.15}$$

Result: The individual had to borrow not only the $2000 to purchase the bonds, but also an additional $1000 to finance the amount he spent over and above what he earned. He is a deficit budget unit who accumulated financial assets, but was still a net borrower to the economy.

Net Lenders, or Surplus-Budget Units (SBUs)

Equation (3.13) also illustrates what constitutes a net lender to the economy, or what is sometimes referred to as a *surplus-budget unit (SBU)*. This individual has positive net savings, such that her earnings exceed her expenditures. She therefore has a net accumulation of financial assets that exceeds her net accumulation of debt.

$$R > E \Rightarrow \Delta FA > \Delta D \tag{3.16}$$

Again a simple example can be instructive.

Example: Suppose an individual's monthly income is $4000 and her expenditures out of this income are $3000, but she also chooses to purchase $2000 in bonds. What is the change in her level of debt? Solving equation (3.13) for the change in debt and plugging in the numbers, her debt level is seen to have risen by $1000, despite the fact that she was a net lender to the economy.

$$\Delta D = E - R + \Delta FA = \$3000 - \$4000 + \$2000 = +\$1000$$
(3.17)

Result: Her desire to accumulate $2000 in financial assets caused her to have to borrow the additional $1000 that she could not cover from the $1000 in her net savings for the month.

3.4 Sectoral Lending and Borrowing in the US Economy

This section takes a look at some data and at the big picture to determine who the big net lenders and the big net borrowers in the U.S. economy were in 2016. Table 3.7 displays the net borrowing and lending to the U.S. economy originating in key sectors. There is a lot of information on this table. Some of the patterns that you see are typical and others are not.

Historically, households are net lenders to the economy as was true during 2016. However, this pattern has changed over the past two decades. U.S. households be-

Sector	Δ FA	Δ D	Net Lenders (+) or Net Borrowers (-)
Households	1,118.6.	528.4	590.2
Nonfinancial firms	1,295.1	1,220.2	74.9
State/Local Govts	117.5	302.0	-184.5
Fed Govt	262.7	890.4	-627.8
International	654.3	411.8	224.4
Financial	2272.3	2049.2	223.2

Table 3.7: Net Borrowers and Net Lenders to the U.S
Economy in 2016, Billions of $
(excluding capital gains and losses)
Source: Federal Reserve

gan to take on unusually high levels of debt in the 1980s
and 1990s, and then this trend became much more
pronounced during the Great Recession. Household
debt has grown somewhat in 2015 and 2016, although
it had in fact been shrinking for several years prior
to 2015, as households tried to pay down their debts
with higher savings to offset the loss in wealth from the
sharply falling house prices and declining stock prices.

In 2016, their financial asset holdings rose considerably, and households were net lenders for the year to the tune of nearly $528 billion.

Nonfinancial firms are normally net borrowers in the economy, as they borrow to expand production, and while the access to borrowed funds became difficult for most firms during the Great Recession, as we will discuss in detail in subsequent chapters, they were actually net lenders in 2016 of some 75 billion dollars as the tight credit markets from the Great Recession have eased.

In recent years, governments at all levels have been net borrowers. The big difference is that state and local governments are less able to run large budget deficits and were on tight austerity programs for several years as a result of the Great Recession. Nonetheless, in 2016, they were net borrowers, with their indebtedness increasing by $185 billion over and above their additional accumulation of financial assets.

The federal government consciously ran sizable deficits for several years in a row to help fight the Great Recession. In 2016, the federal government was still a large net borrower in the economy, absorbing nearly $628 billion of the available credit in the economy. This figure is down considerably from recent recent years, and as a share of GDP is close to the average over the past 50 years. These historical patterns will be examined in more detail in subsequent chapters.

In recent years, important net lenders to the United

States are foreign investors, including foreign governments. However, this was not always the case. Until
households began their surge of indebtedness, particularly during the 1980s and 1990s, there was very little
net borrowing or lending with the foreign sector. However, as household debt grew, the foreign sector became the major source of funds. This net lending completely collapsed during the financial crisis, with the
foreign sector becoming a significant net borrower of
credit from the U.S. economy. This collapse of funding
from abroad has now reversed course as the U.S. economy has recovered from Great Recession. In 2016, the
foreign sector was once again a significant net lender
of more than $224 billion.

A traditional major net lender to the economy is the
financial sector. As Table 3.7 indicates, it contributed
nearly $223 billion to the credit markets. However, in
the depths of the Great Recession, the Federal Reserve
supplied the majority of this lending in their effort to
support the economy. In the past few years, credit
conditions have eased significantly and private financial
institutions are beginning to lend more freely. We will
have much more to say about these and other actions
taken by the Federal Reserve in later chapters.

After many years of unusual conditions in the credit
markets, more normal borrowing and lending patterns
are slowly returning. The principal net lenders to the
economy are once again households and the financial
sector, with essentially no significant role for the Fed-

eral Reserve, and the principal net borrowers are nonfinancial businesses seeking to borrow the funds needed for expansion. However, the federal government's future role in the credit markets is unclear, with a significant amount of political uncertainty surrounding the federal government's budgetary priorities. We will discuss the current status of the government's debt and deficit situation with reference to historical patterns in subsequent chapters.

3.5 Methods of Finance

Lending and borrowing can take place in a variety of ways. For discussion purposes, we can label them *methods of finance*.

Consider the simplest form referred to as *direct finance*. Here the borrower and lender meet up and agree to a financial contract that may be formal or informal. For example, you could borrow $100 from a friend until payday. You know each other and firm up the loan with a handshake.

More formally, you could loan money directly to the federal government by purchasing a newly issued Treasury bill online. The Treasury Department will set up an account for you and ensure both your ownership of the T-bill and your payment when it matures.[1]

---

[1]If you want to learn about this option, go to *treasurydirect.gov*.

A second method of finance is referred to as *semi-direct finance*. In this case, an investor employs the services of a broker or dealer to find the borrower and consummate the contract. There is a significant difference between a broker versus dealer, although you as an investor may not know which it is you are working with.

A *broker* matches up borrowers with lenders, but does NOT take a *position of risk*, in that he never actually owns any stock involved in the transaction. For example, you may go to a stock broker to place an order for Apple's stock. The broker will find a seller, ensure transfer of ownership, and collect his fee.

A *dealer*, on the other hand, manages a portfolio of stock and stands ready to buy and add to the portfolio or to sell from the portfolio. While he is also matching up borrowers with lenders, there is some risk that the stock he owns may lose value before he has a chance to sell it. Of course, he would also make a profit from the stock if its price rose while he owned it.

The final and most pervasive form of finance is *indirect finance*. This method of finance is performed by a *financial intermediary*, such as a commercial bank, that simultaneously writes contracts with the ultimate lenders, such as depositors, from whom it borrows funds, and with the ultimate borrowers, such as small businesses, to whom it loans out the deposit funds, again under contract.

So why do these different methods of finance coexist? Direct finance is simple, but not always practical. Semi-direct finance can be more efficient in that it normally reduces what could otherwise be significant *search costs* for borrowers and lenders to find one another. Indirect finance has an additional benefit for certain risky lending. By collecting, say, a large number of small depositors' funds and aggregating them up and investing in a portfolio of larger loans, the financial intermediary can reduce the risk to the depositors' investments through *diversification*. That is, not all of the loans are likely to fail at the same time, so default on the entire portfolio is unlikely, despite the fact that any one of the loans may carry a measurable risk of default.

3.6 Financial Institutions

To complete this lengthy overview of the financial system, it is useful to get a feel for how important many of the economy's financial institutions are with respect to their role in providing funds for households, businesses, and governments to carry out their economic functions.

A comparison of the the relative size of these institutions is helpful. For example, securities broker and dealers engaged in semi-direct finance have over $3 trillion under management. This is a significant number, but is much smaller than the sum total of assets in the banking system, broadly defined to in-

FINANCIAL INSTITUTION	TOTAL FINANCIAL ASSETS
Semi − DirectFinance	
Securities Brokers/Dealers	3,022.5
IndirectFinance	
Depositories Commercial Banks & Savings Institutions	14,898.5
Credit Unions	1,243.0
Non-Depositories Private Pension Funds	9086.1
State/Local Govt Pension Funds	6096.9
US Govt Pension Funds	3,894.4
Finance Companies	1,385.0
Mutual Funds (Stock & Bonds)	13,615.6
Money Market Funds	2,728.1
Life Insurance Companies	6,863.8
Property-Casualty Ins Cos	1,947.2

Table 3.8: Assets under Management by Type of Financial Institution (in 2016, Billions $)
Source: Federal Reserve

clude all major categories of regulated *depository institutions*: the commercial banks, savings institutions, and credit unions, which aggregate up to more than $16 trillion, with commercial banks and savings institutions accounting for approximately $15 trillion, or about 92 percent of that total.

However, when we turn to *non-depositories*, we see that, while no one institutional category dominates the commercial banking system, there are some sizable contributors helping to meet the specialized financing needs of households, businesses, and governments. For example, pension funds collectively – both private and government-managed – account for nearly $19 trillion, which is somewhat comparable to the commercial banking system. This comparison is also true of mutual funds, when stock and bond funds are combined with money market mutual funds, the total assets under management reaches more than $16 trillion.

These institutions, as well as finance companies and insurance companies, are big players in the financial markets, and understanding their mission is important for any practitioner in the financial markets or consumer of financial services.

3.7 Summary

This chapter completes a rather lengthy overview of the financial system. This overview is intended to provide a framework from which the details of the financial system can be more fully developed in the remainder of the book. As stated in the Introduction, the purpose of this book can be stated very simply: to provide the knowledge necessary to become smarter consumers of financial services. Rather than feeling that the financial system is simply too complicated to understand, which would leave the hapless consumer with this sense of being overwhelmed by it all, the goal should be to put this knowledge to work in order to become a wise consumer of financial services.

Of course, for many of us, there is also the sheer intellectual excitement of figuring it all out, and seeing the strategy behind the numbers, the management decisions, and the policy debates. However, the experience of the Great Recession has certainly taught everyone just how important the financial system is to our individual lives and to the world economy at large.

There has been a great deal written about the financial crisis and the subsequent Great Recession, and there is much more yet to be written. However, the pain that this episode inflicted on so many consumers of financial services has led to a lot of hyperbole and misinformation. Therefore, before probing too deeply into the inner workings of the money, bond, and stock markets or the balance sheets of commercial banks and the Federal Reserve, it is important to sort out what is now known about the causes and consequences of the financial crisis, and to look at what the government is doing to avoid such a catastrophe in the future. Understanding this once-in-a-generation event is essential to a probe into the complexities of today's financial marketplace. Describing the evolution of the financial crisis of 2007-2008 and its aftermath is the task of the next chapter.

Key Terms

net lender
net borrower
financial assets
nonfinancial assets
total liabilities
total assets
owner's equity
capital paid in
retained earnings
accounting identity
net worth
economic stock variables
economic flow variables
net savings
deficit-budget unit (DBU)
surplus-budget unit (SBU)
methods of finance
direct finance
semi-direct finance
broker
dealer
position of risk
indirect finance
financial intermediary
search costs
diversification
depository institutions
non-depositories

3.8 Review Questions

1. Consider two computer companies – Orange and PH – that report current sales receipts of $323 million and $294 million, respectively. Their current operating expenses were $150 million each. Orange issued $5 million in new debt, while PH paid off a $6 million bank loan. What changes in financial assets must have occurred for each during the period? Were either or both a deficit-budget or surplus-budget unit? Explain.

2. A household writes a check that is used to purchase a municipal bond. This results in:

    a) An increase in the household's total nonfinancial assets, and its net worth.
    b) An increase in the household's total liabilities, but there is no effect on its net worth.
    c) No change in the household's total financial assets, and no change its net worth.
    d) No change in the household's total liabilities, but an increase in its net worth.

3. Melvin purchases a computer online for $2,000 with a credit card. His balance sheet shows an increase in:

    a) Nonfinancial assets by $2,000 but no change in net worth.

   b) Nonfinancial assets by $2,000 and an increase in net worth by $2,000.

   c) Liabilities by $2,000 and a decline in net worth by $2,000.

   d) Liabilities by $2,000 and an increase in net worth by $2,000.

4. June received $5,000 in income for the month of September. She spent $6,000 during the month. Which of the following *could* be true?

   a) Her financial assets grew by $1,000 and her debt grew by $2,000.

   b) Her financial assets grew by $2,000 and her debt grew by $1,000.

   c) Her financial assets fell by $1,000 and her debt grew by $2,000.

   d) Her financial assets fell by $2,000 and her debt grew by $1,000.

5. Describe which of the major sectors to the economy listed in Table 3.7 are the *traditional net lenders* and which are the *traditional net borrowers*. Do these patterns differ from those observed in the data for last year? Explain.

6. What is meant by "taking a position of risk"? How do brokers and dealers differ in this regard?

7. How does *indirect finance* differ from *semidirect finance*? What advantages are there to *indirect finance* over *semidirect finance*?

8. Which of the following groups have assets under management that are close in dollar value to those of the banking system? Cite data to support your answer.

    a) Brokers and Dealers.

    b) Pension Funds (including Private, State and Local Government, and Federal Government).

    c) Mutual Funds (including stock and bond funds and money market mutual funds).

3.9   References

"Financial Accounts Guide" to the *Financial Accounts of the United States: Flow of Funds, Balance Sheets, and Integrated Macroeconomic Accounts (Z.1 data release)*. 2017. Board of Governors of the Federal Reserve System. Available at: https://www.federalreserve.gov/apps/fof/ Describes these extensive financial accounts for the U.S. economy that are compiled quarterly by the Federal Reserve.

Data for Economic Flows reported in Table 3.7: *Financial Accounts of the United States: Flow of Funds, Balance Sheets, and Integrated Macroeconomic Accounts (Z.1 data release)*. 2017. Tables: F.101, F.103, F.106, F.107, F.111, F.133. Board of Governors of the Federal Reserve System. Available at: https://www.federalreserve.gov/releases/z1/current/z1.pdf

Data for Economic Stocks reported in Table 3.8: *Financial Account of the United States: Flow of Funds, Balance Sheets, and Integrated Macroeconomic Accounts (Z.1 data release)*. 2017. Tables: L.111, L.114, L.116, L.116, L.118, L.119, L.120, L.121, L.122, L.128, L.130. Board of Governors of the Federal Reserve System. Available at: https://www.federalreserve.gov/releases/z1/current/z1.pdf

Chapter 4

The Financial Crisis and the 2007-2009 Great Recession

In 2007, the United States and other major Western economies were on the brink of the worst *financial crisis* since the *Great Depression* of the 1930s. As occurred in the Great Depression, the crisis would lead to the collapse of major financial institutions, a deep and prolonged worldwide recession, and unprecedented actions taken by governments around the world to offset the macroeconomic consequences of an imploding financial system.

In response to the Great Depression, the U.S. Government created a number of new regulatory agencies and imposed a wide range of reforms in the financial markets designed to deal with what was thought to be the major causes of the financial crisis.[1] However, since that time, there have been rapid developments in information technology and *financial innovation* along with significant institutional changes within the *financial services industry* that have altered the financial markets' landscape.

Today, governments around the globe have had to rethink the relevancy of their systems of regulations and have attempted once again to update and modernize those regulations while taking into account the new technology available to financial institutions that are more highly integrated internationally than ever before in history. As a result, virtually every financial institution in the United States, and most other countries, have been affected with many having to make substantial changes in the way they do business. Therefore, to understand today's financial system, it is essential that we examine the origins and the aftermath of the financial crisis that began to unfold in 2007 and the Great Recession that followed.

---

[1] A concise overview of the events of the Great Depression of the 1930s that is accompanied by a short video can be found at: http://www.history.com/topics/great-depression

4.1 A First Look at the Financial Crisis and the Great Recession

To gain an appreciation of how the the financial crisis in which a *housing bubble* took center stage impacted the *macroeconomy*, it is instructive to observe some data.

The Stock Market

As will be described in detail later, the stock market is one indicator of the future health of the economy, since stocks are bought and sold in anticipation of future corporate earnings. These earnings tend to rise and fall with the ups and downs of the economy. Forward-looking traders therefore form expectations of what the future will bring in order to forecast those future earnings. These forecasts then determine the value that traders place on the stocks in which they trade.

On October 9, 2007, the *S&P 500 stock market index* closed the day's trading at an all-time high of 1565.15. By March 9, 2009 – just 19 months later – the S&P 500 had lost more than half of its value, closing at 676.53 for a decline of 57 percent. In a single month, from October 26, 2008 to November 27, 2008, the S&P 500 lost nearly one-third of its value (30 percent) as the financial market crisis took a sharp turn for the worse. This decline was followed by a second

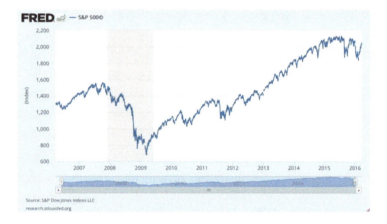

Figure 4.1 S&P 500 Stock Market Index
Source: Federal Reserve Bank of St. Louis

sharp selloff that began in February 2009 of 20 percent
before the S&P 500 finally reached its March 9, 2009
low and the market began to recover. However, it took
more than 5 years for the stock market to once again
reach its previous high.

What factors led to this 19-month decline from late
2007 to the end of the first quarter of 2009? And what
occurred in late October 2008 and February and March
2009 that so rattled the equity markets?

The Housing Market

Before answering those questions, it is helpful to take a
look at what was happening in the housing market dur-

ing this period. Consider this fact: households' principal sources of wealth are equities, held either directly
or indirectly in pension funds and mutual funds, and
the equity that they have in their house.

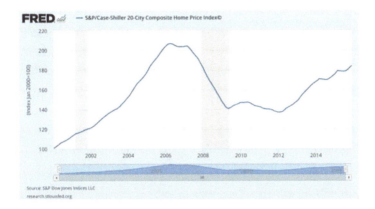

Figure 4.2 Case-Shiller House Price Index
Source: Federal Reserve Bank of St. Louis

Figure 4.2 displays the *Case-Shiller House Price Index* that is widely watched by market participants as
a gauge of the overall supply and demand conditions
of the U.S. housing market. As shown here, according
to the index, house prices peaked in July, 2006 after
more than doubling from the values recorded in January 2000. However, this housing bubble eventually
burst and by April 2009 house prices had declined by
33 percent from their all-time high. What caused this

collapse in house prices? And what impact did it have
on the macroeconomy?

The Macroeconomy: Real GDP

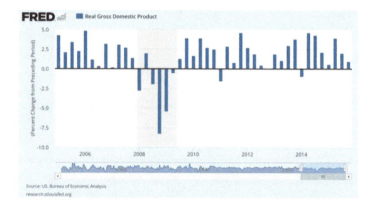

Figure 4.3 Annualized Growth Rate of Real GDP (%)
Source: Federal Reserve Bank of St. Louis

Consumption expenditures of households account
for roughly two-thirds of *GDP*, or the value of goods
and services produced in the United States. The principal factor that determines the level of consumption
expenditures is *household net worth*, or the total value
of their assets minus the value of their liabilities. From
the end of September 2007 through December 2008,
household net worth declined by $13 trillion or by nearly
20 percent. Of this total, about three-fourths was ac-

counted for by the declines in the stock market and house prices.

This sharp downturn in net worth led households to curtail consumption. Businesses experienced these declines in demand for their goods and reduced their investment purchases, which accounts for approximately 15 percent of GDP. By December, 2007 the economy had entered into a recession that included annualized declines in *real GDP* in the first quarter of 2009 of more than 8 percent followed by a second quarter decline of nearly 6 percent, marking the sharpest contraction in the U.S. economy in 75 years.

The Macroeconomy: Unemployment

The falloff in demand for goods and services also forced firms to cut back on production and reduce employment. By October, 2009, the *unemployment rate* had climbed to 10 percent – a figure not seen for more over 30 years – before starting its painfully slow decline as the economy began to recover.

While record-high oil prices during the summer and fall of 2008 shared some of the blame for weaknesses in the economy, the turmoil in the financial markets – with the freezing up of credit markets – brought economic activity in many sectors of the economy to a virtual halt. What caused financial institutions in the United States to curtail lending to such an extent that even the most creditworthy borrowers were often de-

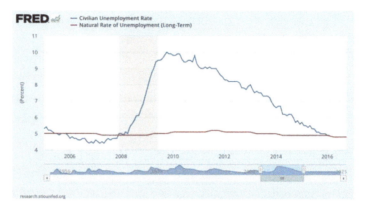

Figure 4.4 Civilian Unemployment Rate
Source: Federal Reserve Bank of St. Louis

nied credit?

Let's turn to the workings of the financial system and seek answers to some of the questions we have posed that concern this extraordinary period in U.S. economic history.

4.2   The Changing Nature of Financial Institutions

For more than two decades, the rapid pace of new information technology fueled financial innovations and the need for many financial institutions to change their delivery of financial services. Many of the Depression-era laws designed to limit competition and risk-taking among financial institutions became largely anachronistic as technology rendered them ineffective.

Policymakers responded by relying more heavily on discipline that a more competitive marketplace would bring to the management decisions of financial institutions. Financial innovations were encouraged, and many new financial assets came into being. They held out the promise of continual improvements in economic efficiency by providing financial intermediaries with new tools to manage risk. Within a short time span, a very large, lucrative segment of the financial services industry sprang up to develop an increasingly complex array of these interdependent financial assets, referred to as *financial derivatives*. However, many of these new financial derivatives were developed in markets with virtually no regulation, no oversight, and no coordination. As will become evident, their very complexity caused them ultimately to succumb to the hidden risks that linked many of them together, so-called *systemic risk*. Once this risk was exposed, the market for these assets began to collapse, their market value began to disappear, and the financial institutions that held them began to implode.

The Banking System

A place to begin is with the banking system and the housing market, and how financial derivatives tied to

the housing market were instrumental in precipitating
the financial crisis.

Asset Side	Liability Side
Assets	*Liabilities*
– Loans	– Deposits
– Investments	– Borrowings
– Other	*Bank Capital*
Total Assets	*Total Liabilities + Bank Capital*

Figure 4.5 Bank's Balance Sheet

While the details of bank balance sheets are described in detail later in subsequent chapters, consider
first the role that these depository institutions play in
the economy as *financial intermediaries*. They raise
most of their money in *deposit markets* by offering safe,
highly liquid, short-term savings assets from households and businesses. The relative safety and liquidity
causes interest rates on deposits to be low. These funds
are then aggregated up into larger less liquid and generally riskier loans and investments that pay a higher
rate of return to the bank.

Over time, a portion of the bank's earnings are reinvested which raises the net worth of the bank, i.e., the
difference between its assets and its liabilities, which
is referred to as *bank capital*. Bank capital plays an
important role in containing the risk that the bank in-
curs. For example, if the bank must "writeoff" an un-

collectible loan, then its assets shrink by the amount of the loan's outstanding balance. Since the bank's balance sheets must balance, this loss must be absorbed on the right-hand side of the balance sheet, and essentially comes out of the bank's capital account. This loss is therefore taken by the bank's owners, thus insulating the depositors' funds from the risks of assets going bad. Obviously, the more bank capital that the bank maintains, the better able it is to absorb the risk in the loans and investments that it makes without threatening depositors' funds. For this reason, a key regulation that banks face is referred to as capital requirements, whereby banks must maintain a certain amount of *bank capital* relative to the size and risk of their asset portfolio.

During the financial crisis that erupted in 2007, many banks found themselves with insufficient bank capital to absorb the massive defaults in their loans and investments that were tied to the housing market. Capital requirements are discussed at length in later chapters, but for now note that they have become a central feature of the recent reforms implemented by nations around the world in their efforts to avoid major financial crises in the future.

Mortgage Markets

Turn now to the mortgage markets, which played such a central role in the financial crisis. Most mortgages in the United States are originated by federally regulated depositories, i.e., commercial banks and savings and loans. These institutions have specialized in assessing the riskiness of the loans by analyzing the mortgage applicant's ability to repay, based on the applicant's salary, debt load, current expenditures and assets, and credit history. The terms of a *traditional mortgage* in the United States are that the borrower must make a minimum downpayment of 20 percent of the sale price and payoff the remainder plus interest – based on a fixed interest rate — on a declining balance as the loan is paid off over a thirty-year period. If the borrower fails to make the payments, the lender can foreclose on the mortgage, take ownership of the house, and place it back on the market.

Beginning in the 1980s, a new breed of mortgages began to appear, referred to as *subprime mortgages*. They were designed to make mortgages more readily available to those who didn't qualify for traditional mortgages. Their terms were very different. Requirements regarding the applicant's income, asset holdings, and credit history that reflect the ability to repay the loan were drastically relaxed. In addition many of the loans reduced the downpayment requirement, in some cases to zero. To keep the monthly payments low initially, so-called *teaser rates* were offered for the first few years of the contract, after which rates could rise dramatically. In addition, some *interest-only loans* were made, whereby the homeowner's monthly payments covered only the interest on the loan, so that no progress was made on reducing the principle and gaining equity in the house over time.

As house prices escalated during the bubble years of the latter part of the 20th century and the first few years of the 21st century, these loans grew in popularity. When the very mild recession hit in 2001, default rates on these loans increased sharply. However, once the economy recovered, subprime mortgages continued to increase their share of the overall mortgage market. Eventually, the housing market bubble burst in 2006, and the subsequent Great Recession caused this market to become extremely vulnerable to massive defaults and foreclosures.

An important question to ask is: were there other factors that spurred the growth of subprime mortgages? The answer is yes. These loans were encouraged by Congress in the hope of increasing home ownership in the United States. Also, interest rates had reached historic lows, placing the loans with reach to a wider range of borrowers. Capitalizing on the bubble, there was a rise in the number of *nonbank mortgage brokers* who failed to screen the loans as thoroughly as traditional bank lenders had done. Finally, there was an extraordinary expansion in the number and complexity of financial derivative contracts ultimately tied to the housing market that fueled the demand for subprime mortgages by financial engineers working in the *investment banking industry*, that we will describe in more

FACTORS CONTRIBUTING TO THE SPREAD
OF SUBPRIME MORTGAGES

Escalating House Prices (The Housing Bubble)
Federal Legislation Designed
to Increase Homeownership
Historically Low Interest Rates
Growth of Non-Traditional Mortgage Lenders
Growth of Financial Derivatives
based on Housing Market

Figure 4.6 The Spread of Subprime Mortgages

detail later, who designed these contracts.

Fannie, Freddie, and Ginnie

To understand the nature of these contracts, it is necessary to first go back to post-World War II America. After the war, there was a strong impetus for Congress to assist in making the American dream of homeownership come true for as many as possible. To achieve this lofty goal, it created three federal agencies: the Federal National Mortgage Association, known as *Fannie Mae*, the Federal Home Loan Mortgage Association, commonly called *Freddie Mac*, and the Government National Mortgage Association, or *Ginnie Mae.* These institutions were authorized to issue government-backed bonds and use the proceeds to purchase mortgages. The mortgage payments were then used to retire the bonds. The idea was to create a more liquid national mortgage market with lower mortgage rates, reflecting the fact that the government bonds were essentially default-free and therefore the lower cost to these agencies of raising money could be passed on to the homeowner.

Eventually, Fannie Mae and Freddie Mac were privatized, and they ultimately grew to hold either directly on indirectly over one-half of the mortgages in the U.S. housing market totaling approximately $7 trillion.[2] Ginnie Mae provides subsidies to low-income families and could not be eligible for privatization. As will become evident, Fannie and Freddie played a major role in the housing bubble and the financial crisis that ensued, as they became heavily involved in financial derivatives, eventually entering into bankruptcy and a takeover by the U.S. Government.

---

[2]The total volume of mortgages outstanding declined from its peak of approximately $14.8 trillion in 2008 in the early stages of the financial crisis to a low of about $13.2 trillion in 2013. It has since rebounded to approximately $14.4 trillion in 2017 as reported by the Federal Reserve.. See https://www.federalreserve.gov/econresdata/releases/mortoutst and/current.htm

Securitization

Traditionally, banks receive most of their income from interest earned on their loans and investments. A portion of this income is used to pay the interest on deposits with the remainder either paid out in dividends to the bank's shareholders or reinvested in new loans and investments.

In recent years, banks began to *securitize* a number of their assets, by which they would pool together a collection of similar assets and sell them to an entity created within the bank, referred to as a *special purpose vehicle* or *SPV*, that issues bonds and uses the proceeds to purchase the pool of assets. In the case of mortgages, the mortgage payments are then pledged to the investors who purchased the bonds, thereby enabling the SPV to retire the bonds.

The benefit to the bank is that it has therefore removed these risky assets from its balance sheet and acquired funds from their sale to make additional investments. Normally, the bank will also retain the servicing rights on the mortgages, whereby it processes the mortgage payments and collects the servicing fees. These bonds issued by the SPV are referred to as *mortgage-backed securities* or *MBSs*, reflecting the fact that their underlying value is tied to the mortgages, which in turn take their value from the houses that the mortgages were used to purchase. Fannie Mae and Freddie Mac also engaged in extensive securitization of their enormous mortgage portfolio by selling MBSs mostly to institutional investors, including commercial banks.

The simplest form of an MBS is a so-called *pass-through MBS*, in which the investors evenly split the mortgage payments on the entire pool of mortgages, referred to as the *portfolio collateral*, and hence equally share in the risk that some portion of the original mortgages will go into default.

It is worth noting that while mortgages form the portfolio collateral for many financial derivatives such as MBSs, they represent only a portion of the portfolio collateral behind a wide range of other financial derivatives that is more generally referred to as *asset-backed securities*, or *ABSs*, many of which derive their value from such financial assets as student loans, home equity loans, auto loans, etc. For now, the focus will be on the financial derivatives based on mortgages as the underlying asset.

Collateralized Mortgage Obligation (CMO)

In the 1980s, a variant of these MBSs came into popularity. It is referred to as a *collateralized mortgage obligation* or *CMO*. It differs in the manner in which the mortgage payments are distributed by creating a set of assets referred to as *tranches* as shown in Figure 4.7, that are differentiated by the priority of claims on the mortgage payments that each possesses. Essentially, the owners of the *high priority tranche* must be paid off first, before any payments are made to the owners of the *medium priority tranche*, who in turn must be paid before any funds are made available to owners of the *low priority tranche*. Obviously, when there are missed mortgage payments the first group of investors to realize the loss is the owners of the low priority tranche. They therefore carry the highest risk with the highest expected rate of return, while the owners of the high priority tranche carry the lowest risk and the lowest expected rate of return.

This financial derivative product has significant economic advantages. It takes a group of risky assets, i.e., the mortgages, and creates three new assets with different risk properties that are then made available to investors. Of course, high risk means high expected rate of return. Investors can therefore choose the amount of risk that they wish to assume in accordance with their own tolerance for risk. This feature of the CMO adds efficiency to the credit markets and can also increase the demand for mortgages overall by giving investors a wider range of assets with different risk-return characteristics from which to choose.

Collateralized Debt Obligation (CDO)

While the portfolio collateral for a CMO is exclusively comprised of a pool of mortgages, a more complicated financial derivative referred to as a *collateralized debt obligation* or *CDO* may have portfolio collateral that

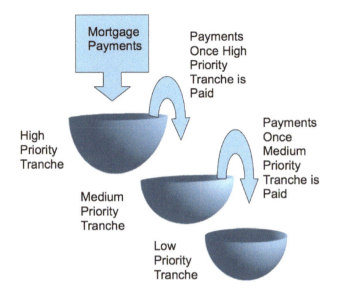

Figure 4.7 Collateralized Mortgage Obligations (CMOs)

consists of pools of various tranches of CMOs, or even of other CDOs. Here is where the lack of transparency in these extremely complicated financial products led to their label during the financial crisis as toxic assets. Essentially a *toxic asset* is one for which a price cannot readily be determined and therefore there is no significant market for the asset.

Consider an example of a complicated toxic asset that was very prevalent during the heady days leading

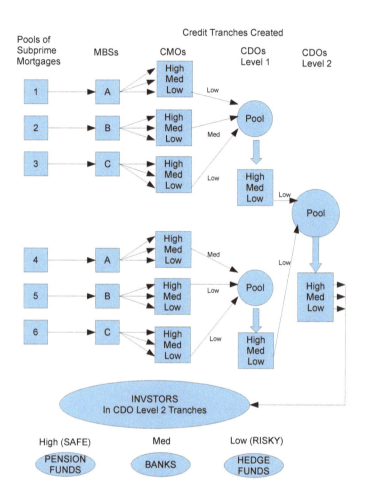

Figure 4.8 Complexity of CDOs

up to the financial crisis. The construction of this asset is displayed in Figure 4.8.

Begin with six different pools of subprime mortgages that are divided up into two separate groups. On each of these pools, pass-through MBS, labeled A through C in each group, are then written. Now suppose that an analyst at an investment bank begins constructing CMOs with various tranches of each of the MBSs in the first group based on the mortgage pools 1-3. Segments of these tranches are then sold to another investment bank that purchases a low tranche from the A and C CMOs and a medium tranche from the B CMO.

This investment bank in turn pools these assets and creates a CDO with high, medium, and low tranches, labeled CDO Level 1. While this is underway, other investment banks were engaging in precisely the same exercise with the underlying pools of subprime mortgages numbered 4 through 6, ultimately arriving at their CDO Level 1.

Finally, another investment bank purchases the low tranche from each of these Level 1 CDOs and creates a new Level 2 CDO and sells the high tranche to a pension fund seeking relative safety, the medium tranche to a bank willing to accept a little more risk, and the low tranche to a hedge fund seeking to reach out to the high risk assets in the hopes of realizing a high rate of return on its investment.

Think about what has been created. Out of a set

of very risky subprime mortgages, a wide range of investors have each attempted get a piece of the return while controlling their individual risk. However, when the subprime mortgage market began to collapse and many of these underlying mortgages began to fail, the task of unraveling who has claims to what became an almost impossible task. Many of the ultimate investors sought to sell the assets and avoid the uncertainty, but failed to find any buyers. There was simply no way to determine a market value for the CDOs, and investors were stuck with nearly valueless toxic assets.

It should be emphasized that this example merely scratches the surface of the complexity of many of the CDOs that were actually created and the volume of these assets was astounding.

Credit Default Swaps (CDS)

To gain some protection against possible default on these very complex assets, many investors sought to purchase insurance whereby they could obtain the value of the assets in the event of default. These contracts are known as *credit default swaps* or *CDSs*.

CDSs can play a useful economic role. Suppose for example that you are managing a pension fund and you purchase a corporate bond from a prominent business, such as GM. Your fiduciary responsibilities prohibit you from buying a bond that has a low credit rating. Suppose that after you purchase the bond, Standard

& Poor's or Moody's downgrades the bond to below investment grade. You have two options. You can sell the bond, in which case you will realize a loss, since the bond's price will fall with the downgrade, or you can hold on to the bond and purchase a CDS from an insurer, thereby shifting the risk of the default from that of GM to that of the insurer, since the insurer must be able to pay off in the event that GM defaults on the bond. If the insurer's bond rating is sufficiently high, then you can maintain your ownership of the GM bond and avoid the fire sale, but at a cost of periodic insurance premiums paid to the insurer.

However, CDSs differ in significant ways from a straight insurance contract. First, to take out insurance you must legally have an *insurable interest* in whatever it is that you are insuring. You cannot take out fire insurance on your neighbor's house, for example. However, CDSs can be taken out by an individual who has *NO* insurable interest in the financial asset that is being insured. Such a contract is referred to as a *naked CDS*. Why would an individual purchase a naked CDS? The answer is *pure speculation*. This investor is guessing that the asset will go into default, in which case he receives the value of the asset specified in the CDS contract. If the asset does not go into default, then the investor loses everything he paid to the issuer of the CDS.

A second major difference between a CDS and a standard insurance contract is that the insurance com-

panies issuing insurance contracts are heavily regulated
and must maintain adequate reserves to meet anticipated insurance losses. This was not the case with
CDSs during the early days of the financial crisis, and
this feature of the CDS market further exacerbated the
financial crisis that ultimately led to the demise of some
of the oldest financial institutions in the country.

4.3   The Financial Crisis Unfolds

We are ready now to take a look at how financial derivatives tied to the housing market ultimately became the
financial weapons of mass destruction, as the legendary
investor Warren Buffet pronounced them years before
their markets imploded and the financial crisis erupted
in full bloom.[3] While this crisis took us to the brink of
a worldwide meltdown that had the potential to rival
the worst days of the Great Depression, we were fortu-
nate that the Federal Reserve and, with Congressional
approval, the Treasury Department took extraordinary
and unprecedented actions to soften the impact of what

---

[3] This reference came in his annual newsletter to shareholders in Berkshire Hathaway in 2003, as reported by Fortune Maga-
zine (and the BBC News) in which he colorfully described financial derivatives as contracts apparently written by "madmen"
that are similar to "hell, easy to enter, but nearly impossible to
exit."

would still become the worst economic recession in 75 years.

Systemic Risk and Too Big To Fail

The credit crisis of 2007-2008 was touched off by the collapse of the subprime mortgage market in the United States. This collapse burst the housing bubble, and as house prices began their sharp decline, the crisis began to spread throughout the world's financial system on the wings of financial derivatives such as MBSs, CMOs, CDOs, and CDSs, that we described above. Financial institutions with a large exposure to the subprime mortgage market were the first to fail.

In the wake of those bankruptcies, other healthier institutions that had credit arrangements through these failing institutions saw their balance sheets weakened and found themselves locked out of the credit markets. Lending dried up. Banks could no longer borrow from other banks; households and nonfinancial businesses could no longer get credit from lending institutions. The only assets that were in high demand were U.S. and Japanese government debt that were the safe havens to which investors around the world were flocking.

This freezing up of the credit markets, with its potential to bring down many other financial institutions worldwide, is an example of what is referred to as *systemic risk* and is often hidden within the interlinkages of financial institutions' obligations to one another. It is an important consideration in the government's regulation of the financial markets and financial institutions. Could one event, such as the collapse of a single market or the bankruptcy of a single firm, cascade throughout the financial markets and threaten the viability of the entire financial system? For example, a failing institution has liabilities that it can no longer honor. Those liabilities are assets to other financial institutions which then must be written off. This writeoff strains the resources of those institutions and puts its liabilities – which again are assets to yet other financial institutions – in jeopardy, and the financial web of credit arrangements among these institutions continues to unravel.

The threat of such catastrophic eventualities presents regulators of financial institutions with perhaps their most difficult decisions: Should a large financial institution be allowed to enter bankruptcy when there is the potential that its strategic relationships with other financial institutions could lead to systemic failures that threaten a financial collapse? Or, should the institution be bailed out by the government and allowed to survive, thus encouraging excessive risk-taking among other financial institutions? We will return to two important related questions that are at the heart of regulatory reform in the wake of the recent crisis: Which financial institutions should be considered *too big to fail*? How should they be regulated?

Investment Banking

Prior to the onset of the financial crisis, there were five large U.S. *investment banks* with worldwide operations: Goldman Sachs, Merrill Lynch, Morgan Stanley, Lehman Brothers and Bear Stearns. These were at the center of the financial implosion and today, none of these firms survive as a stand alone investment bank. Their fates will be examined, but first it is necessary to explain the important difference between an investment bank and a commercial bank.

Investment banks differ from commercial banks in terms of their assets, their source of funds, and the regulations that govern them. As previously stated, commercial banks derive most of their funds from deposit accounts that are federally insured. As a consequence of providing this insurance, the federal government imposes a strict set of regulations on the banks to ensure that they avoid excessive risk taking.

Commercial banks typically have so-called *leverage ratios*, or the value of their loans and investments divided by their capital reserves of roughly 10 to 1, suggesting that for every 10 dollars that is in a bank's loans and investments portfolios, it borrows 9 dollars in the form of deposits and other borrowings.

Investment banks perform a number of important functions in the economy. Essentially they serve as consultants to large corporations and start-up companies desiring to raise money in the capital markets. They advise firms on how best to raise these funds, i.e., whether to issue stock or bonds, and at what price. They often underwrite new securities of firms, thereby guaranteeing the price at which new issues will be sold into the market. They help new companies with their initial public offerings (IPOs) of stock, and investment banks also advise firms on mergers and acquisitions and will actively manage their clients' investments on their behalf.

However, in the years leading up to the financial crisis, investment banks became very active in managing investments for their own accounts, and these investments grew into an extremely lucrative business on the backs of the mushrooming volume of financial derivatives that would ultimately spell their demise.

The severity of the risk they were taking was compounded by the typical leverage ratios for investment banks of approximately 30-35 to 1. Yet, since they held no insured deposits, their chief regulator, the *Securities and Exchange Commission, or SEC*, did not subject them the same strict regulations faced by commercial banks.

In good economic times, investment banks can be highly profitable enterprises by investing in relatively risky, high-return assets with very liquid, short-term, low-interest borrowings, much of which consists of overnight loans. Importantly, these profits are significantly increased with very high leverage ratios. However, in weak economic times, imprudent management decisions can quickly transform large profits into equally large losses and even threaten the viability of the firm.

The Demise of the Large Investment Banks

The first investment bank to come to the brink of failure was Bear Stearns. It had worldwide investments of over $400 billion with many major financial institutions who were creditors to Bear, and as with most investment banks, a major source of funds was overnight loans. During the boom years, when subprime mortgages were rapidly proliferating, Bear was among the many financial institutions that invested aggressively in MBSs, CMOs, and CDOs tied to the subprime mortgage market.

In March 2008, rumors began to circulate that Bear was in trouble with an asset portfolio that was bloated with toxic assets. Many of its creditors in the overnight lending market, as well as its long-term investors, began to pull their money out, and as Bear's stock price tumbled, the flight of funding from Bear accelerated. In just a matter of days, this venerable institution that had been operating since 1923 was on the verge of collapse, as it faced a *bank run*, with many of its major creditors refusing to renew their overnight lending, and Bear was stuck with a portfolio of toxic assets for which there was no market.

In response, the Federal Reserve engineered a "shotgun marriage" between Bear Stearns and its lead commercial bank JP Morgan Chase. Essentially the Federal Reserve made a large loan to JP Morgan Chase to purchase Bear Stearns for approximately $2 per share. Just one year earlier, Bear's stock price stood at $160.

The scenario with Bear played out again, first with Lehman Brothers and then with Merril Lynch. When Lehman, with worldwide assets totaling $691 billion, was on the brink, the Federal Reserve and the Treasury Department sought suitors to purchase the firm, but the subprime mortgage market had dramatically worsened and no buyer could be found. This time, Lehman was seen to have such a weak balance sheet that it was deemed by the Federal Reserve and the Treasury Department to be too far gone, with nothing much left to save, and on September 15, 2008, Lehman filed for bankruptcy. On this very day, Merrill Lynch, also on the brink of collapse, was sold to Bank of America in another fire sale.

This event came to be known as *Lehman Day*. It signaled that the Federal Reserve and the Treasury were not always going to bail out large, troubled financial institutions and it had international repercussions with investors pulling assets first out of the remaining two big investment banks, then spreading to virtually all segments of the stock market, which within a week had fallen by more than 40 percent.

Goldman Sachs and Morgan Stanley were still left standing, but were also seeing a flight of funds from creditors. To forestall bank runs similar to what Bear,

Lehman, and Merrill had experienced, they applied for and were expeditiously granted a change in their charters from investment banks to commercial banks. Under these terms, they would have to abide by the stricter regulations imposed by the Federal Reserve. However, this change enabled them to attract federally insured deposits and shore up their funding source. They also had access to lending facilities at the Federal Reserve, that acts as *lender of last resort* to its member banks. They were assisted with Federal Reserve loans as they began to reduce their leverage ratios from roughly 20-to-1 to the norm for commercial banks of 10-to-1. These provisions reassured Goldman's and Morgan's creditors of the security of their investments, and the withdrawals were halted. However, there were then no longer any large stand alone investment banks operating in the United States.

The Collapse of Fannie and Freddie

There were two other important actors in the financial crisis who played a role in spreading the risk of financial derivatives. The first is the group of *credit rating agencies*, the largest of which are Moody's, Standard and Poor's, and Fitch, whose job it is to assess the level of risk associated with various debt securities. During the boom years that preceded the financial crisis, these credit rating agencies failed to properly evaluate the risk of CMOs, CDOs, and the debt of financial firms with large exposure to what ultimately became unmarketable toxic assets. Many of these securities received ratings of AA – nearly as high as the AAA rating given to U.S. Government debt.[4]

This false assessment of the level of risk of these financial derivatives fueled their creation, as investors were attracted to their high returns for what seemed to be relatively low levels of risk. Large institutional investors whose fiduciary responsibilities preclude them from investing in assets with less than investment grade ratings (of Baa or BBB or higher) also eagerly sought these assets and acquisitions of them began to spread globally. Once the true nature of the risk inherent in these assets began to be revealed, investors quickly tried to unload them on the open market, and their price fell dramatically, as their markets began to dry up.

The second major player that exacerbated the financial crisis was AIG, the largest insurance company in the world. However, AIG is actually comprised of four separate businesses: insurance, management of pension funds, an airline leasing business, and finally an internal investment house. The last of these businesses became a huge profit center for AIG during the pre-crisis boom years, just as it had been for the big investment banks, with massive investments in financial derivatives.

---

[4]The credit ratings are discussed in more detail in a subsequent chapter.

In addition, AIG became the largest supplier of CDSs to firms wishing to hedge their investments in these untested financial products, many of which relied on portfolio collateral that was largely comprised of subprime mortgages. At the time, CDSs were new, unregulated financial assets, and AIG failed on its own to retain adequate capital reserves against the prospects of losses when the housing market began to collapse. When AIG received downgrades on its debt from the credit rating agencies, it could no longer raise funds in the capital markets, and was the subject of a run, as creditors began to withdraw their funds.

In October, 2008, the Federal Reserve, with the support of the Treasury Department, ultimately took ownership of 79.9 percent of AIG's stock and injected $85 billion into the firm. This injection proved to be inadequate, and another infusion of $100 billion was required in March 2009. On both occasions, the stock market took a dive. The economy was in the depths of the Great Recession.

4.4 Troubled Asset Relief Program (TARP)

When the crisis first began to unfold in 2007, Congress, at the request of the Bush Administration, authorized the Treasury Department to spend up to $700 billion in a *Troubled Asset Relief Program* (known by its acronym as *TARP*) to deal with the financial crisis. The original objective was to use those funds to buy toxic assets from the financial firms that possessed them, and thereby preclude the need for investors to withdraw their funds from these institutions due to the weakness that the toxic assets were creating in their portfolios.

The banking system was clearly at the center of the financial crisis and represented the greatest threat to financial stability. During the waning months of the Bush Administration, the largest of these banks were targeted to receive injections of TARP money in the form of collateralized loans to beef up their bank capital. The idea was not only to provide funds needed to absorb assets that would likely have to be written off as uncollectible, but also to restore confidence in the banking system and preclude a bank run.

One indication of how dire the situation had become is the dramatic increase in the number of *bank failures* during the crisis. As seen in Figure 4.9, there were no bank failures during the boom years of 2005 and 2006 and only 3 in 2007. However, this number increased to 25 in 2008, 140 in 2009, and 157 in 2010, before beginning to subside as the crisis eased. By 2015, this number had dwindled to less than 10 per year.

It should be noted that as of 2016, of the $700 billion in TARP money authorized by Congress,[5] only

---

[5]This figure was later reduced to $475 billion in 2010 under

Date	Number
2005 and 2006	0
2007	3
2008	25
2009	140
2010	157
2011	34
2012	51
2013	24
2014	18
2015	8
2016	5
Jan-July, 2017	6

Figure 4.9 Bank Failures in the United States
Source: Federal Deposit Insurance Corporation

about $445 billion was actually projected by the Congressional Budget Office (or CBO) as of July 2017 to be spent, and most of it went to capitalizing the banks and other firms weakened by the financial crisis. Of the $438 billion already spent, $377 billion had been

the financial reform legislation known as Dodd-Frank, which is described in detail in the next section.

repaid and $61 billion was written off as uncollectible.

After all is said and done, the net cost to taxpayers of the massive federal program is projected by the CBO to have been $33 billion or only approximately $100 per person. It could be argued that this is a very small price to pay for the benefits it bestowed on the economy in terms of stabilizing the financial system that was in freefall.

Here is a closer look at the major sources of projected costs to the government, net of repayments:

- $15 billion for the AIG bailout

- $12 billion to the auto industry

- $33 billion to assist homeowners in avoiding foreclosures.

All other expenditure categories associated with TARP yielded profits to the government, with aid to commercial banks accounting for $24 billion in profits. What is often referred to as a "federal bailout of the banks" could alternatively be characterized as a large volume of emergency loans to the banks that was repaid in full with interest. Moreover, when the support to homeowners that enabled them to remain in their homes and avoid foreclosure is subtracted from the remaining net costs of TARP, the remaining net cost to taxpayers of this enormous federal program drops to zero!

4.5 The Path to Normalcy in a New Regulatory Environment

The TARP funds were employed by the Bush and Obama Administrations in confronting the immediate task of stemming the tide of events away from an impending collapse of the worldwide financial system. It was indeed that serious. While there are debates about how well their efforts worked, the worst case scenario was definitely avoided. A principal player in these efforts was the Federal Reserve, and in subsequent chapters we'll discuss how its unprecedented actions were crucial in steering the credit markets back to a state of normalcy, so that the economy could begin its long road to recovery.

However, once the period of crisis came to end in 2009, the Administration and Congress had to shift their attention toward developing long-range plans that would ward off a recurrence of future crises similar to what had precipitated the longest, deepest recession since the Great Depression of the 1930s. Here is how that effort unfolded.

Shortly after taking office, President Obama put forward a set of guidelines that was intended to achieve the following four major objectives designed to deal with the major issues that arose during the financial crisis.

1. Develop a system of oversight that would focus on potential threats to financial market stability before they developed.

2. Enhance consumer protection in financial market dealings.

3. Strengthen regulations on lightly or unregulated financial markets and institutions whose activities were seen to have contributed to the financial crisis.

4. Achieve greater transparency in the actions of financial market participants and in financial contracts and accounting practices.

In July 2010, after extensive hearings and vast amounts of testimony in both the House and Senate, Congress passed the *Dodd-Frank Wall Street Reform and Consumer Protection Act,* commonly known as *Dodd-Frank* after its co-sponsors Senator Christopher Dodd and Representative Barney Frank. This bill ushered in the most sweeping changes to the regulation and oversight of the financial markets and financial institutions in 75 years.[6] The goal of the bill was to provide the template

---

[6]The importance of this bill is reflected in the many summaries of its major provisions on line, including those by the American Bankers Association and Harvard Law School, with the full text including a detailed Congressional summary available at https://www.congress.gov/bill/111th-congress/house-bill/04173.

for achieving financial reform while leaving the details to be worked out by the regulators themselves who have the necessary knowledge to implement the bill's provisions in the most efficient and effective manner.

1. Create the *Consumer Financial Protection Bureau (CFPB)*

   - This bureau is to have an independent director appointed by the President and confirmed by the Senate.

   - The bureau is housed in the Federal Reserve, but is not accountable to the Federal Reserve. It retains independence in carrying out its mandate of establishing and enforcing regulations associated with consumer financial protection.

   - Its function is to examine and enforce consumer protection legislation over all large financial and non-financial firms (with assets over $10B) that are involved in consumer lending by consolidating regulatory oversight previously granted to:

     - Comptroller of the Currency (principal regulator of federally chartered banks)
     - Office of Thrift Supervision (now defunct, principal regulator of S&Ls)
     - Federal Deposit Insurance Corporation (FDIC)

- Federal Reserve
- National Credit Union Administration (principal regulator of Credit Unions)
- Federal Trade Commission (FTC, key agency charged with investigating consumer fraud)

2. Create the *Financial Stability Oversight Council (FSOC)*

- Composition of the Council
  - Chair: Treasury Secretary
  - 9 members drawn from:
    * Federal Reserve
    * Security and Exchange Commission (SEC, principal regulator of the stock and bond markets)
    * Commodity Futures Trading Commission (CFTC) principal regulator of the futures and options markets
    * Federal Deposit Insurance Corporation (FDIC)
    * The recently created Federal Housing Finance Agency (FHFA) that the oversees activities in the housing market, and is currently the government's conservator over Fannie Mae and Freddie Mac

- Their principal responsibility is to monitor developments in the financial markets and identify any potential "systemic risk" problems that could produce instability in the financial system.

- The FSOC then plays an advisory role in which it makes recommendations to the Federal Reserve for increasingly strict rules for suspect firms by raising minimum capital requirements, additional set-aside provisions for adequate liquidity, and the need for enhanced risk management practices on the part of the institutions.

- They are authorized to approve (with 2/3 vote) extending Federal Reserve regulations to non-bank financial firms, if they pose a threat to financial stability (e.g., AIG)

3. Dodd-Frank confronts for perhaps the first time in our nation's history the problem of firms that are deemed to be *Too Big To Fail* labeled *Systemically Important Financial Institutions (SIFI)*.

- One part of the original Dodd-Frank Act was intended to limit the risk taken on by commercial banks by restricting their activities such that they cannot engage many of the riskier investment banking activities. The provision is known as the *Volcker Rule*, named after its influential advocate Paul Volcker, who was a former Chair of the Federal Reserve. It included a prohibition against commercial banks engaging in:

- proprietary *"in-house" trading activities*
- investing in *"hedge funds"*
- investing in *"venture capital"*

These investment banking activities had been off limits to commercial banks under the so-called *Glass-Steagal Act* that was passed in 1933 following the Great Depression. It was "in-house" trading activities in particular that was seen at that time to have contributed to the near collapse of the banking system, as the stock market crash drastically reduced the value of the banks' assets, which at that time could be comprised of corporate stock. Glass-Steagal was repelled in the 1980s as it was generally seen to be an outdated prohibition that posed an undue burden on U.S. commericial banks, since their counterparts in other Western industrialized countries were under no such restriction. However, in the recent recession, it was financial derivatives, particularly related to the housing market that were seen to be the major contributor to weakness in the asset portfolios of many of the nation's major banks.

- The too-big-to-fail problem, of course, extends beyond the banking system. Therefore, Dodd-Frank permits the banking rules to be extended to non-bank financial firms that are seen to threaten the stability of the financial system.

- Another important provision has come to be known as the *Funeral Plans*.

  - Large, complex companies must submit plans for an orderly shut down of their operations, if they were to fail.

  - Sanctions (in the form higher capital requirements, etc.) would be imposed on companies that do not present acceptable plans

  - A *liquidation procedure* for bankrupt SIFI firms must also be developed. The procedure must be agreed by the Treasury Department, the FDIC, and the Federal Reserve and would be Implemented by the FDIC.

  - Dodd-Frank also requires that an industry-based fund that is capitalized by the SIFI firms be established to absorb losses of liquidated firms.

  - Finally, the legislation extends the Federal Reserve's role as "lender of last resort" to support financial firms during

"destabilizing events" but not to prop
up failing institutions.

4. To deal with the issue of *greater transparency
and accountability* of financial derivatives, these
financial products will now come under the Regulatory purview of the SEC and CFTC that will
have authority to regulate trading activities in financial derivatives that are currently unregulated
(such as CDOs and CDSs). In addition:

- financial derivatives will be traded on organized exchanges and cleared at a centralized
  clearing house (such as the *Chicago Board
  of Trade*), thus enabling knowledge of the
  market transactions to be recorded.

- *margin requirements* will be imposed on un-
  cleared trades to prevent the use of excessive
  leverage.

- *swap dealers* and other market participants
  will be subject to capital requirements.

- to enhance transparency, data collection and
  publication will be provided by the clearing
  houses to market participants and to regulators.

5. Securitization became an important issue during the financial crisis, with mortgage originators having the incentive to create volume in the

mortgages without concern for the ability of those receiving the mortgage to repay the loan. Under Dodd-Frank, mortgage originators must:

- maintain some *"Skin in the Game."* That is, the originators of MBSs and other mortgage-related financial products must maintain a minimum of 5 percent credit risk in those financial instruments.

- provide greater disclosure of information needed to analyze the quality of the assets and their inherent risk.

6. *Hedge funds* had previously become a growing and lightly regulated industry that was heavily involved in trading mortgage-related financial derivatives. Dodd-Frank:

- required them to register with the SEC for the first time.

- required them to report trading activities and portfolio holdings to the SEC, which is information to be shared with regulators (particularly the FSOC) and Congress.

- gave states the responsibility for regulating smaller hedge funds, but the size limit is raised from the current $25 million in assets under management to $100 million (which will substantially increase the workload for state regulators).

7. *Credit rating agencies* which failed to adequately assess the risk of many financial derivative products allowing them to proliferate worldwide, will now come under greater scrutiny. An *Office of Credit Ratings* was created and housed within the SEC to oversee activities of the sanctioned credit rating agencies (the so-called Nationally Recognized Statistical Ratings Organizations, NRSROs).

- These NRSROs must report for the time:
    - their methodologies used in obtaining ratings.
    - the use of 3rd party information in ratings.
    - their track record for the ratings (that is, how good they have been).

- NRSROs can be *deregistered* by the SEC for a poor ratings history, which effectively excludes them from selling their ratings, since they cannot be used by firms who NRSRO ratings to issue new debt instruments.

- Individuals are allowed to take legal action against the ratings agencies if they can prove "reckless conduct" or "willful misrepresentation in their ratings" that led to financial losses for the individual.

- NRSROs must also require their ratings analysts to pass qualifying exams.

8. The final set of provisions in Dodd-Frank was designed to strengthen the Federal Reserve's role as a chief regulator of the financial system.

   - The Federal Reserve became the principal regulator over *large, complex financial firms*, the SIFIs, whose operations could pose a *systemic risk* to financial stability.

   - A new "Vice Chair for Supervision" on the Federal Reserve's Board of Governors was created to be appointed by the President and confirmed by the Senate. He or she is charged with:
       - developing policy recommendations for supervision and regulation for the banks.
       - reporting to Congress semi-annually.

   - Given the expanded regulatory powers of the Federal Reserve, Congress felt it necessary to increase oversight over their activities. It added two new provisions:
       - Due to the special roles played by the Federal Reserve Bank of New York within the Federal Reserve System, the President of the Federal Reserve Bank of New York will now be appointed by the President and confirmed by the Senate rather than by the Bank?s directors.
       - The *Government Accounting Office (GAO)* is authorized to audit any emergency

lending facility operated by the Federal
Reserve. As we will describe in detail
later in the course, these facilities played
an extremely important role in the Federal Reserve's response to the frozen credit
markets? during the financial crisis.

Many of the provisions of Dodd-Frank have been
implemented, while others are still under debate. As
their costs and benefits are analyzed, and the financial
system continues to evolve, refinements of the bill will
inevitably be made.

4.6   Summary

Much has been learned and much more will be learned
from the financial crisis and the Great Recession of
2007-2009 that ensued. One thing is perfectly clear.
A healthy, dynamic, and growing economy is fundamentally dependent upon a stable, efficient, and well-
regulated financial sector. However, changing technology and financial innovation will always alter the financial landscape and regulators must be alert to their
consequences. Monitoring these developments and designing appropriate regulations in the future that maintain the proper balance between economic efficiency
and financial stability in a world economy, where international financial linkages are becoming stronger and

deeper every year will be the challenge that future policymakers will have to face.

This chapter provides many of the details of how the financial crisis unfolded and what some of the major steps taken by the government were in response. It then described the major proposed changes to the structure of the U.S. financial regulations contained in the 848-page legislation known as Dodd-Frank. This legislation represents the most sweeping changes that have been undertaken since the 1930s, and affects nearly every facet of the financial system in the United States. Obviously, many of its provisions were controversial and implementation of them, some of which are extraordinarily complicated, have not come quickly.

Omitted in this chapter is a discussion of the critical role played by the Federal Reserve in its response to the financial crisis, in which it took unprecedented actions in attempting to restore normalcy to the financial markets that were so shaken by a series of events that took the entire financial system to the brink of collapse. Those actions will be explained in detail in a subsequent chapter. First, it is necessary lay the ground work for that discussion by providing a more complete description of the workings of the financial markets and institutions that comprise the financial system in which all of us participate on a daily basis.

4.7 Appendix: Consumer Financial Protection Bureau: "Ability-to-Repay"

The housing market played a central role in precipitating the Great Recession of 2007-2009. Hundreds of thousands of mortgages were originated by banks and other mortgage lenders and mortgage brokers for which there was little prospect that the loans would ever be repaid. These free-wheeling lending practices fueled the housing bubble with the subsequent buying frenzy that drove house prices up to unsustainable levels, while vastly expanding the inventory of new houses. When the housing bubble burst, house prices tumbled and loan defaults multiplied, with one-in-three homeowners finding themselves "underwater" on their homes, owing more than their house was worth.

As part of the Dodd-Frank Act passed by Congress in 2010, mortgage lenders were to be made legally responsible for adequately screening applicants to ensure they have the means to handle their loan payments. The newly created Consumer Financial Protection Bureau (CFPB) was tasked with designing the rules that govern this "ability-to-repay" mandate imposed on future mortgage originations. In January, 2013, the CFPB announced the new rules that took effect in January, 2014, that set out guidelines for future lending practices while recognizing the current state of the mortgage market, and the need to deal with past abuses.

Lenders should consider for each potential borrower the following underwriting standards when originating mortgage loans:

1. current or reasonably expected income or assets,

2. curent employment status,

3. the monthly payment on the new loan,

4. the monthly payment on any existing loans,

5. the monthly payment for mortgage-related obligations, such as mortgage insurance or property taxes,

6. current debt obligations, alimony, and child support,

7. the monthly debt-to-income ratio (or residual income), and

8. credit history

However, in recent years, many loans were made with low initial monthly payments that were later adjusted upward. These practices often caused homeowners to face higher future payments that they were not prepared to meet. To deal with the numerous unconventional loans that have been the principal source of foreclosures, the CFPB issued the following set of rules:

1. Monthly payments must now be calculated by assuming that the loan is repaid in "substantially equal monthly payments." This ruling introduces special "calculation rules" that affect all adjustable-rate mortgages, including loans with balloon payments (where the loan must be completely paid off or refinanced at a specified future date), interest-only payments (where no payments are made against the principal of the loan), and negative amortization (where the monthly payment is less than the interest owed, with the difference added to the principal of the loan).

2. Special rules are laid out to encourage the conversion of non-standard mortgages of the type listed in item (1) to standard mortgages with fixed rates for at least 5 years with reduced monthly payments.

The CFPB's new rules affect what are termed "qualified" mortgages. It is expected that nearly all new mortgages will be "qualified" since this designation tends to shield lenders from possible lawsuits by homeowners who default on their mortgage with the claim that the lender violated the "ability-to-repay" mandate in the Dodd-Frank Act.

1. Subprime ("higher-priced") loans that carry higher interest rates than the standard qualified loans (with criteria described below) are more clearly spelled out under the new rules. Unlike standard "qualified loans," for which the lender cannot be sued for failing to meet the "ability-to-repay" mandate, guidelines are provided for legal recourse by borrowers. They must show that at the time the loan was originated the consumer's income and debt obligations (of which the lender was made aware) did not leave sufficient income or assets to meet living expenses.

2. Mortgages with interest-only payments, balloon payments, or negative amortization and with terms exceeding 30 years are prohibited.

3. "No-doc" loans, where the lender fails to verify income or employment status, are prohibited.

4. Points and fees on "qualified mortgages" (with specific guidelines for their calculation) cannot exceed 3 percent of the total loan amount (with some exemptions for prime loans).

5. Monthly payments are based on the highest payment that will apply in the first five years of the loan.

6. The consumer will have a maximum monthly recurring debt payments-to-income ratio of 43 percent.

Finally, the housing market traditionally plays a central role in recoveries from economic recessions. However, despite considerable evidence that the housing market was "on the mend," it was perceived by the CFPB to be in a "fragile state" of recovery at the time the new rules were written. Consequently, the CFPB wanted to avoid the possibility that these new standards would increase the reluctance of lenders to make loans that could not meet the criteria for "qualified mortgages," despite the fact that they may be adequately unwritten. Therefore, a second, temporary category of qualified mortgages was also established with more flexibility, provided the loans remain eligible to be purchased, guaranteed, or insured by either Fannie Mae or Freddie Mac while they are under the conservatorship of the Federal government, or by the U.S. Department of Housing and Urban Development, Department of Veterans Affairs, or the Department of Agriculture or Rural Housing Service. This provision was to be phased out within seven years.

Key Terms

Great Depression
financial innovation
financial services industry
housing bubble
macroeconomy
S&P 500 stock market index
Case-Shiller House Price Index
Consumption expenditures
GDP
household net worth
bank capital
subprime mortgages
teaser rates
interest-only loans
nonbank mortgage brokers
Fannie Mae
Freddie Mac
Ginnie Mae
special purpose vehicle or SPV
mortgage-backed securities or MBSs
pass-through MBS
portfolio collateral
collateralized mortgage obligation or CMO
high priority tranche
medium priority tranche
low priority tranche
collateralized debt obligation or CDO
toxic asset

credit default swaps or CDSs
naked CDS
pure speculation
financial weapons of mass destruction
too big to fail
investment banks
leverage ratio
Securities and Exchange Commission (SEC)
Federal Housing Finance Agency (FHFA)
Troubled Asset Relief Program (TARP)
Dodd-Frank Wall Street Reform and Consumer Protection Act of 2010 (Dodd-Frank)
Consumer Financial Protection Bureau (CFPB)
Financial Stability Oversight Council (FSOC)
Systemically Important Financial Institutions (SIFI)
"in-house" trading activities
hedge funds
venture capital
Glass-Steagal Act (1933)
Funeral Plans
liquidation procedure
greater transparency and accountability
Chicago Board of Trade
margin requirements
swap dealers
Skin in the Game
credit rating agencies
Office of Credit Ratings

Nationally Recognized Statistical Ratings Organizations (NRSROs)

deregistered

large, complex financial firms

systemic risk

Vice Chair for Supervision

Government Accounting Office (GAO)

4.8 Review Questions

1. The collapse of the bubble in the housing market in the United States followed by the selloff in the stock market had a major effect on the U.S. economy in terms of economic growth and unemployment. Explain the linkage between them.

2. Explain the importance of Bank Capital in regulating the banking system.

3. What are the differences between a conventional (traditional) and a subprime mortgage?

4. What was the origin of Fannie Mae and Freddie Mac, how did their mission change over time?

5. What advantages do banks realize when securitizing loans, such as mortgage contracts?

6. A mortgage-backed security (MBS):

   a) is a financial derivative that has no purpose other than to provide a tool for investors to speculate on the housing market?

   b) is similar to a credit default swap (CDS) in that both provide a mechanism for holders of mortgages to insure against default of the homeowners.

   c) differs from a collateralized mortgage obligation (CMO) in that an MBS is composed of a series of risk tranches that can help match up the risk preferences of investors with the level of risk of the tranche in which they choose to invest, while a CMO has no such tranches.

d) is designed to increase funding of mortgages by producing securities that can be sold directly in the financial markets with the proceeds used to purchase mortgages from the institutions that originated them.

7. Credit default swaps (CDSs):

a) have a constructive role to play in the management of portfolio risk for financial firms and have helped to alleviate the financial crisis of 2007-2009.

b) are financial instruments used strictly for speculative purposes, but have nonetheless helped to alleviate the financial crisis of 2007-2009.

c) have a constructive role to play in the management of portfolio risk for financial firms, but they have nonetheless contributed to deepening the financial crisis of 2007-2009.

d) are financial instruments used strictly for speculative purposes, and they have contributed to deepening the financial crisis of 2007-2009.

8. Which of the following statements is true? President Obama's plan for reform of financial market regulation includes proposals to:

   a) create a Financial Services Oversight Council to identify sources of potential systemic risk in the financial markets and coordinate the activities of the various federal agencies that regulate the financial markets to head off systemic failures before they develop.

   b) create a Consumer Financial Protection Bureau with an advisory role to each of the regulatory agencies including the Federal Reserve, the FDIC, and the SEC, on issues relating to consumers' participation in financial markets.

   c) extend federal regulations to private non-bank financial firms (such as hedge funds) that are not currently regulated and ban their practice of continually developing new financial innovations, such as financial derivatives.

   d) Nationalize all financial firms that are deemed to be too big to fail.

9. A collateralized debt obligation (CDO):

   a) has portfolio collateral that must consist exclusively of subprime mortgages or financial derivatives written on subprime mortgages, such as CMOs or MBSs.

b) provides insurance against default on a specified debt. This debt could be a mortgage or a corporate bond or a financial derivative product such as a CDO.

c) can only be issued by financial firms that are subject to government regulations.

d) can produce some highly rated (low-risk) tranches for investors even if the portfolio collateral is entirely "junk," that is, the collateral has the lowest credit rating (and carries the highest risk).

10. How does a Credit Default Swap (CDS) differ from a standard insurance contract? What is a Naked CDS?

11. The news media often uses descriptive terms to capture complex issues. In the credit crisis of 2007-2008, some old and some new such terms have appeared. Explain what is meant by:

a) toxic assets.

b) financial weapons of mass destruction.

c) transparency.

d) bank run.

e) too big to fail.

12. Bear Stearns, Lehman Brothers, Merrill Lynch, and AIG were all firms that teetered on the brink of bankruptcy. What was the fate of each? In what ways were their problems similar? How did they differ?

13. Morgan Stanley and Goldman Sachs converted their charters to become commercial banks rather than investment banks as a result of the credit crisis.

    a) What advantages did they derive from this conversion?

    b) Were there any disadvantages from the change?

14. What role did the NRSROs play in deepening the financial crisis, and what actions have taken in Dodd-Frank to deal with this problem?

15. What was the Troubled Asset Relief Fund (TARP) originally designed to do and how was it ultimately used?

16. What role did AIG play in deepening the financial crisis?

17. What advantages do banks realize when securitizing loans, such as mortgage contracts?

18. How does investment banking differ from commercial banking?

19. How does the problem of "Too Big To Fail" relate to "systemic risk"? In what ways has Dodd-Frank attempted to deal with this problem?

20. What is the objective of creating the FSOC? What authority does it have to carry out its mission?

21. Why is "transparency" such a critical issue in the trading of financial derivatives? How is Dodd-Frank attempting to enhance transparency in those markets?

22. Describe the importance of requiring mortgage originators to retain some "Skin in the Game" when they securitize mortgage pools, that is, how does it alter their incentives when originating mortgages?

23. What steps were taken to strengthen the Federal Reserve? In what ways did Dodd-Frank increase oversight of the Federal Reserve's activities?

Review Questions relating to the Appendix

1. What were the objectives of the new rules issued by the CFPB regarding the underwriting standards for new mortgages?

2. What criteria should a mortgage lender consider when making a new loan and how do they relate

to the "ability-to-repay" mandate of the Dodd-Frank Financial Reform Legislation?

3. What is a "qualified mortgage," and why is it an important designation? Why is there a separate category for "high-priced" subprime mortgages?

4. What are the provisions that new loans must satisfy to be considered "qualified mortgages"? Which abuses of the past lending practices that fueled the housing bubble were these provisions intended to address?

4.9   References

"The Great Depression." The History Channel. Available at: http://www.history.com/topics/great-depression

"Mortgage Debt Outstanding," Board of Governors of the Federal Reserve System, Data Release June, 2017. Available at: https://www.federalreserve.gov/econresdata/releases/mortoutstand/current.htm

"Failed Bank List," 2017. Federal Deposit Insurance Corporation. Available at: https://www.fdic.gov/bank/individual/failed/banklist.html

"Buffet Warns on Investment 1time bomb'," BBC News, March 4, 2003. Available at: http://news.bbc.co.uk/2/hi/2817995.stm

"Report on the Troubled Asset Relief Program – June 2017." Congressional Budget Office. Available online at: https://www.cbo.gov/system/files/115th-congress-2017-2018/reports/52840-tarp.pdf

"Executive Summary: Dodd-Frank Wall Street Reform and Consumer Protection Act." American Bankers Association. July 14, 2010. Available at: https://www.congress.gov/bill/111th-congress/house-bill/04173

"Summary of Dodd-Frank Financial Regulation Legislation," Harvard Law School Forum on Corporate Governance and Financial Regulation, July 7, 2010. Available at: https://corpgov.law.harvard.edu/2010/07/07/summary-of-dodd-frank-financial-regulation-legislation/

"H.R.4173 - Dodd-Frank Wall Street Reform and Consumer Protection Act," 111th Congress,(2008-2011). Available at: http://www.aba.com/Issues /Reg Reform /Pages/RR_ExecSummary.aspx

Suggested Readings relating to the Appendix

Details of the Consumer Financial Protection Bureau's ruling can be found at:

http://www.consumerfinance.gov/regulations/ability-to-repay-and-qualified-mortgage-standards-under-the-truth-in-lending-act-regulation-z/

A particularly useful summary on this website can be downloaded under the heading: "Detailed summary of the rule"

A description of the "debt-to-income" calculation that is part of the rules can be found at:

http://www.fha.com/fha_requirements_debt.cfm

Part II

Asset Pricing and Financial Markets

Chapter 5

Money Market Interest Rates and Corporate Bonds

This chapter begins a more detailed look at the financial markets in the United States. Fundamental to an understanding of the operation of these markets is how interest rates and asset prices are determined. Of course there is a wide range of assets available in the marketplace, and a number of different ways in which interest rates can be computed. The goal of the next few chapters will therefore be to examine the pricing and interest rate determination for specific classes of financial assets that have previously been discussed. This information can then be used to compare these various financial assets both from the investor's point of view and from the perspective of the issuers of the assets.

Determining the prices and interest rates on stocks, bonds, or money market assets is the job of financial analysts. The objective here is to understand how they approach their task. Whether the goal is to become a financial analyst or merely a savvy investor, one must not only be up on the wide range of factors that affect the value of financial assets, whether that is technology, the economy, natural disasters, or politics, but one must also have a sharp pencil. Small mistakes in the math can lead to large financial losses.

5.1   Money Market Interest Rates

A good place to begin is to determine how interest rates are computed on assets with shorter maturities, or *money market assets*. There are two important methods of calculating money market interest rates and both of these measures are used in the markets so an investor will need to be able to go back and forth between them. The first is referred to as the *investment rate* (which we'll label *IR*). It is the actual annualized rate of return that is of concern to the investor. The second is the *bank discount rate* (which we'll label *DR*). This interest rate is used by traders when offering to buy or sell these assets.

It is easiest to understand these calculations by way

of a simple example: Suppose an investor purchases a $100,000 *U.S. Treasury Bill* that matures in 180 days. For this asset, the ONLY payment will be the *face or par value* of $100,000 that is received at *maturity*. The T-Bill is therefore said to be "*sold at a discount*" to its face value.

Assume:

1. the investor paid $98,000 for the T-bill today, and

2. the investor plans to hold it until it matures.

What is the *rate of return* on this investment?

Investment Rate (IR)

Begin by computing the investment rate, IR. There are two parts to this calculation. First, what rate of return does the investor receive up to maturity, and second, how do we *annualize* that rate of return? Here is the formula:

$$\text{Investment Rate (IR)} = \underbrace{\frac{\text{Interest Income}}{\text{Investment Base}}}_{\text{Rate of Return to Maturity}}$$

$$\times \underbrace{\frac{\#\ \text{Days/Year}}{\#\ \text{Days to Maturity}}}_{\text{Annualized Rate of Return}} \qquad (5.1)$$

where the *Interest Income* is the Face (Par) Value received at maturity minus the initial *Purchase Price*, and in this case, the *Investment Base* is the actual amount invested, or the Purchase Price.

$$\text{Interest Income} = \text{Par Value - Purchase Price} \quad (5.2)$$

and

$$\text{Investment Base} = \text{Purchase Price} \quad (5.3)$$

Substituting from (5.2) and (5.3) into (5.1), the expressions for IR becomes:

$$\text{Investment Rate (IR)} = \underbrace{\frac{\text{Par Value - Purchase Price}}{\text{Purchase Price}}}_{\text{Rate of Return to Maturity}}$$

$$\times \underbrace{\frac{\text{365 Days/Year}}{\text{\# Days to Maturity}}}_{\text{Annualized Rate of Return}} \quad (5.4)$$

The first part of this calculation represents the actual rate of return on the investment up to maturity, assuming the asset was not sold. Annualizing that rate of return essentially asks: What would be the rate of return on this investment, if the investor could stay invested in this asset for one year? This is an important calculation, since interest rates on ALL assets are quoted as annualized rates of return so that comparisons across assets can be easily made.

In this example, we then find the IR by plugging in the numbers:

$$\text{IR} = \frac{(\$100{,}000 - \$98{,}000)}{\$98{,}000}\left(\frac{365}{180}\right) = 0.0414 = 4.14\%$$

$$(5.5)$$

Bank Discount Rate (DR)

Now, compute the bank discount rate (DR) on this same asset. It differs from the IR in 2 ways:

1. It uses the Par Value as the Investment Base.

2. It annualizes the rate of return based on a 360-day year.

We therefore have this expression.

$$\text{Bank Discount Rate (DR)} = \underbrace{\frac{\text{Par Value - Purchase Price}}{\text{Par Valuee}}}_{\text{Rate of Return to Maturity}}$$

$$\times \underbrace{\frac{360 \text{ Days/Year}}{\# \text{ Days to Maturity}}}_{\text{Annualized Rate of Return}} \qquad (5.6)$$

Plugging in the numbers, we obtain the DR for this asset:

$$DR = \frac{(\$100,000 - \$98,000)}{\$100,000}\left(\frac{360}{180}\right) = 0.0400 = 4.00\%$$
(5.7)

When comparing the investment rate (IR) with the bank discount rate (DR), note that the IR is ALWAYS greater than the DR. This is true since both of the changes in the calculation of DR versus the IR lower the computed interest rate. Also note that the DR is NOT the actual rate of return to the investor, but as discussed in detail in a subsequent chapter, the DR is what dealers quote one another when trading the asset. Therefore, investors must be able to go back and forth between to the two rates.

These calculations will be revisited in a subsequent chapter when current data for one of the most important financial markets in the world, the market for *U.S. Government debt*, is examined in detail.

5.2   Present and Future Value Calculations

Next, turn attention to the capital markets, where longer term assets , i.e., stocks and bonds, are traded.

Ownership of these assets represents a stream of claims that the owner expects to receive in the future, which may differ in both the amount and the timing of when they are received. Therefore, to price these assets, today's value of each of the claims must be determined. This valuation is accomplished by the "workhorse" tool of finance: *present value calculations*.

A simple example best illustrates how these calculations are made:

Example: Suppose you win a prize and have a choice between two assets in receiving your winnings:

1. Asset A is a claim on $100 today, while

2. Asset B is a claim on $105 that is to be received with certainty one year from today.

To decide which of the two you would choose, assume that you don't need the money today and that you have available to you a risk-free investment option on which you could earn 7%. To compare the investments, you must compare their values at the same point in time.

Future Value. First, compare their values at a future date, say one year from today.

If you received the claim on Asset A and invested it in the safe asset at 7%, you can then compute its *future value* at that date as:

$$\text{Future Value (A)} = \$100(1.07) = \$107 \qquad (5.8)$$

However, the future value of Asset B is simply the claim received on that date, or:

$$\text{Future Value (B)} = \$105 \qquad (5.9)$$

<u>Conclusion</u>: Obviously, you would choose Asset A with the higher future value.

Present Value. Now compare those two assets by determining today's value of the claims.

Today's value of Asset A is simply the claim received today, or:

$$\text{Present Value (A)} = \$100 \qquad (5.10)$$

For Asset B, we have to ask the question: How much would you have to invest today at 7% in order for that investment to grow into $105 after one year, which is the value of the claim represented by Asset B to be received one year from today.

Let x_B denote this Present Value (B). Then,

$$x_B(1.07) = \$105 \Rightarrow x_B = \frac{\$107}{1.07} = \$98.17 \qquad (5.11)$$

Note what this calculation reveals: As the investor, you would be indifferent between receiving $98.17 today versus a claim on $100 to be received with certainty one year from today.

<u>Conclusion</u>: Again, when we compare the present values of the two claims, we would choose Asset A, since it has the higher present value.

This is a very simple example, but it illustrates an extremely useful tool in placing a value on very complicated investments that may have future costs as well as future benefits. One simply computes the present value of all expected receipts and subtracts the present value of all future expected costs. If that difference is positive, the investment is said to have a *positive net present value* and would be a worthwhile investment, provided the funds are available to make the investment after accounting for other possible uses of those funds.

5.3   Corporate Bond Pricing

This section illustrates how the price of standard *corporate bonds* is determined. We can begin with the plan vanilla corporate bond that represents claims to: (i) a series of semi-annual *coupon payments* received throughout the life of the bond plus (ii) the *face or par value* received at maturity.

Example: A 10-year corporate bond represents 21 future payments: 20 semi-annual coupon payments and the par value received at maturity. ALL of these payments are known at the time the bond is purchased. Assuming the corporation doesn't default on the bond, these payments will NEVER change throughout the life of the bond. Therefore, to price the bond, the investor must determine the present value of each of those claims and sum them up.

There 2 generic types of corporate bonds: *pure-discount or zero-coupon bonds* and the *standard coupon bonds*.

Zero-Coupon Bonds

Start by pricing a zero-coupon bond, which is the simpler of the two. As the name implies, the issuer of the bond does not pay any coupons, and the bond therefore represents only one claim, which is to the par value to be received upon maturity.[1] A simple example is instructive.

Example: A firm issues a 2-year zero-coupon bond with a par value of $1000. Assume that the market demands

---

[1]A discussion of the potential advantages of investing zero-coupon bonds can be found at the website of The Securities Industry and Financial Markets Association: http://www.investinginbonds.com/learnmore.asp?catid=6&id=46

an annualized rate of return of 6% based on the perceived level of risk of default, the bond's liquidity, and
expected inflation. What is the bond worth?

Let B_0 be today's value of the bond, i.e., the bond
price. An investor who agrees with the market assessment of the risk and liquidity of the bond and the expected rate of inflation in the future must therefore
expect the amount he or she pays for the bond to grow
into $1000 in two years assuming a rate of return of
6%.

Therefore, after one year the investment would grow
to $B_0 \times (1.06)$ and this principal plus interest would all
then stay invested at an additional 6% for the second
year. We have this calculation:

$$\underbrace{\underbrace{[B_0(1.06)]}_{\text{value after one year}} \quad (1.06)}_{\text{value after two years}} = \$1000 \qquad (5.12)$$

$$\implies B_0 = \frac{\$1000}{(1.06)^2} = \$890 \qquad (5.13)$$

Then, the bond price B_0 must be $890. Note that
this figure is simply the present value of the one future
claim that the investor is purchasing, i.e., the par value
of the bond to be received at maturity.

Now, take this example one step further.

Example: Suppose that the investor bought the 2-year zero-coupon bond of the previous example when it was initially issued and then, after one year, sold it at the prevailing market price. What would be the sale price of the bond and the initial investor's realized rate of return on this one-year investment, given that the markets have reassessed the default risk associated with the bond?

Consider three different scenarios. Suppose the markets have factored new information on the level of risk into this bond's price and arrived at an expected rate of return consistent with that risk assessment of: case (a) 5%, case (b) 6%, and case (c) 14%.

Case (a): Let B_1^a be the bond price after 1 year (denoted by the subscript) under the case (a), indicated by the superscript. After one year, there will be one year left on the bond. Therefore, the investor who purchases the bond demanding a 5% required rate of return on the bond must expect to see his investment grow into $1000. We therefore have this present value calculation:

$$B_1^a(1.05) = \$1000 \Rightarrow B_0^a = \frac{\$1000}{1.05} = \$952.38 \quad (5.14)$$

What was the original investor's rate of return on this one year investment, denoted r^a? Essentially, determine the capital gain by subtracting the purchase price from the sale price, then divide by the amount invested, or the purchase price, to determine the rate of return on the investment. (Note that the rate of return does not have to be annualized, since it is a one-year investment.)

$$r^a = \frac{\text{sale price - purchase price}}{\text{purchase price}} \times 100\%$$

$$= \frac{\$952.38 - \$890.00}{\$890.00} \times 100\% = 7.01\% \qquad (5.15)$$

In this case (a), the original investor had expected a rate of return averaging 6% over two years. However, the lowering of the risk assessment on the bond caused the subsequent buyer to require only a 5% expected rate of return and therefore he or she was willing to pay more for the bond. The initial investor therefore realized a capital gain that boosted the return to over 7%.

Case (b): Now consider similar calculations for case (b), with the bond price denoted B_1^b and the realized rate of return to the initial investor given by r^b.

$$B_1^b(1.06) = \$1000 \Rightarrow B_0^b = \frac{\$1000}{1.06} = \$943.40 \qquad (5.16)$$

$$r^b = \frac{\text{sale price - purchase price}}{\text{purchase price}} \times 100\%$$

$$= \frac{\$943.40 - \$890.00}{\$890.00} \times 100\% = 6.00\% \qquad (5.17)$$

In this case (b), the risk assessment hadn't changed from the time the bond was initially issued, but the bond price still rose. The higher bond price was simply due to the fact that the new investor was one year closer to receiving the $1000 par value, and therefore discounted it less, i.e., by (1.06) rather than $(1.06)^2$. Meanwhile, the original investor received precisely the 6% expected rate of return that he or she anticipated when the bond was initially purchased.

Case (c): Finally, for the extreme case (c), the risk assessment rose substantially, and the required rate of return increased to 14%. The original investor can sell the bond at the end of one year at the prevailing market price that discounts the $1000 par value back one year at 14%, or:

$$B_1^c = \frac{\$1000}{1.14} = \$877.19 \qquad (5.18)$$

The original investor's realized rate of return is now seen to be negative in this case:

$$r^c = \frac{\$877.19 - \$890.00}{\$890.00} \times 100\% = -1.44\% \qquad (5.19)$$

The investor realized a capital loss of $22.81 for an annualized rate return on his $890 investment of -1.44 percent.

Result: This exercise produces an important general conclusion: As expected rates of return on bonds rise, bond prices fall.

Coupon Bonds

The vast major of corporate bonds pay coupons. They are more complicated to price than zero-coupon bonds since their price represents the value of a stream of future payments, not just a single payment received at maturity. Again, their pricing is best illustrated by way of a simple example:

Example: A firm issues a 3-year bond with a par value of $1000 and a coupon rate of 5%. What is the market price of the bond, assuming that the market demands a 6% rate of return. This rate of return is referred to as the bond's *yield to maturity (YTM)*. An investor who agrees with the market's assessment of risk, liquidity, and inflation as they relate to the bond, would therefore expect to receive this rate of return, if he were to buy the bond at its current market price and hold it to maturity.

For simplicity, assume that the coupons are paid annually rather than semiannually. Therefore, the bond price is the sum of the present value of 4 future payments: 3 annual coupon payments and the par value paid at maturity.

First, it is necessary to determine the size of the coupon payments. This value is found by using the *coupon rate* and the bond's par value.

$$\text{Coupon Payment} = \text{Coupon Rate} \times \text{the Par Value}$$

In the example, the annual coupons are:

$$\text{Coupons} = 0.05(\$1000) = \$50 \qquad (5.20)$$

Let x_1, x_2, x_3, and x_m be the present values of the first 3 coupons and the par value, respectively. Then, the current bond price is given by:

$$B_0 = x_1 + x_2 + x_3 + x_m. \qquad (5.21)$$

The present values of the future payments are computed as was done previously.

$$x_1 = \frac{\$50}{1.06} = \$47.17 \qquad (5.22)$$

$$x_2 = \frac{\$50}{(1.06)^2} = \$44.50 \qquad (5.23)$$

$$x_3 = \frac{\$50}{(1.06)^3} = \$41.98 \qquad (5.24)$$

$$x_m = \frac{\$1000}{(1.06)^3} = \$839.62 \qquad (5.25)$$

Therefore, the bond price is $B_0 = \$973.27$.

Note that, in this example, the coupon rate is greater than the yield to maturity and that the bond price is less than its par value, when the bond is said to be *selling below par*. There is an important general result here:

$$\text{When a bond sells} \begin{pmatrix} \text{Below} \\ \text{At} \\ \text{Above} \end{pmatrix} \text{Par}$$

$$\implies \text{ its YTM is } \begin{pmatrix} \text{Above} \\ \text{Equal to} \\ \text{Below} \end{pmatrix} \text{ the Coupon Rate.}$$

5.4   The Primary Market for Corporate Bonds

When a corporation engages an investment bank to assist in the initial offering of its bonds, the investment bank will:

1. Set the par (face) value of each of the bonds.

2. Assess the market demand for the bonds to determine the rate of return (YTM) that reflects the expected rate of return to be demanded by the market.

3. Set the coupon rate = expected YTM once the bonds are introduced into trading.

Note that if the coupon rate were set too low, the bonds will sell below par and the firm will not raise as many funds as expected.

To avoid this problem, the investment bank will often *underwrite* the bond issue by essentially guaranteeing that the firm will receive the amount of funds that the bond issue would raise had the bonds sold at par. This activity is normally very profitable, but it can be a very risky undertaking. That is, if the bond issue raises less than expected, then the investment bank will have to make up the difference and take the loss.[2]

5.5 The Secondary Market for Bonds

Once corporate bonds have been issued, trading takes place in the secondary markets. Importantly, the coupon payments and the par value of the bonds will

---

[2]Investment banks have a strong incentive to properly price new issues, as their reputation for acquiring relevant (often sensitive) information is on the line with each transaction. See Morrison and Wilhelm (2007) who discuss the changing nature of investment banking in the face of technological change and globalization of the financial marketplace.

not change, but bond prices do change in response to changes in the YTM that is demanded by investors. These altered expectations of the market could occur as a result of:

1. a change in the general structure of interest rates (for example, when the risk-free rate rises, perhaps due to an increase in inflation expectations, causing ALL interest rates to rise), or

2. the markets change their collective perception of risk that the issuing firm will default on the bond.

We could characterize this risk-return relationship as follows:

$$\text{YTM (Corp Bond)} = \text{Risk-Free Rate} + \text{Default Risk Premium} \quad (5.26)$$

A graph of the YTM versus default risk may appear as shown in Figure 5.1.

A measure of the *risk-free rate* for a given maturity of the bond is the corresponding U.S. Treasury security of that same maturity. That is, when comparing the YTM on the corporate bond with the YTM on the U.S. Treasury security, the maturities of the two assets must match. In this case, the difference between them is the *default risk premium.*

Example: In Figure 5.1, the risk-free rate is given by the yield to maturity on the Treasury Note, which is seen to be 3.5 percent. Identifying the level of default risk of the corporate bond A (which is assumed to be of

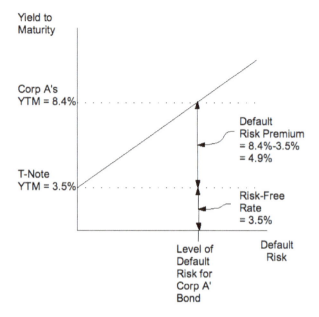

Figure 5.1: Default Premium in Corporate A Bond

the same maturity as the T-Note) along the horizontal axis allows you to determine the YTM of the corporate bond. It can be read directly from the the graph to be 8.4%. Therefore, the default risk premium for this bond is:

$$\text{Default Risk Premium} = 8.4\% - 3.5\% = 4.9\%. \tag{5.27}$$

5.6 Credit Rating Agencies

Obviously, an assessment of default risk is an important factor in determining the value of corporate bonds. The *credit rating agencies* specialize in this activity.[3] The two largest ratings agencies are Moody's and Standard & Poor's. The highest ratings are Aaa (Moody's) and AAA (Standard & Poor's), while the lowest ratings are C, although Moody's does rate bonds that are currently in default with a D designation.

	Moody's	Standard & Poor's
Investment Grade	Aaa	AAA
	Aa	AA
	A	A
	Baa	BBB
High-Yield (or Junk) Bonds	Ba	BB
	B	B
	Caa	CCC
	Ca	CC
	C	C
Bonds in Default	D	–

Table 5.1: Bond Ratings Categories

Their ratings include broad categories of bonds rated as *investment grade*, corresponding to ratings Aaa to

---

[3]For a good overview, see "The ABCs of Credit Ratings," published by the Securities and Exchange Commission.

Baa (Moody's) and AAA to BBB (Standard & Poor's) and those rated as *high-yield*, often referred to as *junk bonds* with ratings Ba to C (Moody's) and BB to C (Standard & Poor's). The distinction is important, as many pension funds and other investment houses have fiduciary responsibilities that prohibit them from investing in junk bonds. Therefore, a firm that receives a junk bond rating will see the demand from these large institutional investors dwindle. Those institutions that own them may be required to sell them, with the added supply in the market further weakening their price.

In all cases, lower ratings mean a higher default premium that increases the yield to maturity on the bonds demanded by investors, and the bond price will fall.

5.7 Daily Information on Bond Trading

Investors in the bond market must understand how the financial news media reports information on corporate bonds.[4] A sample of some data for Investment Grade Corporate Bonds reported in the *Wall Street Journal* on March 22, 2016 is shown in Table 5.2.

---

[4]For an overview of considerations for bond investing, see "Bond Basics Tutorial," at http://www.investopedia.com /university/bonds/.

Most Active Investment Grade Bonds

Issuer Name	Symbol	Coupon	Maturity	Moody's/S&P/Fitch	High	Low	Last	Change	Yield%
COMMONWEALTH BK AUSTRALIA NY BRH MEDIUM	CBAU4104785	1.125%	03/13/2017	Aa2//AA-	100.01400	99.88600	99.91400	-0.059000	1.214402
CITIGROUP INC	C4325406	3.700%	01/12/2026	Baa1//A	102.47900	101.51900	102.00200	-0.042000	3.456955
BANK AMER CORP	BAC4273622	3.875%	08/01/2025	Baa1/BBB+/A	104.87309	102.47460	103.24000	-1.825987	3.465999
COCA-COLA FEMSA S A B DE C V	FMX4072789	3.875%	11/26/2023	A2//A	103.42500	102.90100	103.42500	0.297000	3.364229
MORGAN STANLEY	MS4329522	3.875%	01/27/2026	A3//A	104.86000	103.19700	103.34000	-0.037000	3.471023
MORGAN STANLEY	MS3832844	4.750%	03/22/2017	A3/BBB+/A	103.74200	102.75000	103.74200	0.286000	0.960017
JPMORGAN CHASE & CO	JPM4340142	2.550%	03/01/2021	A3//A+	101.99600	100.20700	100.46200	-0.147000	2.448469
SUMITOMO MITSUI BKG CORP	SMFG4029099	1.450%	07/19/2016	A1//	100.19100	100.12400	100.12400	-0.025000	1.067705
ORACLE CORP	ORCL3919232	1.200%	10/15/2017	A1/AA-/A+	100.54100	100.35900	100.44100	-0.004000	0.914247
APPLE INC	AAPL4336435	2.250%	02/23/2021	Aa1//	102.78200	101.29500	101.72800	0.203000	1.874150

Table 5.2: *Walll Street Journal*: Most Actively Traded Corporate Bonds, March 22, 2016

There are several observations to be made regarding Table 5.2. Reading across the top row reveals the information that is being provided for each bond.

In the first column is the *name of the corporation* issuing the bond, followed by the bond's *trading designation*. Continuing to read from left to right gives the bond's *coupon rate*, the *month the bond matures*, and the *bond ratings*. The remaining columns provide information on the trading activity for the day. Listed first are the *highest and lowest price per $100 in par value* that the bond traded at throughout the day. The *last (or closing) price per $100 in par value* is followed by the *change in the last price* from the previous day's close. Finally, the *YTM* associated with the last price is displayed in the final column.

5.8 Exercises Based on Table 5.2

From Table 5.2, a great deal can be learn about the bonds listed.

1. Based on the *Last* price, which of the bonds traded above par and which below par?

   To answer this question, simply compare the reported *Last* price with $100. All of the bonds listed here, except for the COMMONWEALTH BANK OF AUSTRALIA traded above par.

2. Suppose an investor didn't have the *Last* price for the COMMONWEALTH BANK OF AUSTRALIA bond, CBAU 4104785. How could he or she answer the question of whether the last trade recorded for this day was above or below par?

   What is known is that some of the trades for the day were above par, since the *High* was $100.14 per par value of $100, while some trades were below par, since the *Low* was $99.886 per $100 in par value. Note that its *Yield %* is 1.214%. Then, the investor could answer the question by comparing the YTM with the *Coupon* rate. Knowing that the YTM for the *Last* trade > *Coupon* rate (1.125%), establishes that the bond traded below par in the *Last* trade of the day.

3. What happened to the bond price and the yield on the Apple Inc bond (AAPL336435), over the course of the day's trading?

   Look at the *Change*. Red numbers (preceded by a negative sign) indicate how much the bond price fell from the previous day's *Last* price, while green numbers indicate how much the bond price rose. In this example, it rose by 20.3 cents per $100 in par value, so the previous day's *Last* price was $101.728-$0.203 = $101.525. Since the bond price rose, then the YTM fell over the course of the day's trading.

4. Was the YTM on the Sumitomo Mitsui Bank bond, SMFG 4029099, for the last trade of the day at his highest or lowest for all of the day's trades?

   You can answer this question, since the price for the last trade of the day was the lowest price for any trade during the day. Therefore, its yield was the highest for the day.

5. Which of these bonds has the highest and which has the lowest ratings? Note that recently, the rating agencies have refined their ratings by adding

1,2,3 (Moody's) and +/- (S&P and Fitch) to the ratings listed in the previous table of categories.

Using Moody's rating, the Apple bond had the highest ratings with a Aa1 Rating. While all of the Citigroup and Bank of America bonds had the lowest, with Baa1 ratings, which is near the bottom of the investment grade category.

6. The data may also allow comparisons across bonds to be made. While the comparison is not valid unless the bonds have the same issue and maturity dates, just for the sake of argument, assume that both the Oracle bond, ORCL391 9232, and the Apple bond, AAPL4336435, DO have the same issue and maturity dates. Also, assume that both bonds initially sold *at par*. Which was seen by the market to be riskier when they were issued? Which is seen by the market on *Last* trade of the day to be riskier?

To answer these questions, one need only compare YTMs for the 2 bonds. When issued at par the YTM for the Oracle bond was 1.20% (the *Coupon* Rate) and for the Apple bond, the YTM was 2.25%. Therefore, the Apple bond carried the higher *default premium* and was seen to be the riskier of the two bonds. On the *Last* trade on March 22, 2016, the YTM on both bonds had fallen, with the YTM on the Oracle bond of 0.91427% and on the Apple bond of 1.87415. Therefore, the default premium is still higher on the Apple bond.

5.9 Summary

This chapter describes some of the essential tools needed to understand how financial markets determine interest rates on money market assets and how they arrive at the price of corporate bonds. This knowledge will be needed for much of the material contained in the remainder of the book. It will be particularly important in a subsequent chapter that describes the great variety of money market assets available to investors along with a detailed discussion of various aspects of one of the most important financial markets in the world: the U.S. Treasury market, which is the market for U.S. government debt.

Corporations raise money in both the money and bond markets, but they also rely on another important capital market: the *corporate equity market*. Question: How does this market arrive at prices for shares of corporate stock? With an answer to this question, it is possible to begin to discuss how corporations decide on how many shares to issue, what their dividend policy should be, and whether they should rely on stocks or bonds when they are in need of funds to pay for new or existing projects that could alter the value of their company. These issues, that are taken up in the next chapter, are important considerations for investors, who must make choices of how to invest to achieve their financial objectives. Those objectives differ from one individual to another, and are subject to change over one's lifetime.

Key Terms

money market assets
investment rate (IR)
bank discount rate (DR)
U.S. Treasury Bill
par value
maturity
sold at a discount
annualize return
interest income
purchase price
investment base
U.S. Government debt
future value
present value
positive net present value
corporate bonds
coupon payments
pure-discount or zero-coupon bonds
standard coupon bonds
yield to maturity (YTM)
coupon rate
selling below par
selling at par
selling above par
risk-free rate
default risk premium
credit rating agency
Standard & Poor's

Moody's
investment grade bonds
high-yield or junk bonds

5.10   Review Questions

1. Calculate the bank discount rate of return (DR) and the YTM-equivalent for the following money market instruments:

   a) Purchase price, $96; par value, $100; maturity, 90 days.

   b) Purchase price, $96; par value, $100; maturity, 180 days.

   c) Purchase price, $97.50; par value, $100; maturity, 270 days.

   d) Purchase price, $975; par value, $1,000; maturity, 270 days.

2. What is the price of a zero-coupon bond that has a Par Value of $10,000, a yield-to-maturity of 5 percent, and five years to maturity?

3. Suppose you had bought the bond described in Question 2. If you sold the bond after one year when its yield-to-maturity had risen to 6 percent, what would the bond sell for? What would your actual realized one-year rate of return be on this investment?

4. A corporate bond has a Par Value of $100,000, a coupon rate of 7 percent, and 3 years to maturity. If these coupons are paid annually, what is

the price of bond if the market is demanding a 6 percent rate of return on the investment?

5. Suppose you had bought the bond described in Question 4. If you sold the bond after you collected the first coupon payment at the end of one year when its yield-to-maturity had fallen to 5 percent, what would the bond sell for? What would your actual realized one-year rate of return be on this investment?

6. A firm receives a bond rating of BAA on its newly issued bonds. After one year the firm's earnings were below expectations and the rating agencies lowered the bond rating to BBB. Would the yield-to-maturity on the bond rise or fall? Why?

7. Firm A had a bond rating of AA and had to pay 6 percent to raise money in the capital markets. Firm B is a competitor to Firm A. It needed to raise $1,000,000 in the bond market and issued bonds with a Par value of $1,000 and with a coupon rate of 6 percent. However, the rating agencies gave it a rating A. Which could be true?

   a) The bond sold below par and the yield-to-maturity exceeded the coupon rate.

   b) The bond sold below par and the yield-to-maturity was below the coupon rate.

   c) The bond sold above par and the yield-to-maturity exceeded the coupon rate.

    d) The bond sold above par and the yield-to-maturity was below the coupon rate.

8. Firm XYZ issued 3-year bonds that if they sold at Par would raise $10,000,000. The bonds had a Par Value of $1,000 and a coupon rate of 4 percent. If the market prices the bonds such that they carried a yield-to-maturity of 5 percent, how much did the firm actually raise with the new bond issue? Assume the coupons are paid annually.

9. When an investment banker advises a firm to issue bonds to raise funds in the capital markets, what detailed information must the investment banker give the company in order for it to offer the bonds in the market? Who faces the consequence of poor advise? Explain.

5.11   References

Morrison, Alan D. and William J. Wilhelm, Jr. "Investment Banking: Past, Present, and Future," 2007. *Journal of Applied Corporate Finance.* 19(1): 8-20.

"Putting Compound Interest to Work: With Zero Coupon Bonds," 2005-1013. The Securities Industry and Financial Markets Association. Available at: http://www.investinginbonds.com/learnmore.asp?catid=6&id=46

"The ABC of Credit Ratings," Office of Investor Education and Advocacy of the Securities and Exchange Commission. Available at: https://www.sec.gov/investor/alerts/ib_creditratings.pdf

"Bond Basics Tutorial." 2010. from Investopedia.com. Available at: http://www.investopedia.com /university/bonds/.

Chapter 6

Corporate Stock

The previous chapter described the manner in which interest rates are determined in the money markets and how prices are determined in the bond market. This chapter examines the pricing of another important class of financial assets: *corporate stock or equities*.

After an initial look at the exchanges where stocks are traded, this chapter seeks to answer the basic questions: Exactly what are is an investor purchasing when he or she buys a share of stock? What are the fundamental determinants of the value of a share of stock? To answer these questions, stock analysts primarily attempt to arrive at reasonable estimates of corporate profits and project how well the firm will fare in the future. This task is far from simple. There are many factors that enter into an assessment of whether a stock is a "buy" or a "hold" or a "sell." Not only must the analyst understand the markets in which the firm operates and the overall state of the economy, but also the knowledge of what the firm's dividend policy is and how it is likely to change are basic to arriving at a reasonable valuation for the stock.

Finally, this chapter closes with another look at inflation. What happens when there is an "inflation scare" on Wall Street? That is, what happens when inflation expectations are raised in light of some new information on the economy or revised expectations about government policy or growth projections elsewhere in the world?

The purpose of this chapter is to leave the reader with a sense that investments in the stock market are subject to significant volatility, as they are buffeted each day by news from a wide range of sources. This makes naïve investment in the stock market very risky. However, informed investment in the stock market can bring substantial rewards.

6.1   Short-Selling

Suppose a stock market analyst believes that a given stock is overpriced. Is there a way he can invest in that belief? The answer is "yes." The stock could be *sold short* by borrowing it from someone who owns it with an agreement to return the stock on a pre-specified day in the future, along with a fee for the use of the stock. The stock could then be sold in the market at the current price – thought to be too high – then repurchased in the future at the price that prevails at that time – expected to be lower than the current price – and the shares returned to their original owner.

The investor makes a profit if the market price of the shares at the time he or she sold the stock exceed the market price when the stock was repurchased plus the fee that must be paid for temporary use of the stock. If the investor guessed wrong and the stock price rose, then he or she stands to loose.[1]

$$
\text{Investor} \begin{pmatrix} \text{makes a profit} \\ \text{breaks even} \\ \text{suffers a loss} \end{pmatrix} \text{ if the market price at}
$$

which the shares were sold is

$$
\begin{pmatrix} \text{greater than} \\ \text{equal to} \\ \text{less than} \end{pmatrix} \begin{bmatrix} \text{the repurchase price} \\ + \\ \text{the fee} \end{bmatrix}
$$

There are many other market mechanisms in addition to short-selling that can add efficiency to the

---

[1]Kelley and Tetlock (2017) provide evidence that short-selling tends to forecast negative returns in individual stocks as well as negative *excess returns* in those stocks relative to the overall market. Consequently, analysts often view a high overall volume of short selling as one indication that the stock market is overvalued and poised for a decline.

equity markets by allowing individuals to make investments that are in keeping with their own analysis which may suggest that current valuations of stock, that is the current market prices, are either too high or too low. With thousands of savvy investors attempting to exploit information that is relevant to the value of individual stocks, the question naturally arises: Is it possible to "beat the market" by constructing an asset portfolio utilizing only publicly available information that can outperform an investment in a simple index fund whose return mirrors that of the overall stock market?

Many studies over the years have asked this question in a attempts to detect systematic inefficiencies in the market.[2] They have generally concluded that such informational inefficiencies do not exist. This result is generally referred to as the *semi-strong form of market efficiency*. The *strong form of market efficiency* would hold if all public and private information could not be exploited for profit. However, this form of market efficiency fails, which is why *insider trading* that is based on private information is illegal in the United States. The conclusion is that U.S. stock market is a relatively *competitive equity market* in which small investors are not significantly disadvantaged, at least

---

[2]These studies began appearing in large numbers after the classic paper written by Eugene Fama (1970). The brief note by John Cochrane (2014) is highly recommended to understand the flavor of informationally efficient markets and why that are consistent with what appear to be bubbles and crashes that are obviously present in the stock market.

with respect to realizing returns on their investments over a longer investment time horizon? The *Securities and Exchange Commission (SEC)* monitors trading activities very closely and is generally charged with rooting out any trading practices that disadvantage one party or another in their investments in the market.

6.2 Organized Stock Exchanges

How do these buy or sell orders for stocks actually get placed? There are essentially two broad categories of stock markets: One is the *organized stock exchanges*, such as the *New York Stock Exchange* or the *American Stock Exchange*.[3] These exchanges are among the oldest in the world and are located in the major financial centers around the globe, including New York, San Francisco, Tokyo, Hong Kong, Frankfurt, and London, among others.

Traditionally, trades take place in a centralized location on the floor of the exchange through what is referred to as *open outcry auction markets*, where buyers and sellers call out buy and sell orders to the *specialists* who are strategically located at *trading posts* on the floor of the exchange. The NYSE, for example, currently has 20 trading posts. In each trading

---

[3]A brief history of the New York Stock Exchange can be found at: https://en.wikipedia.org/wiki/New_York_Stock_Exchange. For a more complete history that ends prior to the recent spate of mergers involving the NYSE, see Geisst (2004).

post are the specialists, who control the trading in specific stocks, such as IBM. All buy and sell orders must pass through this one individual for the stock for whose trade he is responsible. He keeps an *order book* of the orders called out to him and matches up the buy orders with the sell orders in terms of both the price and quantity of stocks for each transaction.

These orders are placed by traders on the floor of the exchange who are continuously receiving buy and sell orders, both electronically and over the phone, at booths which are also located on the floor of the exchange. For the NYSE, there are some 1500 such booths.

The specialists act as both brokers and dealers, by buying and selling for other brokers and for their own accounts. They are responsible for maintaining *orderly trading* and must intervene and buy for or sell from their own account when there is an imbalance in the buy and sell orders that they are receiving. For example, when there is an inordinate number of sell orders that are driving down the price, they must become the buyer so that the stock price will gradually decline rather than plummet.

Recently, *electronic trading* has displaced much of the open outcry auction markets as the major organized exchanges have had to adjust to the information technology revolution of the past fifty years that has transformed the world's stock exchanges. These changes are continuing to take place today.

6.3 Over-the-Counter (OTC) Stock Markets

Most trading in stocks worldwide is done on so-called *over-the-counter (or OTC) markets*. Unlike the organized exchanges, OTC markets are decentralized. The trades on these platforms are largely conducted electronically, with traders quoting *bid prices* at which they are willing to buy the stock and *asked prices* at which they will sell. These traders act as *principals* for selected stocks in that they *take positions of risk* by maintaining portfolio holdings of those stocks, whose price could, of course, rise or fall. These markets are very efficient, since a broker can observe all of the bid and asked prices of every trader in the market, which are being continuously updated throughout the trading day, and can easily find the best price for his client.

One example of an OTC market is the *National Association of Securities Dealers Automated Quotation, or NASDAQ*. It is a private organization that sets rigorous standards to which traders must adhere. Currently, there are some 5000 brokerage firms and more than 650,000 securities representatives who operate in this market. On any given day, the trading volume on NASDAQ could exceed that of the New York Stock Exchange. However, the average share price on NASDAQ is significantly lower, so the dollar value of those trades may be less.

Unruly OTC markets are not controlled by special-

ists. However, after the mini-stock market crash in
1987, in which the stock market fell 23 percent on a
single day, the major exchanges in the United States
– both organized and OTC – put into place so-called
circuit breakers that would halt all electronic trades if
market prices began to fall too sharply. The idea is
to prevent a series of *preprogrammed electronic trades*
from inducing a cascade of sell orders that can be suc-
cessively triggered as prices fall. This *programmed trading* was blamed in large measure for turning a significant market decline into the 1987 mini-stock market
crash. However, the economic fundamentals were relatively strong, and unlike the stock market crash ac-
companying Great Depression of the 1920s, after which
the stock market took 25 years to reach a new high, the
market recovered much more quickly following the 1987
mini-crash, reaching a new high in just two years.

6.4   Listing Requirements

To be traded on the world's most prestigious exchange,
the New York Stock Exchange, firms must meet so-
called *listing requirements*. Essentially, the firms must:
(i) disclose their financial condition, (ii) publish quarterly earnings reports, and (iii) help to maintain an active market in their stock. They must also be large,
with sufficient investor interest as measured by the
daily trading volume. Initial listing requirements include a minimum of 1.1 million shares worth at least

$100 million. Firms may be *delisted* if their stock price falls sufficiently that the total value of the company drops below this threshold. All other exchanges around the world also have listing requirements, although the NYSE is among the most stringent.

The advantage to a firm of having its stock listed on a major exchange is that it can vastly improve the *liquidity of the stock*. As discussed earlier, the greater is the liquidity for any asset, the lower is the required rate of return demanded by investors. This lower required rate of return translates into a higher stock price and a lower cost to the firm of raising money in the equity market.

Technology has dramatically altered the structure of stock exchanges. In the past, listing on one exchange precluded trading in the stock on any other exchange. However, this restriction is no longer true. There are many stocks that have multiple listings on exchanges with new electronic *trading platforms* such as *electronic communication networks or ECNs* that are rapidly extending trading hours and accelerating the speed with which orders are filled, both of which are adding to the trend toward worldwide trading 24/7.

In addition, mergers of stock exchanges around the globe are enhancing this practice of multiple listings. A major example is the merger in 2006 between the *NYSE Group* and *Euronext*, where the latter was the largest exchange operating in Europe, with operations in France, the Netherlands, Belgium, and Portugal.

The new firm, NYSE Euronext subsequently merged with the American Stock Exchange in 2008, only to be acquired by Intercontinental Exchange (ICE) in 2017.

These developments in the marketplace have placed a heavier burden on the chief regulators of the equity markets, which in the United States is the *Securities and Exchange Commission or SEC*, that is charged with maintaining an efficient and fair trading environment, devoid of fraudulent or deceptive trading practices that could put small investors at a competitive disadvantage. Computer technology has compounded this problem, with the enhanced ability to trade quickly on information leading to *"front-running,"* whereby traders get wind of a large block trade by on of their clients, and quickly trade from their own accounts prior to placing the client's order, thereby realizing a quick profit. *High frequency trading (HFT)* has also introduced problem into the normal functioning of the market, with HFT traders employing computer algorithms to engage in thousands of trades per day, with ownership of individual shares lasting perhaps only a few milliseconds. HFT has generally been seen as a source of increased volatility in the stock market, and that in turn has enabled these brief equity positions to produce large profits for its practitioners.

Regulatory agencies in the United States, Europe, and Japan are all looking closely at the computer-enhanced trading activities such as front-running along with other practices of HFT traders. They are working toward esablishing a clear set of regulations that do not inhibit the benefits of HFT, such as added market liquidity, while avoiding the adverse consequences of additional market volatility, and possible manipulation of the price discovery process that could disadvantage small investors.

6.5 Stock Valuations

Now, turn to the pricing of stocks. To understand what determines the price of a share of stock, it is firs necessary to consider what an investor is purchasing when he or she buys a share of stock. Obviously, it represents a share of ownership in the corporation, but how does the investor expect to benefit from this ownership?

Income Statement

Essentially, the investor has claims over a share of the firm's profits. To think this through, consider the standard *income statement* for the firm.

At the top is the firm's *Sales* from which is subtracted tthe *Cost of Goods Sold* to obtain the *Gross Margin*. From this Gross Margin, the firm's *Operating Expenses* are taken out to get to the firm's *Earnings Before Interest and Taxes (EBIT)*. Since *Interest Expenses* of the firm are tax deductible, they are subtracted first to obtain *Earnings Before Taxes (EBT)*.

Firm's Income Statement
Sales
(less) Cost of Goods Sold
Gross Margin
(less) Operating Expenses
Earnings Before Interest and Taxes (EBIT)
(less) Interest Expenses
Earnings Before Interest (EBT)
(less) Taxes
Net Income or Earnings

Table 6.1 Typical Income Statement

Then, *Corporate Income Taxes* are paid and what remains is *Net Income or Earnings*. Shareholders divide
up claims on these *corporate profits*.

Dividends

However, it is management's decision on how to divide
earnings up between *dividends* to be paid out to the
current shareholders versus *retained earnings*, which
are used to reinvest in the firm. Obviously, successful *reinvestments* by the firm should increase earnings
in the future and enhance the firm's ability to pay even
higher dividends to its shareholders. In response, the
markets could respond by bidding up the firm's stock
price today. That is, as a shareholder, the investor has

purchased nothing more than claims to current and future dividends to be paid by the firm.

The price of the stock is therefore given by the present value of the stream of current and future dividends. If the shareholder sells the stock, he or she may realize a capital gain if the stock price appreciated while he or she owned it. However, this capital gain should reflect nothing more than an increase in the market's expectations of the future dividend payments, as would be expected of a company that is making low dividend payments and reinvesting a lot of the firm's profits. Or, the stock price could rise if the market lowered its required rate of return needed to invest in the stock. A detailed look at this math is taken up later in the chapter. However, first, an understanding of how the dividend process works is essential..

Dividends are typically paid each quarter to shareholders. There are significant dates attached to the timing of those dividend payments that affect the stock price.

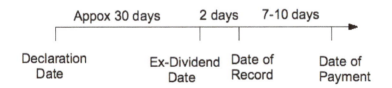

Figure 6.1 Important Dividend Dates

The first important date is the *Declaration Date*, when the *Board of Directors* announces the upcoming dividend, i.e., the amount of the dividend and when it is to be paid. Once declared, the company is obligated to pay the dividend. The firm also announces an important "ex-dividend date," which usually follows the *Declaration Date* by about 30 days. Trading on or after this date excludes a claim on the upcoming dividend. Obviously, the value of the stock drops on this date by exactly the amount of the announced dividend. The *Date of Record* follows the *Ex-Dividend* date by about 2 days, and is when the firm establishes ownership of the stock when it went ex-dividend to determine who has claim to the upcoming dividend. Payment is made approximately 7 to 10 days after the *Date of Record*.

Determining the Stock Price

There are three essential ingredients needed to determine the fundamentals of pricing stocks:

1. a forecast of dividends,

2. a required rate of return to make the investment, and

3. knowledge of how to perform present value calculations.

They can now be used to establish the mathematics of stock prices: Let d_t denote the dividend payout at date t. Note that if the firm doesn't go bankrupt, then what we'll need is a projection that includes its current dividend at date $t = 0$ and all future dividends as time goes to infinity. The current dividend is known, but expectations of future dividends must be formed. which can denoted by $E[d_t]$, for $t = 1 \ldots \infty$. Forming these expectations is one important and very difficult job of the stock market analyst.

A second important matter is to determine the amount risk associated with the investment (which means how uncertain the analyst is about his or her dividend forecast) and the liquidity of the stock. As always, the greater the risk and the less liquid is the stock, the higher will be the required rate of return to make the investment. Denote the required rate of return by r.

For simplicity, assume that the dividends are paid annually. Then, the stock price is simply the present value of the current and future expected dividend payments.

$$S_0 = d_0 + \frac{Ed_1}{(1+r)} + \frac{Ed_2}{(1+r)^2} + \cdots + \frac{Ed_t}{(1+r)^t} \ldots \quad (6.1)$$

where use can be made of the summation sign to simplify the notation:

$$S_0 = d_0 + \sum_{t=1}^{\infty} \frac{Ed_t}{(1+r)^t} \quad (6.2)$$

Note that when the stock goes ex-dividend, its price, denoted S_0^E, excludes d_0, and is given by this expression:

$$S_0^E = \sum_{t=1}^{\infty} \frac{Ed_t}{(1+r)^t} \tag{6.3}$$

From equations (6.2) and (6.3), this relationship between the stock price inclusive of the dividend and the *ex-dividend price* can be obtained:

$$S_0 = d_0 + S_0^E \tag{6.4}$$

These formulas are still very complicated, but they can be used to examine a useful special case: one for which the dividend payments are expected to grow at a constant rate. Let that growth rate be denoted by g. Then, given the current dividend, d_0, it is a simple matter to compute the remaining dividends, assuming the analyst's expectations of dividend growth are correct.

The expected dividend at the end of one year is $Ed_1 = d_0(1+g)$. At the end of 2 years, the expected dividend is $Ed_2 = d_0(1+g)^2$, and so on. Therefore, taking the general formula for the ex-dividend price first, the infinite sum becomes:

$$S_0^E = \sum_{t=1}^{\infty} \frac{Ed_t}{(1+r)^t} = \sum_{t=1}^{\infty} \frac{d_0(1+g)^t}{(1+r)^t} = d_0 \sum_{t=1}^{\infty} \left(\frac{1+g}{1+r}\right)^t \tag{6.5}$$

Moreover, for $g < r$, the infinite sum converges to $\left(\frac{1+g}{r-g}\right)$ and a simple expression for the ex-dividend price results:

$$S_0^E = \frac{d_0(1+g)}{r-g} \tag{6.6}$$

A little algebra reveals the stock price that includes the current dividend to be:

$$S_0 = d_0 + S_0^E = \frac{d_0(1+r)}{r-g} \tag{6.7}$$

An alternative use can be made of these stock price formulas to find the expected growth rate of dividends consistent with the current stock price, the current dividend, and required rate of return. That is, solving equations (6.6) and (6.7) for the growth rates yields the following expressions:

for S_0:

$$g = \frac{rS_0 - d_0(1+r)}{S_0} \tag{6.8}$$

for S_0^E:

$$g = \frac{rS_0^E - d_0}{S_0^E + d_0} \tag{6.9}$$

News and Stock Prices

These formulas indicate that the stock price will rise if projected profits of the firm increase, since that would enable the firm to pay higher dividends in the future. The stock price could also rise if the expected rate of return required by investors falls, due to a decline in the risk-free rate or the risk that the projected dividends will not meet expectations.

Many analysts parse the factors affecting these variables in the stock pricing formulas into three broad categories:

1. News affecting the individual firm, such as the introduction of a new product or a turnover in management personnel.

2. News affecting the industry group of which the firm is a part, such as new legislation affecting industry-specific regulations or innovations within the industry that could affect its cost structure, such as a cheaper more powerful computer chip that could affect the computer industry.

3. Finally, perhaps the most important factor is: news about the economy. Signs of a stronger

economy will generally suggest higher corporate profits and give a boost to all stocks.

Obviously, there is a lot to consider when analyzing stocks to determine where the best place to invest might be.

6.6 Analyzing Information Reported in the Financial Press

What summary information is available in the financial news on a daily basis that covers the trading activity in the stock markets and what can be gleaned from its analysis?

Begin by xamining this information for the Trading Day: April 19, 2017 for International Business Machines or IBM stock which is recorded in Table 6.2.

The ticker symbol is just IBM. The first trade of the day is recorded as OPEN at $161.76 and the last trade of the day is the CLOSE of $161.69. The NET CHANGE records the amount by which the stock price changed from the previous day's CLOSE. On this day, the stock price fell dramatically by $8.36 for a large percentage change (% CHG) of -4.92%. The last column in the first row of the Table reports the total VOLUME, or number of shares traded throughout the day, which for April 19, 2017 was nearly 19 million shares.

STOCK	OPEN	CLOSE	NET CHG	% CHG	VOL (1000s)
IBM	161.76	161.69	-8.36	-4.92	18,857
52 -WK HI	52-WK LO	YTD % CHG	DIV	YLD %	PE
182.79	142.50	-2.59	5.60	3.46	13.29

Table 6.2 Information for the Trading Day:
April 20, 2017

The second row in the Table gives additional information that enables some analysis of the stock to be made. The high (HI) and low (LO) over the past year indicate a trading range for the stock between $182.79 and $142.50. To see what has happened to the stock price since the December 31, 2016, the year-go-date percentage change (YTD) indicates that the stock price has fallen by 2.59%.

These figures suggest that there was a significant change in the stock price on this particular trading day, and moreover that the stock is fairly volatile with such a wide trading range over the past year. Overall, it was not a strong performer in the early months of 2017, when it substantially underperformed the overall stock market, which on April 19, 2017 was up approximately 4.2 percent for the year-to-date.

Analysis of the Firm's Dividend Policy

Now examine the firm's dividend policy by way of example. Knowledge of a firm's *earnings or net income* is available to management, who must decide how much to pay out in dividends versus how much of those earnings to reinvest in the company, and dividends are an important determinant of the stock price.

Referring back to Figure 6.2, the annual dividends that IBM pays for each share of stock is recorded here as DIV = $5.60 per share. Note that dividends are normally paid quarterly, however, DIV represents the annualized dividend. This annual dividend represents a *Dividend Yield (YLD DIV)* of 3.46%, which can be found by dividing the annual dividend by the closing price and multiplying by 100%.

$$\text{DIV YLD} = \frac{\text{DIV}}{\text{CLOSE}} * 100\% \qquad (6.10)$$

This figure (of 3.46%) could be interpreted as *the return an investor in IBM would receive over the next year strictly in the form of dividends, if he purchased the stock at the close of trading, and IBM chose not to alter the dividend payout over the course of the next year.*

To get a feel for how much the management chooses to reinvest its earnings in the company versus pay dividends to its shareholders, use can be made of the PE ratio, which is the closing price divided by the *Earnings Per Share (EPS)* over the previous 12 months.

$$PE \ = \ \frac{CLOSE}{EPS} \qquad\qquad (6.11)$$

For IBM the PE Ratio is seen in Table 6.2 to be 13.29. As indicated in Table 6.1, total earnings are on the bottom line of the income statement. Earnings per share, therefore, represents the portion of the firm's profits over which the the shareholders have claims.

Many stocks are purchased primarily for their dividend income, while others are purchased primarily for their growth potential. Stocks with high dividend payout, that is, the share of earnings paid to shareholders, are typically for firms that have a relatively stable sales growth and are chosen by investors seeking a relatively steady income from their investment. Stocks with a high reinvestment rate, that is, the share of earnings that are retained by the firm and reinvested by the firm in order to raise future earnings, are typically riskier investments, but with a potential for higher returns, and are chosen by investors primarily seeking capital gains from their investment. That is, if the reinvestments made by the firm are successful, earnings will grow in the future and as the stock pricing formulas of the previous section demonstrate, this higher earnings growth would be reflected in a higher stock price.

With IBM's total earnings divided between dividends and retained earnings, equation (6.11) can be solved for the EPS in terms of the PE ratio and the closing price to find that IBM earned $12.17 per share.

$$EPS = CLOSE/PE = 161.69/13.29 = \$12.17$$

To determine IBM's total earnings requires knowledge of the number of shares outstanding. For IBM there are 943.21 million shares in the market. Therefore, IBM earned a total of $11.48 billion over the previous year, or:

$$Total\ Annual\ Earnings = \$12.17(943.21\ million)$$
$$= \$11.48\ billion$$

Of that total, it paid out $5.28 billion, or 46.0% of its total earnings in dividends.

$$Total\ Annual\ Dividend\ Payout = \$5.60\ (943.21\ million)$$
$$= \$5.28\ billion$$

Therefore, its retained earnings for the previous 12 months tallowed it to reinvest $6.20 billion, or 54.0% of its total earnings back into the firm.

$$Retained\ Earnings = Total\ Annual\ Earnings$$
$$- Total\ Annual\ Dividend\ Payout$$
$$= \$11.48\ billion - \$5.28\ billion$$
$$= \$6.20\ billion$$

Analysis of the Firm's Stock Price

Return now to the stock pricing formulas to see how they may be used. Suppose an analyst is tasked with making a recommendation on IBM stock. He wants a

6 percent rate of return to make the investment and projects that dividend growth will be approximately constant at 3 percent. Would he recommend a buy or a sell? Assume the stock is selling ex-dividend.

Use the symbol S_0^{E*} to represent the analyst's valuation of the share price. Then, using the stock price formula (6.6), and plugging in the numbers gives his valuation of the share price to be $178.53.

$$S_0^{E*} = \frac{d_0(1+g)}{r-g} = \frac{\$5.60(1.03)}{0.06-0.03} = \$192.27$$

However, since the stock is selling at $161.69, he believes it to be undervalued, and he would recommend a buy.

There is another approach that the investor could take in arriving at this recommendation. Based on the stock price, the investor can ask: what is the dividend growth rate anticipated by the market that would be consistent with a 6 percent required rate of return?

The alternative formulation of the stock price formula, equation (6.9), that is solved for the dividend growth rate indicates that the market anticipates an average growth rate of dividends of:

$$g = \frac{S_0^E - d_0}{S_0^E + d_0} = \frac{0.06(161.69) - 5.60}{161.69 + 5.60} = 0.0245 \text{ or } 2.45\%$$

which is below the investor's forecast. This explains why the market has placed a lower valuation on the stock than the investor.

6.7 Sources of Funds for Long-Term Growth

Healthy firms are always in need of funds to invest in building new production facilities, financing inventories, or acquiring additional financial assets. Long-term investments are usually financed with a combination of retained earnings, referred to as *internal finance* and new stock and/or bond issues, referred to as *external finance.*

Normally, the cheapest source of finance among these options is retained earnings and it represents, by far, the primary source of these funds for most firms. However, if the available retained earnings are insufficient to meet their investment needs, firms will switch from internal to external finance.

Bonds have an important tax advantage over stocks, as suggested by the firm's income statement displayed in Table 6.1. That is, the interest expense is tax deductible. This tax feature biases firms toward heavier debt loads than would otherwise be the case, and a key financial ratio for a firm is the *debt-to-equity ratio,* which is the amount of debt the firm owes divided by the value of its stock outstanding.

The implication of firms loading up on debt as they increase their reliance on bond financing, is that the probability of default increases with the additional debt burden. The bond rating agencies will lower the firm's ratings, and this drives up the interest rate demanded by new bond investors, which in turn increases the cost of raising capital by issuing bonds. At some point, the additional interest cost more than offsets the tax advantage and the firm will switch to the equity market and issue new stock.

As the firm then increases its reliance on new equity issues, it realizes both costs and benefits. The cost is a dilution of earnings. That is, with more shares of stock outstanding the claims on the firm's earnings are spread across a larger number of shareholders, such that the fraction of profits that each share represents is reduced. The share price will therefore fall, and the amount of funds raised by issuing new stock is hindered.

The advantage of issuing new stock is that the firm's debt-to-equity ratio is reduced. The rating agencies will see this financial ratio as an indication that the probability of default is reduced, since the shareholders will be absorbing any potential revenue losses rather than the bondholders, and the borrowing costs to the firm will fall.

Each firm determines its own optimal mix of retained earnings, stock, and bonds used to finance its long-term investments. Firms with relatively stable sales revenues, such as utilities companies, will typically rely more on debt than equity, since the predictability of their sales diminishes the likelihood of a revenue shortfall that would cause them to miss payments to the bondholders and enter into a default-induced bankruptcy. Firms that rely heavily on equity finance include those firms with strong growth potential, such as new start-up companies, like Facebook, and high tech firms, such as the big biotech firm Genentech. These firms will often spend many years with no debt, and without ever having paid a dividend to shareholders. They reinvest ALL of their earnings in the company and issue additional new shares of stock to investors seeking investments in stocks that are expected to realize strong capital gains. One example was Microsoft that never paid a dividend and maintained no debt for the first 20 years of existence. Its employees often received low salaries, but took compensation in the form of shares in the company. Many of the early employees of Microsoft became quite wealthy in the early days of the firm, as it grew to become the largest company in the world, measured by the value of outstanding shares of stock. Ironically, that claim today is held by Microsoft's rival, Apple Computer.

6.8 Stock Buybacks

In recent years, many firms have undertaken a strategy of buying back their own stock and thereby reducing the number of shares outstanding. Why would a company engage in these *stock buybacks*?

To make these purchases, firms must use their retained earnings, which are the profits over which shareholders have claims. Therefore, if the management of the firm is acting in the interests of its shareholders, it would only engage in stock buybacks if it felt that they were the best investment that it could make.

There may be several advantages to shareholders: For one, it may be seen by the markets as signaling that the firm's own internal analysis suggests that its stock is undervalued in the marketplace. To the extent that markets believe this to be the case, they would bid up the stock price in response. Of course stock buybacks also reduces the dilution of earnings, which again could also cause the stock price to rise.

There are potential disadvantages to a stock buyback. The reduction in shares will likely cause the firm's debt-to-equity ratio to rise, thus increasing the probability of default, adversely affecting the firm's bond rating, and increasing its borrowing costs. Also, the markets could take a different view of management's decision to spend its retained earnings on purchasing its own stock rather than making investments that could grow the companies earnings in the future as an admission that management doesn't see any good investment opportunities. This view would cause a sell-off of the stock and the stock price would fall.

6.9 Inflation Scares on Wall Street

In previous discussions, attention has been drawn to how inflation can affect any financial asset, since those assets generally represent claims to be received in the future that are typically denominated in domestic currency units such as the U.S. dollar. News often hits the financial markets that can cause an *inflation scare*: when the markets believe that inflation in the future is going to be higher than they had previously thought. How do the markets typically respond to an inflation scare?

Begin with a very useful expression, that has already appeared in fa different context: the, so-called Fisher equation named after the early 20th century economist Irving Fisher.

Market Rate(R)=Real Rate(r)+Expected Inflation(Eπ)

It states that the nominal or market interest rate on a financial asset is approximately equal to the real interest rate plus the expected rate of inflation. It acknowledges that investors want to be compensated dollar for dollar for any loss of purchasing power on the returns to their investments due to higher inflation.

An inflation scare implies that the expected rate of inflation has increased, which in turn indicates that the interest rate demanded by the market on financial assets will rise. As described in the last chapter, this higher required nominal rate of return coincides with an increase in the yield-to-maturity on the bond and a fall in the bond price.

Conclusion: An inflation scare always results in a sell-off in the bond market.

How about stocks? There is a slightly different story here. Whereas, for bonds the future claims of bondholders are fixed in, say, dollars which are expected to be worth less as expected inflation rises, for stocks, the future claims are dividend payments that the firm can alter. In general, when inflation rises, firms can increase the dividend payments somewhat and cushion the stockholders' payments form the higher inflation that reduces the purchasing power of those dividends. This is not to say that inflation is good for stocks. History does not support that conclusion. However, an inflation scare on Wall Street will have a greater negative effect on bond prices than on stock prices.

So what is an investor to do when there is an inflation scare? Often the markets will seek liquidity as investment portfolios adjust by attempts to get out of bonds, and to a lesser extent out of stocks, and into money market funds.

As this chapter suggests, there is a lot of information that can affect the stock market, and savvy investors need to be well informed if they are to be successful in this sometimes chaotic marketplace.

6.10 Summary

In this chapter, the basic difference between organized and over-the-counter stock exchanges is described, and along with the requirements a business must meet in order to be listed on one of the exchanges. The most fundamental questions were then addressed: What is an investor purchasing when he or she buys a share of stock, and what determines the share's value? It was discovered that the stock price reflects nothing more than the present value of all future dividends that the firm is expected to pay. Therefore, arriving at a stock price requires a projection of the path of future dividends for the company based on its expected earnings and dividend policy and an assessment of the level of risk attached to those projections. The less certain the investor is about those projections, the riskier the investment appears to be, and the higher is the rate of return required by the investor to make the investment.

It is a non-trivial exercise to form reasonable forecasts of the future performance of a stock, since corporate profits are subject to so many factors, some of which are under the control of management and others, such as natural disasters, political events, or other factors that could weaken the performance of the overall economy and thereby affect the demand for the firm's products, are beyond the control of management.

Turning to the investor, managing the risk and liquidity of one's investments is an important task. Liquidity can generally be enhanced by investments in money market assets that are of very short maturity or by acquiring U.S. Treasury securities, which are actively traded in very *deep* markets. Money market assets also tend to carry lower risk than stocks and bonds, and Treasury securities are devoid of default risk. For this reason, nearly every significant professional portfolio manager in the world holds some money market assets and some U.S. Treasury securities. Various aspects of these important markets are described in the next two chapters.

Key Terms

corporate stock or equities
price discovery process
competitive equity markets
semi-strong form of market efficiency
strong form of market efficiency
insider trading
short-selling
organized exchanges
New York Stock Exchange
American Stock Exchange
Intercontinental Exchange
open outcry auction market
specialists
order book
orderly trading
electronic trading
over-the-counter (OTC) markets
bid prices
ask prices
bid-ask spreads
principals
position of risk
National Association of Dealers Automated Quotation (NASDAQ)
circuit breakers
preprogrammed electronic trades
programmed trading
listing requirements

delisting
liquidity of a stock
trading platforms
electronic communication networks (ECNs)
NYSE Group
Euronext
Securities and Exchange Commission (SEC)
stock valuation
income statement
sales revenues
cost of goods sold
gross margin
operating expenses
earnings before interest and taxes (EBIT)
interest expense
earnings before taxes (EBT)
corporate income taxes
net income (or earnings)
corporate profits
dividends
retained earnings
reinvestments
declaration date
board of directors
date of record
ex-dividend date
ex-dividend price
dividend yield
price-earnings (PE) ratio

earnings per share (EPS)
internal finance
external finance
debt-to-equity ratio
stock buybacks
inflation scare

6.11   Review Questions

1. What constitutes a *competitive equity market*? How does it relate to the semi-strong and strong forms of market efficiency?

2. Why is insider trading illegal in the United States? Who polices the equity markets?

3. An increase in the market's perception of the riskiness of a public corporation's future earnings will cause the firm's stock price to fall because investors:

   a) will increase the required rate of return for investing in the stock, thus lowering the present value of the its future expected dividends.

   b) will decrease the required rate of return for investing in the stock, thus lowering the present value of the its future expected dividends.

   c) will decrease the required rate of return for investing in the stock, thus increasing the present value of the its future expected dividends.

   d) will increase the required rate of return for investing in the stock, thus increasing the present value of the its future expected dividends.

USE TABLE 1 TO ANSWER QUESTIONS 4-8.

Table Q1: Stock Market Trading Day: November 12, 2010

STOCK (SYMBOL)	DIV	YLD %	PE	CLOSE
GOOD-BUY (GB)	1.50	6.00	10	25.00
Amer Elec Pwr (AEP)	1.84	5.04	13.78	36.52
Coca-Cola (KO)	1.76	2.80	19.36	62.92
H & R Block (HRB)	0.60	4.67	8.86	12.85

STOCK (SYMBOL)	CHG	NET % CHG	YTD % CHG
GOOD-BUY (GB)	unch	0.00	-3.00
Amer Elec Pwr (AEP)	-0.02	-0.05	4.97
Coca-Cola (KO)	0.12	0.19	10.39
H & R Block (HRB)	0.05	0.39	-43.19

4. An investor choosing stocks only for their dividend income would:

   a) choose GB since it has the highest YLD %.

   b) choose AEP since it has the highest DIV.

   c) choose KO since it has the highest CLOSE.

   d) choose HRB since it has the highest % CHG.

5. Investors George and Alice each purchased the same dollar amount of each of the four stocks listed in Table Q1. However, George bought his as the last trade of the day on December 31, 2009 and Alice purchased hers as the last trade of the day on November 11, 2010. Which of the following is TRUE?

   a) George and Alice agree that KO was their best buy.

   b) George and Alice agree that HRB was their worst buy.

   c) George was happiest with KO and Alice was happiest with HRB.

   d) George was happiest with HRB and Alice was happiest with KO.

6. Duke is deciding whether to purchase HRB and/or AEP He does his homework and believes that both HRB and AEP will pay dividends that will grow at a rate of 2 percent per year. When he assesses the risk of the investment, he feels that he needs at least a 6 percent expected rate of return to make either

investment. Assume the stock prices listed in Table Q1 are inclusive of the current dividend. He will decide to:

    a) purchase AEP, but not HRB.

    b) purchase HRB, but not AEP.

    c) purchase both HRB and AEP.

    d) purchase neither HRB nor AEP.

7. Assuming there are 1 million shares of GB outstanding, which of the following is TRUE?

    a) The percentage of earnings paid out in dividends during the previous 12 months 40 percent.

    b) The total amount of earnings reinvested in the company during the previous 12 months was $1 million.

    c) Its market capitalization is $1 million.

    d) Its earnings per share is $2.50.

8. KO is selling ex-dividend on November 12, 2010. If the market requires a 6 percent rate of return to invest in the stock, what dividend growth (assume the growth rate to be constant) is the market expecting KO to pay out?

    a) 3.12 percent.

    b) 3.03 percent.

c) 2.80 percent.

d) 4.45 percent.

9. Zeno Corporation had earnings per share for the quarter of 25 cents. It currently pays an annual dividend of 20 cents per share for each of its one million shares outstanding. I would like to make a $100,000 investment in the current quarter. Discuss the pros and cons of funding the investment with: (a) retained earnings; (b) debt: or (c) new equity issues.

10. A common stockholder of Milton Corporation is entitled to a *pro rata* share of any new stock issued by the company. If the firm plans to issue 300,000 new shares at a price of $10 per share and this particular stockholder currently holds 1.5 percent of all Milton's shares outstanding, how many new share is this shareholder entitled to purchase? At what total cost?

11. Riter-Cal Corporation has preferred shares outstanding carrying a $50 par value and promising a 6 percent annual dividend rate. Daniel Smith holds 150 shares of R-C's preferred stock. What annual dividend can he expect to receive if the company's board of directors votes to pay the regular dividend? Suppose R-C's preferred stock consists of *participating* shares, with preferred stockholders participating equally in net earnings with the firm's common stockholders. If the company declares a $5 per share common stock dividend, how much in additional per-share

dividends will each of its preferred shareholders receive?

12. When a firm needs to raise funds to invest in production facilities, it can issue new shares of stock, issue new bonds, or rely on its retained earnings. In considering these options:

   a) most firms rely principally on stocks, despite the fact that increasing the amount of share outstanding dilutes earnings.

   b) most firms rely principally on bonds, since its interest expense is tax deductible.

   c) most firms rely on retained earnings, despite the fact that this represents after-tax income.

   d) there is very little difference across firms with respect to how much they rely on the three principal sources of long-term finance.

6.12   References

Cochrane, John H. 2014. "Eugene F. Fama, Efficient Markets, and the Nobel Prize" (May 20). Available at: http://review.chicagobooth.edu/magazine/winter-2013/eugene-fama-efficient-markets-and-the-nobel-prize

Fama, Eugene F. "Efficient Capital Markets: A Review of Theory and Empirical Work." 1970. *The Journal of Finance* Vol. 25, No. 2, Papers and Proceedings of the Twenty-Eighth Annual Meeting of the American Finance Association New York, N.Y. December, 28-30, 1969 (May): 383-417

Geisst, Charles R. 2004. Wall Street: A History ? From its Beginnings to the Fall of Enron. Oxford University Press.

Kelley, Eric, K. and Paul C. Tetlock. 2017. "Retail Short Selling and Stock Prices." *Review of Financial Studies*, Vol 30(3), 801-834.

For a brief history of the New York Stock Exchange, go to: https://en.wikipedia.org/wiki/New_York_Stock_Exchange

Chapter 7

The Money Markets

In subsequent chapters, we want to examine the important roles that *depository institutions*, most notably *commercial banks*, play in the economy. It is clear that a healthy banking system is essential to a vibrant economy, but why is it so important? To answer this question, an examination of the details of their balance sheet is required, along with an understanding of the nature of the regulations on this most heavily regulated sector of the economy.

However, before plunging into the accounting, it is important to take a look at some of the financial markets in which the banks operate. Most of these markets are *money markets* involving short-maturity assets. These money markets have been among the most innovative – apart, perhaps, from the derivatives markets – over the past 30 years, and those innovations have had a profound influence on the banking sector and on the regulations designed to seek that ever-changing balance between financial stability on the one hand and economic efficiency on the other.[1]

7.1   Money Market Mutual Funds (MMMFs)

A new set of financial institutions was created in the 1970s that competed directly with depository institutions. These firms are the *money market mutual funds*. At the time, *commercial banks* were prohibited by law from paying interest on their *checking accounts*, and *savings and loans, or S&Ls*, could not even offer checking accounts. In addition, the savings accounts of banks and S&Ls were subject to *interest rate ceilings* that were 5% for banks and 5-1/4% for S&Ls. The higher rate for the S&Ls was intended to give them an advantage in this market, although they were required to channel most of those deposits into the housing market by offering *mortgages* on more favorable terms.

In the late 1970s, inflation rose dramatically, eventually peaking at around 14% per year in 1980. Households with deposit accounts in the banks and S&Ls were therefore seeing the value of those assets eroding very quickly with nearly double-digit negative real returns. In response, households began to pull their deposits in search of higher returns.

---

[1]The classic reference to the money markets is Stigum and Crescenzi (2007), now in its 4th edition.

Cropping up to fill the void were money market mutual funds (MMMFs). Their role is to accept deposits (which are not federally insured), aggregate those funds, and invest in a portfolio of short-term money market assets which were not subject to the interest rate ceilings that existed at the time on deposits in banks and S&Ls. The money funds extract a fee for managing the investment portfolio, and pass along the remaining interest income to investors. The value of assets under management is referred to as the money market mutual fund's *net asset value, NAV.*

Since investments by MMMFs are restricted to short-term money market assets, where there is no room for capital gains, the NAV should reflect a stable market value of the those investments. Typically, the firm pays dividends to investors that are computed daily, reflecting the income earned on its investments less administrative fees, such that it maintains a NAV of $1.00 per share (equal to the amount of money invested in the fund where each share is worth $1.00). Money market mutual funds rarely lose money, but a combination of low short-term money market interest rates and bad investments could cause the value of the fund's NAV to fall below $1.00, in which case, it is said to be *"breaking the buck."* Money market mutual funds are regulated by the *Securities and Exchange Commission (SEC),* which enforces strict accounting rules to ensure that investors' funds are properly managed to avoid the scenario of a "broken buck."

The flight of funds from the depository institutions into MMMFs that occurred during the 1970s is referred to as *disintermediation*, and was creating a major threat to the viability of those institutions. In the early 1980s, Congress passed two major pieces of banking legislation. The first was referred to by the long title of *Monetary Institutions Deregulation and Monetary Control Act of 1980* and the second was the *Garn-St Germain Acto of 1983* that were primarily intended to address this problem. They repealed the regulations that placed interest rate ceilings on deposit accounts of depository institutions, thus allowing banks and S&Ls to pay market rates of interest on their accounts. They also allowed S&Ls to offer checking accounts and to make business loans for the first time, thus *leveling the regulatory playing field* across depository institutions.

However, in those years leading up to the deregulation of deposit interest rates, hundreds of money funds had started up and attracted $1 trillion from investors. Since their creation, they have become a mainstay in the financial markets by offering investment options with the following characteristics:

1. The assets are very liquid – they can be easily converted into cash without large costs.

2. Investors earn a market rate of return from the portfolio (less the money funds' fees) and achieve *diversification* by investing in a range of money market assets.

3. They open up markets to small investors by investing a portion of their assets in an important set of money market assets that require large (million dollar) minimum investments.

4. Since all of the money funds' assets are short-term money market assets that carry a relatively low level of risk, large institutional investors, such as pension funds, can use these money funds to achieve their desired balance between risk and return in their overall investments, which generally include more risky assets, such as corporate stock.

5. Of particular note with regard to major investors in MMMFs is the fact that pension funds in the United States have grown tremendously in recent years. In 2015, the total value of their assets under management computed to nearly 80 percent of GDP or over $23 trillion. This growth has been spawned by the shift in pension plans of firms and governments from *defined benefits programs* (which guarantee a monthly retirement payment based on the number of years of service and the average salary over the last 3 or 4 years of service) to *defined contribution plans* (where the employer invests the retirement money on behalf of the employee, who directs how those funds are to be invested). The liquidity and risk characteristics of money funds allow them to play a significant role

in the management of these *retirement accounts*.

As noted in a previous chapter, there are more than $700 billion in *retail money market mutual funds* with accounts below $100,000, but the larger accounts in excess of $100,000 that are collected in so-called *institution-only or IO MMMFs* have more than $1.8 trillion dollars in them. While the number of MMMFs operating in the United States has declined in recent years to a little over 400, they have clearly established for themselves an important niche in the financial market, serving investors and portfolio managers who are interested in placing some of their financial wealth in the money markets.

Let's take a look at some of the money market instruments in which money funds invest.[2]

7.2   Treasury Bills

Approximately one-half of the money market funds in the United States restrict their investments to government securities, primarily issued by the Treasury Department. Moreover, one of the principal assets in which virtually all money market mutual funds invest is short-term U.S. government debt, or *Treasury bills*

---

[2]Detailed statistics on MMMFs can be found at the Securities and Exchange Commission's website at: https://www.sec.gov/divisions/investment/mmf-statistics/mmf-statistics-2017-6.pdf

(T-bills). The *Treasury Department* is authorized by Congress to issue debt securities with maturities up to one year that have the following characteristics:

1. They are currently issued in maturities of 4-week, 3-month, 6-month, and 1-year.

2. All T-bills are sold at discount to face value, which is the value paid to investors upon maturity.

3. As with all U.S. government debt, T-bills are backed by the taxing authority of the U.S. government and are thus free of default risk.

4. The market for T-bills is one of the deepest of all financial markets such that T-bills are among the most liquid of all financial assets. Facilitating the ease of trading in these securities is the fact that all T-bills are *paperless securities* whose ownership must be registered on the computers of the Federal Reserve. The importance of this feature of T-bills is discussed in detail in subsequent chapters.

5. Due to their relatively low risk and high liquidity, T-bills generally carry a low expected rate of rate which forms an anchor or benchmark against which all other short-term interest rates with higher risk and less liquidity are compared.

The pricing of T-bills was encountered in previous chapters. Because of the relative importance of the market for U.S. Treasury securities, including Treasury notes and bonds as well as T-bills, a separate chapter will be devoted to the details of how they are traded and the roles they play in facilitating short-term finance and portfolio management.

7.3   Commercial Paper

A central asset in the portfolios of prime money funds is *commercial paper*. Commercial paper is often referred to as a "corporate IOU." In their earliest form, these assets were uncollateralized short-term debt sold at a discount.[3]

They are analogous to T-bills, except that they: (i) carry a higher risk of default, and (ii) are much less liquid, generally traded in relatively "thin" markets (or markets with a low volume of trading). Both the higher risk and the lower liquidity suggest that they carry a higher expected rate of return than T-bills of comparable maturity.

Their other asset properties include:

- A minimum investment of $1 million is normally required.

---

[3]Data on the commercial paper market is compiled by the Federal Reserve and available online at: https://www.federalreserve.gov/releases/cp/

- They range in maturity from 30 to 270 days. The upper limit here is due to the SEC requirement that firms must post filings at some cost to them of future debt issues with maturities in excess of 270 days.

- The market is very sensitive to risk, and the volume of commercial paper falls dramatically during recessions.

- The fact that commercial paper is sold at a discount implies that the investor receives nothing on his or her investment until it matures.

- The primary market for commercial paper is comprised of: (a) *direct paper*: that is sold by the issuing firm (normally financial firms) directly to the investor, and (b) *dealer paper* (normally issued by non financial firms) which is sold through an intermediary, usually a broker that finds a buyer for the commercial paper for a fee.

- One of the largest buyers of commercial paper is the group of prime money market mutual funds (MMMFs), for whom commercial paper represent the riskiest asset and therefore the highest expected rate of return in the portfolios that MMMFs manage.

To deal with the additional risk of uncollateralized commercial paper, the markets have relied on the following:

- Only firms with high credit ratings, so-called *blue chip firms*, such as General Electric or IBM, can issue commercial paper.

- Even high quality firms must maintain a *backup line of credit* at a commercial bank, with the idea that if sales fell and they didn't have the funds to retire maturing commercial paper, they could tap their commercial bank for a short-term loan to make good on their debt obligations.

- *Covenants* in a bank's line of credit agreement include provisions for closing the line of credit if the firm's *financials* deteriorate too much. For example, the firm must maintain a minimum ratio of current (short-term) assets to current liabilities. Falling below this minimum may terminate the loan agreement.

- *Credit enhancements* have also been offered by banks to some lesser quality firms (but still with good credit ratings) whereby the bank would essentially guarantee payment on maturing commercial paper, if the firm was unable to do so.

Given that firms usually have alternative ways to raise funds, why would they choose to issue commercial paper? There are several potential reasons.

- Funds raised with commercial paper are often used to satisfy short-term financing needs. It takes precedence over bank loans, which are the major alternative source of short-term funding, since commercial paper is much cheaper than bank loans, carrying substantially lower interest rates.

- Commercial paper may also be used for so-called *bridge financing* of longer-term investments. It may be that the firm believes that the market would not be very receptive to any new stocks or bonds that it might issue, and the firm could issue commercial paper and continue to "roll-it-over," that is, issue new commercial paper as the outstanding commercial paper matures, until a more favorable market environment presented itself.

- Some firms may choose to rely on a sort of leverage by shortening the average maturity of its debt. The firm may see that short rates are significantly below long rates, thereby enabling lower average cost funding by relying more heavily on shorter-term credit. Of course, this firm runs the risk of rising short rates in the future and the need for refinancing at higher short rates as they roll-over those commercial paper offerings to the public. This practice is referred to as *playing the yield curve*. A complete description of the yield curve will be coming up in the next chapter.

The growth in commercial paper has been phenomenal, at least up until the onset of the Great Recession.

Here are some figures: In 1970, the amount of commercial paper outstanding was $33 billion. By 2007, prior to the Great Recession, it had grown to $2.2 trillion! As we stated, this market is very sensitive to risk and economic conditions, and during the Great Recession, the commercial paper market contracted severely. By 2010 the volume of commercial paper outstanding had fallen to $1 trillion, which is roughly where it stands today. Note that this implies that firms which had relied on the commercial paper market for funding suddenly saw $1.2 trillion of funding withheld by the market! These funds had to be drawn from somewhere else. Obviously, commercial paper played an important role in the credit crisis. This phenomenon will be discussed later in connection with the unprecedented actions taken by the Federal Reserve to restore liquidity to the economy during this difficult period.

7.4 Large Negotiable Certificates of Deposit (CDs)

The group of regulated *depository institutions* comprised of *commercial banks, savings & loans (S&Ls)*, and *credit unions* obtain the bulk of their funds in the money markets. Subsequent chapters will detail the decisions that bank managers must make on which of these potential sources to choose, and how they make

those decisions. For now, simply note that money
market mutual funds purchase liabilities of these depository institutions to hold in the portfolio of money
market assets that they are managing. Among those
liabilities is the *large negotiable certificate of deposit
(CD)*.[4]

Since the portfolios of MMMFs contain exclusively
short-term financial assets, they must be actively managed, as many of those assets mature each day. Therefore, MMMF managers are always on the lookout for
good short-term investments. Large negotiable CDs
have a number of properties that are particularly attractive to money fund managers.

1. The minimum denomination of these large CDs
   is $100,000; however, the majority of issues have
   a minimum of $1 million, making them a market
   that small investors can access only through a
   mutual fund.

2. As a liability of depository institutions that are
   covered by the *Federal Deposit Insurance Corporation (FDIC)*, they are insured up to $250,000
   per account, which mitigates their risk.

3. Unlike many other money market assets, large
   negotiable CDs are not sold at a discount to face
   value. Instead, the interest rate that is often

---

[4]See Summers (1980) for a description and a history of the
negotiable CD market.

quoted on the CD is computed on the principal (amount invested) on a "CD basis," which is based on a 360-day year.

Example: To determine the total return (principal plus interest) on a 90-day, $1,000,000 CD paying 3 percent on a CD basis, the formula is:

$$\text{Total Return} = \text{Amount Invested}$$

$$\times \left[1 + \left(\frac{\text{Days to Maturity}}{360 \text{ days/yr}} \right) \text{CD rate} \right] \quad (7.1)$$

or,

$$\$1,000,000 \left[1 + \left(\frac{90}{360} \right) 0.03 \right] = \$1,075,000 \quad (7.2)$$

To compute the actual annualized rate of return, r^{CD}:

$$r^{CD} = \frac{\text{Total Return} - \text{Amount Invested}}{\text{Amount Invested}}$$

$$\times \frac{\text{Days to Maturity}}{365 \text{ days/yr}} \quad (7.3)$$

$$\Rightarrow r^{CD} = \frac{\$1,075,000 - \$1,000,000}{\$1,000,000} \times \frac{365}{90}$$

$$= 0.03042 \text{ or } 3.042\% \qquad (7.4)$$

4. Payment to the holder of the CD is normally not made until the asset matures, although some issuing depository institutions pay semi-annual interest payments.

5. Being negotiable, these assets have a relatively high degree of liquidity, although many purchasers tend to buy and hold the assets until maturity, which is normally one year or less from the date of issuance.

Variable-Rate CDs

An alternative variant of the large negotiable certificate of deposit is the *variable-rate CD* or *floating-rate CD*. As the name implies, these assets carry an interest rate that is adjusted over time to market rates. The interest rate on a newly issued variable-rate CD is generally set as a spread over a market rate, such as a given T-bill rate or a market average of newly issued CDs. To compute the interest earned on the CD, the length of the maturity of the CD is divided into periods of fixed length, such as one to three months. At the end of each period, the interest rate is reset.

The maturity of these CDs is typically a little longer – at 18 months to two years – than those of the more traditional large CD. This feature makes them particularly attractive to money market mutual funds, which represent the largest buyers of these assets, as it enables them to maintain a market interest rate on those investments, while avoiding the need of continually reinvesting maturing assets. In addition, the *Securities and Exchange Commission (SEC)*, which restricts the average maturity of money fund investment, allows the money funds to compute the average maturity of their portfolio of investments by treating the maturity of variable-rate CDs as the period over which the rate is reset.

Eurodollar and Yankee CDs

Large negotiable certificates of deposit are often used by banks to raise funds internationally. Large commercial banks with multinational operations can tap markets in locations where their branch offices are operating outside of their country of origin. U.S. banks with branches in London or Tokyo, for example, may issue dollar-denominated CDs in foreign countries where those branches are domiciled. These CDs are referred to as *Eurodollar CDs*, reflecting the facts of both their origin (Europe) and the currency in which they are traded. The buyers are often large multinational corporations who are engaged in markets, such as oil, where transactions are primarily conducted in dollars. Large foreign banks, such as Barclay's bank in London, also find Eurodollar CDs to service the same set of multinational clients.

From the U.S. perspective, foreign banks also wish to service multinational corporations through the operations of their branches in the United States. A significant portion of the funds they raise in deposit markets in the United States is derived from large negotiable CDs. These CDs are referred to as *Yankee CDs*. These branch banks are subject to the regulations of the U.S. bank regulatory agencies, principally the Federal Reserve.

7.5 Repurchase Agreements (Repos or RPs)

A *repurchase agreement*, often referred to as a *repo* or an *RP*, is comprised of two transactions that mimic a collateralized loan, where the collateral is usually a Treasury security, such as a 3-month T-bill. Normally, the maturity of these RPs is overnight. The interest rate is referred to as the *RP or repo rate*. It is a bank discount rate that is typically very low, reflecting the low risk involved in these assets (about which more will be said) and the very short maturities which implies that monies invested in an RP are relatively liquid.

The simplest example of an RP can illustrate the

mechanism at work behind what amounts to a very short-term loan.[5]

Example: One typical issuer of RPs is a large bank that may be in need, say, of about $1 billion quickly in order to meet loan requests by its major corporate clients, such IBM or GE, to draw on their lines of credit with the bank. Suppose the bank possesses a T-Bill with a market value of $1 billion. One option it has in raising the funds is to sell the T-bill and use the proceeds to make the loans. However, it could decide instead that this is a temporary shortage of funds, and rather than sell the T-bill outright, it could enter into a repurchase agreement whereby it agrees to sell the T-bill today, and repurchase the same T-bill back tomorrow at a price that includes the sale price plus an interest payment. How does the process work?

The bank must first find a *counterparty* to the RP, who would be an investor with funds for which he or she needs to find a short-term, relatively low-risk investment, that of course is going to carry a relatively low rate of return. One such buyer is another commercial bank that may have seen an unusual inflow of deposits coupled with maturing assets which leaves the bank with excess funds that it would like to invest. When commercial banks are on both sides of the transaction, the contract is referred to as a *bank RP*.

---

[5]A full description of the repurchase agreement market is can found in Stigum (1988).

The timing of the transactions is, of course, very important since the loan is of such short maturity, i.e., less than 24 hours. Here is the mechanism by which transactions take place.

First note that all T-Bills are paperless securities with ownership registered on computers at the Federal Reserve. The sale of a T-bill can be accomplished electronically by shifting the ownership claims to the owner's agent, which is a commercial bank that is a member of the Federal Reserve System, to the agent of the new owner. In the case of a bank RP, both the borrower and the lender are commercial banks and are likely members of the Federal Reserve. The decision to become a member of the Federal Reserve is discussed later, when the structure of the U.S. banking system is examined. For now, note that these transactions take place over the double-entry bookkeeping and *electronic funds transfer (EFT)* system known as Fedwire. Fedwire transactions will also be described in more detail in the next chapter..

These transactions are referred to *"delivery-versus-payment", or DVP transactions* in which the party possessing the T-bill is in control of the timing of the transactions. Initially, the borrowing bank has the T-bill and "sends" the T-bill electronically to the lending bank. This action triggers the flow of funds electronically from the lending bank to the borrowing bank. The amount sent represents the amount of the loan. The next day, the lending bank has fulfilled its loan

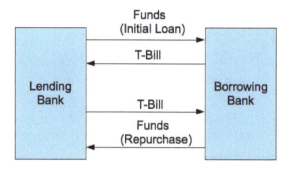

Figure 7.1: Bank RP Transaction

commitment and possesses the T-Bill, so it wants to receive its funds back as soon as possible. It is now in control of the timing of this second transaction and "sends" the T-bill electronically back to the borrowing bank. As in the earlier transaction, this action triggers a flow of funds from the borrowing bank to the lending bank. The amount sent is referred to as the *repurchase price* that equals the amount loaned plus interest.

Given the amount of collateral represented by the T-bill, how much would the lending bank be willing to loan? There is some risk that the borrowing bank will not repurchase the T-bill once the RP contract is fulfilled. Such RPs are labeled *fails*. They usually only occur for some technical reason that caused the transaction to be unfilled. Nonetheless, when they do occur, there is some chance that short-term interest rates could have risen overnight and the value of the collateral, or the market price of the T-bill, has declined. The lending bank is therefore incurring some *interest rate risk* in making the loan.

To protect the lending bank from this interest rate risk, the loan amount will not reflect the full market value of the T-Bill. Instead, the lending bank will base the *loan amount* on a repurchase price that is less than the market value of the T-bill. This reduction, which is usually a percentage of the market value of the T-bill, is referred to as a *haircut*. Obviously, this haircut provides an additional incentive for the borrowing bank to repurchase the T-bill when the RP matures to avoid what would otherwise effectively amount to selling the T-bill at a loss.

Computing the Amount of the Loan

For our example, let's compute the loan amount that a bank may receive when issuing an *overnight RP* against the $1 billion T-bill, when the lending bank demands an RP rate on its investment of 2% and is instituting a haircut that is 1% of the market value of the T-Bill. We can use the discount rate formula (from Chapter 5) to determine how much money the bank can raise by issuing this RP. The only change is that the par or face value is replaced by the repurchase price which reflects the haircut, or:

$$\text{RP Rate} = \frac{\text{Repurchase Price - Loan Amount}}{\text{Repurchase Price}}$$

$$\times \frac{360 \text{ days}}{1 \text{ day to maturity}} \qquad (7.5)$$

where:

$$\text{Repurchase Price} = \text{Face Value of the T-bill}$$

$$\times (1 - \% \text{ Haircut}) \qquad (7.6)$$

Plugging in the numbers:

$$0.02 = \frac{\$1 \text{ billion } (1-.01) - \text{Loan Amount}}{\$1 \text{ billion } (1-.01)} \times 360 \qquad (7.7)$$

and solving for the Loan Amount:

$$\text{Loan Amount} = \$989,945,000 \qquad (7.8)$$

We can now compute the interest income that the lending back should receive on this loan:

Interest Income = Repurchase Price − Loan Amount

$$= \$1,000,000,000 - \$989,945,000 = \$55,000 \quad (7.9)$$

The annualized rate of return on this loan can be found by answering the question: What would the lending bank receive if it were able to roll-over the original investment in this overnight loan for 365 days and receive the same daily return? In this case, the total return would be 365 ×$55,000, or $20,075,000. The annualized rate of return on the investment can be computed as:

$$\text{Annualized Rate of Return}$$

$$= \frac{\text{Total Return per Year}}{\text{Loan Amount}} \times 100\%$$

$$= \frac{\$20,075,000}{\$989,945,000} \times 100\% = 2.028\% \quad (7.10)$$

The Role of Government Securities Dealers

It is typical of this market that RP transactions are carried out by the use of a *Government Securities Dealer*

(GSD). They manage portfolios of Treasury securities and make markets for those assets in the same way that dealers on the NASDAQ are market makers for stocks, as described Chapter 6.

As we'll discuss in more detail in the next chapter, GSD's quote *bid and ask discount rates* for T-bills that they hold in their portfolios. They stand ready to buy selected T-bills at a price that guarantees the buyer a discount rate coinciding with the bid rate. They also stand ready to sell the same T-bills from their portfolio at a price that guarantees the GSD a discount rate given by the ask rate.

They are also market makers for RPs in which they quote bid and ask (discount) RP rates. As is the case for T-Bills, the bid rate is higher than the ask rate, which enables them to realize a profit for making the market.

GSDs prefer to act as brokers in the RP market by netting out their RP sales with their RP purchases. However, when they find themselves unable to sell all of the RPs they have purchased, they must find an alternative financing source. That source is usually a commercial bank, where the GSD takes out what is referred to as a *demand loan*, which normally carries a higher rate than does the RP that they have issued, causing the GSD to lose money on the transactions.

Continuing Contracts

While banks rely on RPs for short-term funding as well as managing the liquidity and risk in their asset portfolios, which we will discuss in greater detail in subsequent chapters, there are other players with financing and investing needs who turn to the money markets, and often to the RP market. One important institution is the money market mutual fund (MMMF) that is continually seeking to reinvest its maturing assets. Many of these businesses rely on the RP market for a continued source of funds.

To achieve this regular source of funding, these businesses can establish a working relationship with buyers and enter into what are referred to as *continuing contracts*. Continuing contracts are essentially RP contracts that are automatically renewed each day until one of the two parties decides to terminate the contract. The RP rate is updated each day and interest accumulates on the contract until termination. This arrangement avoids the transactions costs associated with the sale and resale of the securities.

The overnight RP market is vast, with over $500 billion in loans made each day. It also serves as the principal market in which the Federal Reserve conducts its purchases of government bonds when it implements its monetary policy decisions. These transactions will be described in detail later in Chapter 10.

7.6   Banker's Acceptances

A *banker's acceptance* is a short-term debt instrument, much like a Treasury bill, where the issuer is a commercial bank rather than the federal government. It is sold at a discount to face value and carries a maturity that is typically between 30 and 180 days. Once issued, the banker's acceptance can be resold in the secondary market, and is therefore a relatively liquid, low-risk, short-term debt instrument that makes it an ideal investment for money market mutual funds.

Banker's acceptances are used by large firms for the payment of intermediate goods used in their production process, and are most frequently utilized in international trade involving import-export transactions. Their value in this regard is best illustrated by way of example.

Example: Suppose a U.S. import/export firm wished to purchase coffee from Brazil and resell it to a coffee processor in the United States. The coffee producer in Brazil will not release the coffee for shipment until he receives payment, but the U.S. importer does not wish to pay for the coffee until he has sold it to a coffee processor in the United States. However, the coffee processor will not pay for the coffee until it is received, that is, after it has been shipped from Brazil, which is a process that may take a few weeks. Essentially, the coffee importer needs to finance the purchase for the duration of the shipment while the coffee is in transit.

We assume that the coffee importer has a good credit history and a long-standing relationship with a commercial bank in the United States. The coffee importer could go to the bank and request a banker's acceptance (BA), which is a note obligating the bank to make payment to the bearer of the note at a future date. The coffee importer agrees to provide the bank with funds to honor the BA prior to its maturity in an amount equal to the face value of the BA plus interest. The importer can then sell the BA in the open market to, say, a MMMF for cash. The cash is transferred to the Brazilian coffee producer and the coffee is shipped.

When the coffee arrives in the United States, the coffee importer sells it to the U.S. coffee processor for cash. The amount received from the sale must be equal to the Brazilian exporter's sale price plus the funds needed for shipping, handling, and any duties that may apply, plus the importer's profits from the transaction. That is, they must be sufficient for the coffee importer to make the required payment to the bank, thus fulfilling his obligation to the bank, plus additional funds that he retains as a net profit from the sale.

In the meantime, the BA may have been bought and sold several times in the open market (although they are usually held to maturity by the original buyer). Upon maturity, the bearer of the BA redeems it with the bank, receiving interest on the loan. The bank made a profit by issuing the banker's acceptance, not by loaning out any funds, but by guaranteeing repay-

ment of the loan. In essence, the risk of the loan incurred by the investor (the MMMF) was shifted from
the coffee importer to the commercial bank.

7.7   Summary

Money market mutual funds came into existence in the
1970s as a result of regulations imposed on commercial
banks and savings institutions that limited the interest rates those institutions could pay on various deposit accounts. When the United States experienced
double-digit inflation, these interest rate ceilings were
significantly below the general rate of inflation, causing depositors to earn a negative real rate of return on
their deposits. As a result, the depository institutions
subject to those regulations experienced a shrinkage of
the deposit base, as customers withdrew their funds
and placed them in the burgeoning money market mutual funds that were under no such limitations on the
interest they could pay.

In the early 1980s, these interest rate ceilings were
lifted and this process of disintermediation ceased. However, money market mutual funds had gotten a foothold
in the process of financial intermediation in the United
States. They received a further boost by the movement
to replace so-called defined benefit retirement programs
with defined contribution plans, whereby pension funds
that were managing those accounts invested portions
of the funds in money market mutual funds, as well

as stock and bond funds. These MMMFs in turn purchased portfolios of Treasury bills, commercial paper, certificates of deposit, repurchase agreements, and banker's acceptances, thus providing an important source of funding for the issuers of these money market assets. As described in upcoming chapters, commercial banks are among those institutions that rely on these funds to meet their short-term financing requirements.

Key Terms

depository institutions
commercial bank
money markets
money market mutual funds (MMMFs)
checking accounts
savings and loans (S&Ls)
interest rate ceilings
mortgages
net asset value (NAV)
breaking the buck
Securities and Exchange Commission (SEC)
disintermediation
Monetary Institutions Deregulation and Monetary
    Control Act of 1980
leveling the regulatory playing field
diversification
defined benefit versus defined contribution retire-
    ment plans
retail money market mutual funds versus
    institution-only (IO) money market mutual funds
U.S. Treasury bills
Treasury Department
paperless securities
commercial paper
direct paper versus dealer paper
blue chip firms
backup line of credit
covenants

financials
credit enhancements
bridge financing
playing the yield curve
credit unions
large negotiable certificate of deposit (CD)
Federal Deposit Insurance Corporation (FDIC)
"CD basis"
variable-rate or floating-rate CD
Eurodollar CD
Yankee CD
Repurchase Agreement or Repo or RP
bank RP
electronic funds transfer (EFT)
delivery-versus-payment or DVP transaction
repurchase price
fails
interest rate risk
loan amount of an RP
haircut
overnight RP
Government Securities Dealer (GSD)
bid and ask RP rates
demand loan
continuing contracts
banker's acceptances

7.8   Review Questions

1. Explain when and why money market mutual funds came into existence in the United States.

2. What is meant by a MMMF's NAV?

3. How does a MMMF make money?

4. What is meant by "breaking the buck," and why is it so important?

5. Explain the advantages to households that retail MMMFs offer as a savings asset.

6. Who are the major suppliers of funds to the IO MMMFs? What advantage do these MMMFs have for these investors?

7. How has the change in retirement plans of firms and governments tended to support the MMMFs?

8. What are the principal characteristics of U.S. Treasury bills as investment vehicles?

9. Compare commercial paper with T-bills as investment instruments?

10. Why is the maturity of commercial paper limited 270 days?

11. Why do MMMFs find commercial paper so attractive relative to other money market assets?

12. Discuss the importance of risk associated with investments in commercial paper and the ways in which the markets deal with that risk.

13. What advantages are there for firms issuing commercial paper as opposed to relying on alternative sources of funding?

14. You invest $500,000 in a 6-month, large negotiable CD paying 2 percent on a CD basis.

    a) What is the total return from your investment?

    b) What is the actual annualized rate of return on this investment?

    c) Could you lower the risk you are taking while continuing to investment in large, negotiable CDs?

15. What is the advantage to a money market mutual fund of investing in a variable-rate CD? What do you suppose making the CD a variable rate versus a fixed rate has on the interest rate? Does this advantage or disadvantage the issuing bank, S&L, or credit union that issued the CD?

16. What are Eurodollar CDs, and why do they exist? How do they differ from Yankee CDs?

17. Describe how a bank wishing to raise money in the RP market would go about it?

18. What is the purpose of a "haircut" when applied to a repo contract? How does it affect the likelihood of repayment? Explain.

19. A bank wishes to raise funds in the overnight RP market against a T-bill that it owns which has a market value of $100,000.

    a) If the bank is offered a 3% repo rate with a 2% haircut, how much can it raise by issuing the RP?

    b) What is the interest income that the lender to this bank would make on this overnight loan?

    c) What is the actual annualized rate of return that the lender would receive on this investment?

20. Describe the role of Government Securities Dealers in the market for repurchase agreements.

21. Continuing contracts represent an important segment of the repurchase agreement market.

    a) Describe such a contract and why they may be advantageous to both the lender and the borrower?

    b) How are interest rates determined in the continuing contract?

    c) When is the interest income received by the lender?

22. Banker's acceptances are often used to finance the purchase of international commodities while they are in transit.

    a) When a banker's acceptance is used for international transactions, who is the ultimately lender for these purchases?

    b) What risk does the lender run when making this investment?

    c) What risk does the issuer of the banker's acceptance run?

    d) Why might they be a good investment for a MMMF?

7.9   References

Stigum, Marcia and Anthony Crescenzi.. 2007 *Stigum's Money Market*, 4th ed. McGraw-Hill Education: New York. Available as a free download at: https://archive .org/stream/MarciaStigum/Marcia%20Stigum%2C%20 Anthony%20Crescenzi-Stigum%27s%20Money%20Mar- ket-McGraw-Hill%20%282007%29#page/n1/mode/2up

Stigum, Marcia. 1998. *The Repo and Reverse Markets*, McGraw-Hill Companies: New York.

Summers, Bruce. "Negotiable Certificates of Deposit," 1980. *Economic Review*, Federal Reserve Bank of Rich- mond (July/August).

"Money Market Fund Statistics." 2017. Securities and Exchange Commission. (June 30). Available at: https: //www.sec.gov/divisions/investment/mmf-statistics/ mmf-statistics-2017-6.pdf

"Commercial Paper Rates and Outstanding Summary" 2017. Board of Governors of the Federal Reserve Sys- tem. Available at: https://www.federalreserve.gov/re- leases/cp/

Chapter 8

The U.S. Treasury Market

In previous chapters, we have discussed the money markets, the corporate bond market, and the stock market. Portfolio managers typically combine investments in assets drawn from each of these markets. However, they must be able to achieve a balance of risk and expected return in the assets that they have under management. One of the principal tools that they rely on is the U.S. Treasury market.

U.S. Treasury securities have three important properties that make them exceptionally valuable for helping to achieve this balance. The first is that they are free of default risk. To date, the U.S. government has never defaulted on its debt. This fact has been rewarded by the markets by driving down the interest rate the government must pay to raise funds in the debt markets. This feature is important to portfolio managers, since they can adjust the overall level of risk in their portfolios by adding or selling off U.S. Treasurys. This important property is enhanced by the fact that U.S. Treasurys are very liquid, with a high volume of trading taking place each day. They can be easily bought and sold without having to pay large transactions costs. Finally, there is a broad range of maturities from which investors may choose, ranging from 4 weeks to 30 years. Not only does this feature of the market enable portfolio managers to achieve the desired balance in the maturities of their assets and liabilities, it also provides a foundation for all interest rates economywide across all maturities and tends to provide a forecast of overall economic activity.

For these reasons, the market for U.S. government debt deserves an especially close look.

8.1   Historical Background

A look at some historical data can put the current fiscal situation of the U.S. government into perspective. This perspective requires a good sense of the growth of government, the size of the federal deficit and federal debt, and the current outlook for the future. This information is available from the non-partisan *Congressional Budget Office, or CBO*, that is responsible for advising Congress on the consequences of legislation that affects the levels of spending and revenues of the federal government.

Of course, as the economy expands, government expenditures and revenues will also grow. Therefore, a meaningful measure of the size of government is federal expenditures and revenues relative to the size of the economy, or as a percentage of *Gross Domestic Product, or GDP*, which is the value of all domestically produced goods and services. Figure 7.1 indicates that by these measures the federal government has not grown much over the past 50 years. Whether measured by expenditures or revenues, the size of government in 2017 is projected by the CBO to be roughly what it was in 1968, and close to the 50-year average of 20.3 percent in terms of expenditures and 17.4 percent in terms of revenues.

The difference between *federal expenditures* and *government revenues* is the *federal deficit* and this deficit adds to the *federal debt*. When federal revenues exceed federal expenditures, the government is running a *government surplus* and the federal debt is shrinking. Federal deficits are the norm for the U.S. economy. As Figure 7.2 shows, the only period of sustained surpluses in the past 50 years was during the Clinton Administration from 1997-2000. Periods of economic recession typically exacerbate federal deficits as a result of shortfalls in tax revenues to the federal government, while government expenditures on support programs, such as unemployment insurance, rise. This phenomenon is particularly evident during the severe recessions of

Figure 7.1 Federal Government Expenditures and
Revenues as a percentage of GDP
Source: Congressional Budget Office

1975-6, 1981-2, and the Great Recession of 2007-2009, as well as during the milder recession of 1991-2.

Taking a longer look at how cumulative federal deficits have translated into federal debt, it is evident from Figure 7.3 that the federal debt relative to the size of the economy tends to rise during times of war as well as during economic recessions. The peak in the debt-to-GDP ratio was during World War II, when the federal debt rose to 106 percent of GDP. The average since 1940 is 47 percent. By way of comparison, by the end of 2017, that number is projected to be 77 percent, its highest level since 1950. Moreover, under current law, the CBO projects very rapid growth in debt in the fu-

Total Deficits and Surpluses

Percentage of Gross Domestic Product

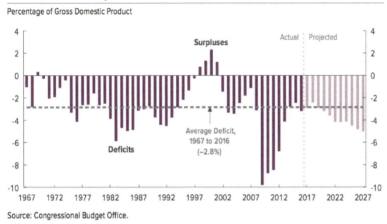

Source: Congressional Budget Office.

Figure 7.2 Federal Deficits (Surpluses) as a
percentage of GDP
Source: Congressional Budget Office

ture, with revenues falling further behind expenditures.
The principal factors contributing to this projection
include: a slowdown in the growth of the labor force
and an aging of the population, with the "baby boom"
generation placing increasing pressure on social security and Medicare and Medicaid, along with a slower
rate of productivity growth, and continued increases in
interest payments on the burgeoning debt. The federal
debt is projected to be 89 percent of GDP in 2027 and
141 percent by 2046, far exceeding its historical peak.

While war and economic recessions put heavy pres-

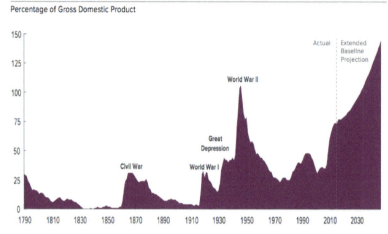

Federal Debt Held by the Public

Figure 7.3 Federal Debt as Percentage of GDP CBO
Jan 2017
Source: Congressional Budget Office

sure on federal budgets, the so-called long-run *structural deficits* caused by legislation that systematically produces underfunding of federal expenditures has been the culprit in recent years. Beginning with the Reagan Administration in 1981, Figure 7.2 shows how deficits grew substantially for many years following the end of the recession. This mismanagement of the federal budget was the result of a belief that severe cuts in federal income taxes would so stimulate the economy that they would be self-financing. It was finally acknowledged that this optimistic scenario was not going to unfold, and the succeeding Administrations of George H.W. Bush and Bill Clinton raised taxes. Ultimately, with the aid of the "tech boom," in the late 1990s, the federal deficits turned to surpluses.

However, deficits soon returned. Two large tax cuts and the onset of the Great Recession during the George W. Bush presidency, followed by the government's massive fiscal stimulus program under the Obama Administration to fight the Great Recession led to the ever-widening deficits, as seen in Figures 7.1and 7.2, with the attendant rise in the debt-to-GDP ratio that we observe today.

The deficit relative to GDP has subsided to historical levels in recent years with the economic recovery and the initial slowdown in health care expenditures due to provisions in the *Affordable Care Act*. However, these gains are not expected to be lasting. The projected ballooning of the debt, as depicted in Figure 7.3, is expected to occur absent a combination of slower growth in government spending and higher taxes. The CBO cautions that the following significant negative consequences are likely to result:[1]

- Federal spending on interest payments would increase substantially as a result of increases in interest rates, such as those projected to occur over the next few years.

---

[1] *The Budget and Economic Outlook: 2017 to 2027.* Congressional Budget Office, January 2017.

- Because federal borrowing reduces total saving in the economy over time, the nation's capital stock would ultimately be smaller, and productivity and total wages would be lower.

- Lawmakers would have less flexibility to use tax and spending policies to respond to unexpected challenges.

- The likelihood of a fiscal crisis in the United States would increase. There would be a greater risk that investors would become unwilling to finance the government's borrowing unless they were compensated with very high interest rates; if that happened, interest rates on federal debt would rise suddenly and sharply.

As of this writing, the current budget proposals of the Trump Administration include tax cuts that exceed those enacted during the Reagan and George W. Bush Administrations that led to sustained structural budget deficits (see Figure 7.2). Without significant reductions in federal spending, these proposals, if enacted into law, would lead to a very significant increase in the structural deficit and exacerbate an already dire outlook for the economy due to continued inattention to the government's fiscal health.

8.2 Composition of U.S. Treasury Debt

The principal interest of this book in U.S. government debt is on how the U.S. Treasury market influences the inner-workings of the financial markets generally.

Type	Billions of $	% of Debt
U.S. Government Debt Held by Public	**14,293**	**72**
Marketable	13,928	
Nonmarketable	365	
Intragovernmental Holdings	**5,553**	**28**
Marketable	22	
Nonmarketable	5,530	
Total U.S. Government Debt	**19,846**	**100**

Table 7.1 Composition of U.S. Government Debt,
April 30, 2017
Source: U.S. Treasury Department

Begin with a look at the composition of U.S. Treasury securities in the marketplace. As of April 30, 2017, federal debt in the hands of the public totaled approximately $14.3 trillion. Of that total, about $13.9 trillion is traded in the marketplace and is referred to as *marketable securities*. The remaining $400 billion or so are *nonmarketable securities* held in various trust accounts where they will remain until they mature. There is an additional \$5.5 trillion of intragovernmental holdings such as in the *Social Security Trust Fund*, for a total of \$19.8 trillion.

Focus attention on the marketable Treasurys, which total \$13.9 trillion. As shown in Table 7.2, the short-maturity *Treasury bills* comprise approximately 12 percent of the total, or \$1.7 trillion. T-bills are money market instruments with a year or less in maturity and are all *sold at a discount* to their face or par value.

Type (maturity)	Billions of \$	% of Marketable Debt
Bills (1-yr or less)	1,740	12
Notes (> 1-yr & ≤ 10-yr)	8,710	63
Bonds (> 10-yr)	1,902	14
Inflation-Protected Securities	1,238	9
Floating Rate Notes	338	2

Table 7.2 Breakdown of U.S. Government Debt,
April 30, 2017
Source: U.S. Treasury Department

Treasury notes or T-notes with maturities exceeding 1 year and up to and including 10 years represent approximately 2/3 of marketable Treasurys, or $8.7 trillion, with *Treasury bonds* or T-bonds having maturities in excess of 10 years and up to and including 30 years, comprising about 13 percent of marketable Treasurys, or $1.9 trillion. T-notes and T-bonds are coupon securities priced identically to corporate bonds as described in Chapter 5.

Treasury Inflation-Protection Securities (or TIPS) are coupon securities with a special feature that is intended to provide their owners a means of avoiding losses due to inflation by systematically adjusting the coupon payments and the par value upwards for inflation as measured by the CPI. Currently there are approximately $1.2 trillion in TIPS outstanding.

The Treasury Department chooses which maturity classes of securities to issue. Currently, they issue T-bills nearly every week in combinations of 4-week, 3-month, 6-month, and 1-year maturities. T-notes are issued each month in various maturities of 2-years, 3-years, 5-years, 7-years, and 10-years. The only T-bonds that are currently being issued have a maturity of 30-years.

8.3   "On-the-Run" Treasurys

At any point in time, there are several securities of each maturity category that are being traded in the marketplace. However, the financial markets have focused more intently on the most recently issued security from each maturity class, referred to as the *on-the-run Trea-surys*.

These securities comprise only about 10 percent of all marketable Treasury securities, but represent approximately 50 percent of the trading in Treasurys that takes place throughout the day. As a consequence of being the most actively traded, they therefore tend to have the highest liquidity and the lowest rates of return of all securities in their maturity class.

While all of the on-the-run Treasury securities have important roles to play in the economy, there are 2 rates that are exceptionally important. The 3-month T-bill rate is a key short-term interest rate in the economy to which other short rates, such as credit card rates, are tied. The yield on the 10-year T-note is similarly a key long-term interest rate, with mortgage rates very closely tied to this yield. That is, an increase in the yield on the 10-year T-note for whatever reason will generally lead to a similar rise in the 30-year mortgage rate. One reason for this latter relationship is that most mortgages are paid off before they mature, and on average are retired after approximately 10 years.

8.4   Trading U.S. Government Securities

This section takes a look at how information on trading in Treasury securities is reported in the financial press, and what can be learned from it.

Treasury Bills

Important players in these markets are *Government Securities Dealers*, who manage portfolios of Treasury securities. They *make a market* for Treasury bills by posting a *Bid Rate*, which is a bank discount rate that the dealer must receive in order to buy the T-bill and add it to his or her portfolio, and an *Asked Rate*, which is a bank discount rate that an investor who purchases the T-bill from the dealer would receive if the T-bill is held to maturity.

"On-the-Run" T-Bill	Maturity Date	Days to Maturity
3-month	Aug 3 17	87
1-year	Apr 26 17	353

'On-the-Run" T-Bill	Bid	Asked	Chg	Asked Yield
3-month	0.863	0.853	-0.007	0.866
1-year	1.095	1.085	0.015	1.112

Table 7.3 Information on Trading Activity for May 8, 2017 as reported in the *Wall Street Journal*

Shown Table 7.3 is information on the final trade of the day for May 8, 2017 for two "on-the-run" T-bills: the 3-month and 1-year bills. The *maturity date* along with *days to maturity* are listed. Also listed are the bid and asked rates quoted by the dealer. Note that the *bid rate* is ALWAYS higher than the *asked rate*, which ensures a profit for the dealer if he could acquire the T-bill at the higher bid rate – which corresponds to a lower price – and sell it at the lower asked rate, or higher price.

Note that we are living in an historically low interest rate environment. In some countries, short-term interest rates have actually turned negative, implying that the lender is paying the borrower to hold his money! These very low, and sometimes negative interest rates have been a side effect of the Great Recession, as central banks around the world have attempted to prop up their weak economies by pushing short-term interest rates to historic lows.

The so-called *bid-asked spread* for T-bills is the bid rate minus the asked rate, which indicates the reward to the dealer for making the market. It tends to be low for highly liquid assets. These on-the-run T-bills are among the most liquid of financial assets in the world. This spread for the 3-month T-bill is 1-100th of a percent! Obviously, there is not much room for dealers to make mistakes in these postings, which they must constantly update as conditions in the market change.

The next column in the Table is labeled Chg and represents the amount by which the asked rate changed relative to the previous trading day's close. For example, this change for the 3-month T-bill was a -0.007 implying that the asked rate on May 5, 2017 (bond markets were closed on May 6-7 for the weekend) was 7/1000 of percentage point higher, or 0.873%.

Remember that T-bills are sold at a discount to their face or *par value*, so as long as interest rates are positive, they will always sell below par, and tend to rise in price up to the par value at the time of maturity. Therefore, as a result of trading on this day, the price of the 3-month T-bill tended to rise due to the lower asked rate, and it was also higher due to the tendency for the T-bill price to rise as there was one less day to maturity. The *Asked Yield* listed in the Table is the *investment rate* or *yield to maturity* that corresponds to the asked discount rate.

Exercise using Information on Daily Trading in T-Bills

It' useful to perform an exercise whereby the asked yield is computed for the 1-year T-bill using the remaining information in the Table. There are two steps involved:

Step 1: First, compute the price per $100 in par value for which the T-bill sold in the last trade of the day.

Remembering the formula (Equation 5.6 in Chapter 5) for computing the *discount rate (DR)*:

$$DR\ (Asked) = \frac{Par\ Value - Purchase\ Price}{Par\ Value}$$

$$\times \left(\frac{360\ Days}{\#Days\ to\ Maturity}\right) \qquad (7.1)$$

Everything in this equation is known except the *Purchase Price*, which is also the market price of the T-bill. Substituting in the numbers and solving for the purchase price, the *market price* is found to be $98.936 per $100 in par value:

$$0.01085 = \frac{(100 - Market\ Price)}{100}\left(\frac{360}{353}\right)$$

$$\Rightarrow\ Market\ Price\ =\ \$98.936 \qquad (7.2)$$

Step 2: Now use the investment rate (IR) formula (Equation 5.4 from Chapter 5) to compute the asked yield:

$$IR\ (Asked\ Rate) = \frac{Par\ Value - Purchase\ Price}{Purchase\ Price}$$

$$\times \left(\frac{365\ Days}{\#Days\ to\ Maturity}\right) \qquad (7.3)$$

Plugging in the numbers and solving for the asked yield, gives the 1.112 percent shown in Table 7.3:

$$IR = \frac{100 - 98.936}{98.936}\left(\frac{365}{353}\right) = 0.01112, \text{ or } 1.112 \text{ percent.}$$
$$(7.4)$$

Obviously, this could have been done in reverse. That is, the asked rate could have been computed given the asked yield and the number of days to maturity, by first computing the market price per $100 in par value from the investment rate formula, then plugging that number into the discount rate formula.

Treasury Notes and Treasury Bonds

Government securities dealers also make tthe markets for Treasury notes and Treasury bonds. However, unlike the market for T-bills, dealers quote *Bid* and *Asked Prices*. The quotes shown in Table 7.4 are for prices per $100 in par value.

For example, for the 10-yr on-the-run T-note maturing on February 15, 2027 that carries a coupon rate of 2-1/4 or 2.250 percent, the dealer is willing to pay $98.9141 per $100 in par value in order to add that T-note to his portfolio. He also stands ready to sell that same security for $98.9297 per $100 in par value. The bid-asked spread is then measured as the asked price minus the bid price, which again represents the profit margin to the dealer for making the market. These spreads are typically very narrow. For example, for the benchmark 10-yr T-note, the bid-asked spread is slightly over 1.5 cents per $100 in par value.

T-Note/ T-Bond	Maturity Date	Coupon
2-year	Apr 30 17	1.250
3-year	Apr 30 20	1.375
5-year	Apr 30 22	1.750
7-year	Apr 30 24	2.000
10-year	Feb 15 27	2.250
30-year	Feb 15 47	3.000

T-Note/ T-Bond	Bid	Asked	Chg	Asked Yield
2-year	99.8359	99.8516	-0.0313	1.326
3-year	99.5078	99.5234	-0.0547	1.539
5-year	99.1719	99.1875	-0.1172	1.922
7-year	98.7969	98.8125	-0.1641	2.184
10-year	98.9141	98.9297	-0.2031	2.374
30-year	99.6641	99.6953	-0.5313	3.016

Table 7.4: Information on Trading Activity for May 8, 2017 as reported in the *Wall Street Journal*

As with corporate bonds, the *Coupon* shown in Table 7.4 is the *coupon rate*. For example, for the 10-yr T-note, the annual *coupon payments*, given by the coupon rate times the par value, is $2.250 per $100 in par value.

The two remaining columns in Table 7.4 reflect the outcome of trading that took place on May 8, 2017. Chg represents the amount by which the asked price at the end of the day's trading changed relative to the previous trading day's close. For example, on May 5, 2017 (with the market closed on May 6-7 for the weekend), the closing price for the 10-yr T-note was 20.31 cents per $100 higher than at the close on May 8, 2017, or $99.1318 per $100 in par value. Finally, investors are primarily interested in the asset's yield to maturity. For the 10-yr T-note, the asked yield for the last trade of the day was 2.374 percent. This yield is the actual annualized rate of return that an investor would receive if he bought the T-note at the end of trading on May 8, 2017 and held it until it matured.

Exercises Using Information in Table 7.4

Using Table 7.4, there are a number of questions concerning the trading activity in these securities that can be quickly answered.

1. *Which of the T-notes and T-bonds are selling above, at, or below par at the close of trading?*

   This question can be answered in two ways.

   a) First, is the Asked Price > or = or < 100?

b) Second, is the coupon rate above, equal to, or below the asked yield? Only if the coupon rate equals the asked yield is the bond selling at par. If the coupon rate > asked yield, the bond is selling above par, and vice versa, if the coupon rate < asked yield, the bond is selling below par.

<u>On this date</u>: All of the on-the-run Treasury notes and the Treasury bond were selling below par.

2. *If the securities had been issued at par initially, then have their yields fallen, remained unchanged, or risen since they were issued?*

a) Again, this question could be answered by comparing the asked price with 100. If the security is selling above par, the yield has fallen, and if it is selling below par, the yield has risen.

b) Alternatively, the asked yield could be compared with the coupon rate. If the coupon rate is above the yield, then the yield has fallen, and if it is below the yield, then the yield to maturity has risen.

<u>By the end of trading on this day</u>: The yields on ALL of the on-the-run T-notes and the T-bond listed in Table 7.4 have risen since the securities were initially issued.

3. *We can also determine the previous day's closing price and whether the yield had risen or fallen as a result of the day's trading by examining the change in the asked price.*

Table 7.5 lists the previous trading day's closing prices. Since the change is negative for all on-the-run T-notes and T-bonds, their yields all rose. Only the 30-year T-bond was trading above par at the close on the prior trading day.

T-Note/ T-Bond	Asked	Chg	Prior Trading Day's Close	Yield's Change
2-year	99.8516	-0.0313	99.8829	⇑
3-year	99.5234	-0.0547	99.5781	⇑
5-year	99.1875	-0.1172	99.3047	⇑
7-year	98.8125	-0.1641	99.9766	⇑
10-year	98.9297	-0.2031	99.1328	⇑
30-year	99.6953	-0.5313	100.2266	⇑

Table 7.4: Information on Trading Activity for May 8, 2017 as reported in the *Wall Street Journal*

4. *Finally, we can ask what a trader's annualized rate of return on each of the securities would have been had he or she purchased the security at the close of trading on the previous day and sold it at the close on May 8, 2017.*

For example, for the 30 T-bond, we can use the investment rate (IR) formula to compute the annualized rate of return using today's asked price from Table 7.3 as the sale price and yesterday's closing asked price from Table 7.4 as the purchase price, and recognize that the number of days the asset was held was one.

$$\text{IR} = \frac{99.6953 - 100.2266}{100.2266}\left(\frac{365}{1}\right)$$

$$= -1.93 \text{ or } 193\% \text{ annualized loss!} \qquad (7.5)$$

In this case, the annualized rate of return computes to a 193 percent loss!! Obviously, with this kind of volatility in prices, trading bonds day by day can be very risky indeed.

8.5   Treasury Inflation Protection Securities (TIPS)

As emphasized in previous chapters, unexpected increases in the inflation rate cause bond prices to fall. In recent years, the Treasury Department has been issuing bonds that allow investors to receive some protection from inflation. These so-called Treasury Inflation Protection Securities, or TIPS bonds, essentially have their coupon payments and face or par value systematically increased for inflation in accordance with the *CPI inflation rate.* In addition to being one of the few ways that investors can avoid inflation risk, these securities also can be used to obtain reasonable values for the market's expectation of future inflation by comparing their yields with the yields on standard coupon bonds of comparable maturity.[2]

Using TIPS to Approximate Market Expectations of Inflation

When traders have the option to buy a standard coupon bond or a TIPS of the same maturity, they will price those investments differently based on their expectations of future inflation. It turns out to be a simple matter to use the outcome of that trading to approximate market expectations of future inflation by comparing their asked yields. The asked yield for the standard coupon bond is the nominal interest rate, while the asked yield on the TIPS is a real, or inflation-adjusted, interest rate.

Example: Table 7.5 provides data on the asked yields of the 30-year standard coupon bond and the 30-year TIPS for the trading day May 9, 2017.

Refer again to the *Fisher equation*, where the nominal or market rate of interest is approximately equal to the real interest rate plus the expected rate of inflation.

---

[2]See Sack, Brian, and Robert Elsasser.(2004) for a review of the history of TIPS.

T-Bond	Maturity	Coupon	Asked Yield
30-yr Std Coupon	Feb 15 47	3.00	3.038 (R)
30-yr TIPS	Feb 15 47	0.875	1.043 (r)

Table 7.5: Yields on the 30-year Coupon Bond and
the TIPS on May 9, 2017

Fisher Equation:

Nominal Interest Rate (R) = Real Interest Rate (r)

$$+ \text{ Expected Inflation Rate}(E\pi) \qquad (7.6)$$

The yield on the standard coupon bond is the market rate, while the yield on the TIPS bond is the real rate. Therefore, using the Fisher equation we can compute the market's expectation of long-run future inflation and, under the assumption that the bonds were initially issued at par, how that expectation has changed since the bonds were issued on February 15, 2017.

$E\pi$(as of the close of trading on May 9, 2017)

$$= \text{ Asked Yield on Std Coupon Bond (R)}$$

$$-\text{Asked Yield on TIPS (r)}$$

$$= 3.038 - 1.043 = 1.995\% \qquad (7.7)$$

To determine how these expectations have changed since the bonds were initially issued, first compute expected inflation for February 15, 1947. If the bonds were issued at par, their yields would have been equal to the coupon rate. Therefore, the difference in their coupon rates should yield an estimate of expected inflation at that time.

$$
\begin{aligned}
&E\pi(\text{as of February 15, 2007}) \\
=\ &\text{Coupon Rate on Std Coupon Bond} \\
&-\text{Coupon Rate on TIPS} \\
=\ &3.00 - 0.875 = 2.125\% \qquad (7.8)
\end{aligned}
$$

These calculations indicate that long-run inflation expectations fell slightly between February 15, 2017 and May 9, 2017:

$$
\begin{aligned}
&E\pi(\text{as of the close of trading on May 9, 2017}) \\
&\quad -\ E\pi(\text{as of February 15, 2007}) \\
&\quad = 1.995\% - 2.125\% = -0.130\% \qquad (7.9)
\end{aligned}
$$

8.6 Primary Market for U.S. Treasurys

The previous sections have described how Treasury securities are traded in the *secondary market*. This section describes the *primary market* for Treasury securties,or how they are introduced into the economy in the first place.

There is a need for new issues of Treasurys for several reasons:

1. As existing issues of Treasury securities mature, they need to be replaced with new issues, if the government wishes to maintain the existing level of U.S. government debt.

2. Seasonal fluctuations take place in both the expenditures and the revenues of the federal government. Typically, federal expenditures fluctuate less than revenues, with large swings in tax receipts occurring primarily in April, but also as many households and businesses make quarterly tax payments throughout the year. In order to meet any temporary shortfalls in revenues, the Treasury Department will issue Treasury securities, usually of short maturity.

3. Structural deficits, as described previously, when there is a systematic shortfall in revenues relative to expenditures, will have to be met with additional borrowing by the federal government, requiring new issues of Treasury securities.

On those rare occasions when the government was running annual budget surpluses, the Treasury Department had to reduce its debt outstanding. It did so through a combination of minimizing the amount of maturing debt that it replaced or "rolled-over" and buying back outstanding debt by conducting so-called *reverse auctions*, whereby holders of selected U.S. Treasury securities could make offers to sell that debt back to the U.S. government.

Treasury Auctions

Since the government typically runs budget deficits, it is normally the case that new Treasury securities are auctioned off each week in so-called *single-price or Dutch auctions*. There are two parties involved in carrying out the auctions:

- The U.S. Treasury Department decides on the amount of funds that need to be raised and, under consultation with the Federal Reserve, decides on the composition of the Treasurys to be auctioned in terms of maturities and whether any TIPS should be included.

  A public announcement of the upcoming auction is then made, with coupon securities priced to SELL AT PAR based on the expected reception in the marketplace.

- The Federal Reserve Bank of New York then conducts the auctions.

The process of auctioning off new issues of U.S. Treasury securities has evolved over time. The goals are to ensure adequate participation in the auction to meet the government's borrowing needs at the lowest possible cost (interest rates), and avoid collusion by market participants who are purchasing the debt.

Structure of the Dutch Auction of U.S. Treasury Securities

1. The Federal Reserve accepts sealed competitive bids on the announced offerings, where the bidders commit to purchasing a certain quantity of the new securities, by bidding a discount rate on T-bills or a price/$100 in par value for T-notes or T-bonds.

2. The Federal Reserve also receives *noncompetitive tenders*, whereby investors agree to purchase a certain quantity of the new securities at the rates for T-bills or prices for T-notes and T-bonds as determined by the auction.

   - Many of these noncompetitive tenders are made online through the website: treasury-direct.gov

   - It is an inexpensive way to invest for anyone interested in purchasing U.S. Treasurys, as there are no brokerage fees to pay. The Treasury opens and manages an account for the investor.

3. Once all bids are received, the Federal Reserve subtracts the noncompetitive tenders from the total amount of securities being auctioned.

4. The competitive bids are then ordered: for T-bills, the bid rates are ordered from low to high, and for T-notes and T-bonds, the bid prices are ordered from high to low.

5. Orders are then filled beginning with the highest bidder (highest price) until the entire offering is exhausted.

6. The highest discount rate for T-bills or the lowest price for T-notes and T-bonds that is accepted determines the auction rate for T-bills and the auction price for T-notes and T-bonds that ALL successful bidders, including the noncompetitive tender offers, receive. The price paid for these securities is often referred to as the *stopout price*.

Auction Results

The results of the auction are published online. Figure 7.4 displays the result of a recent auction of the 3-month T-bill.

On this date, the Treasury issued 3-month T-bills maturing in 91 days in the amount of $39 billion (in par value). Of the total, $693 million were purchased through non-competitive tenders, $200 million of which

TREASURY NEWS

Department of the Treasury • Bureau of the Fiscal Service

For Immediate Release
March 20, 2017

CONTACT: Treasury Securities Services
202-504-3550

TREASURY AUCTION RESULTS

Term and Type of Security	91-Day Bill
CUSIP Number	912796JX8
High Rate [1]	0.760%
Allotted at High	41.98%
Price	99.807889
Investment Rate [2]	0.772%
Median Rate [3]	0.730%
Low Rate [4]	0.700%
Issue Date	March 23, 2017
Maturity Date	June 22, 2017

	Tendered	Accepted
Competitive	$119,607,677,500	$38,307,441,500
Noncompetitive	$492,933,300	$492,933,300
FIMA (Noncompetitive)	$200,000,000	$200,000,000
Subtotal [5]	**$120,300,610,800**	**$39,000,374,800** [6]
SOMA	$0	$0
Total	**$120,300,610,800**	**$39,000,374,800**

	Tendered	Accepted
Primary Dealer [7]	$104,340,000,000	$24,050,340,000
Direct Bidder [8]	$4,345,460,000	$3,845,460,000
Indirect Bidder [9]	$10,922,217,500	$10,411,641,500
Total Competitive	**$119,607,677,500**	**$38,307,441,500**

Figure 7.4 Results of the 3-month Treasury Bill
Auction, March 20, 2017
Source: U.S. Treasury Department

were acquired by foreign international monetary authorities (FIMA). The remainder of the issue was sold through competitive auction. The Treasury received $199.6 billion in bids and accepted $38.3 billion, resulting in a *bid-to-cover ratio* of 3.12 dollars bid for each dollar of the issue (in par value). The stop-out price was $99.808 per $100 in par value, for an investment rate of 0.772%. In the Figure, *SOMA* represents the purchases made by the Federal Reserve through its *System Open Market Operations*. The Federal Reserve is authorized to participate in Treasury auctions (through non-competitive tenders) to replace maturing government debt in its portfolio. For this particular auction, the Federal Reserve made no purchases.

A similar online publication of the results of a 10-year T-note auction is shown in Figure 7.5. For this auction of $20 billion in 10-year T-notes (in par value), there were $53.1 billion in bids, of which $19.99 billion were accepted for a bid-to-cover ratio of 2.66 dollars bid for each dollar in par value that was issued. The coupon rate, labeled *Interest Rate*, was set at 2-1/4 percent. However, the stop-out price of $97.297 was below par, so the actual yield to maturity (*High Yield*) was 2.560 percent, slightly above the coupon rate. For this auction, there were no purchases by either the foreign international monetary authorities (*FIMA*) or the Federal Reserve (*SOMA*).

TREASURY NEWS

Department of the Treasury • Bureau of the Fiscal Service

For Immediate Release
March 08, 2017

CONTACT: Treasury Securities Services
202-504-3550

TREASURY AUCTION RESULTS

Term and Type of Security	9-Year 11-Month Note
CUSIP Number	912828V98
Series	B-2027
Interest Rate	2-1/4%
High Yield [1]	2.560%
Allotted at High	85.47%
Price	97.296773
Accrued Interest per $1,000	$1.74033
Median Yield [2]	2.510%
Low Yield [3]	2.449%
Issue Date	March 15, 2017
Maturity Date	February 15, 2027
Original Issue Date	February 15, 2017
Dated Date	February 15, 2017

	Tendered	Accepted
Competitive	$53,099,900,000	$19,990,395,000
Noncompetitive	$9,671,600	$9,671,600
FIMA (Noncompetitive)	$0	$0
Subtotal [4]	**$53,109,571,600**	**$20,000,066,600** [5]
SOMA	$0	$0
Total	**$53,109,571,600**	**$20,000,066,600**

	Tendered	Accepted
Primary Dealer [6]	$32,715,000,000	$3,709,102,500
Direct Bidder [7]	$4,420,000,000	$3,136,025,000
Indirect Bidder [8]	$15,964,900,000	$13,145,267,500
Total Competitive	**$53,099,900,000**	**$19,990,395,000**

Figure 7.5 Results of the 10-year Treasury Note
Auction, March 8, 2017
Source: U.S. Treasury Department

8.7 The Term Structure of Interest Rates

There is one final and very important topic to cover in this chapter. Investors in government securities are essentially investing in assets that are all free of default risk, but investors have choices to make regarding what maturities they wish for their investment. These facts imply that, since all of these assets are available in the marketplace, there is likely some important underlying relationship between the interest rates or yields on these various Treasury securities. This relationship is referred to as the *term structure of interest rates*.

Unbiased Expectations Hypothesis

The term structure of interest rates is essentially a mathematical relationship between the rates of return (or interest rates) on assets that differ only by their term to maturity, i.e., they are all drawn from the same risk class. To understand this relationship, begin with an appeal to a theory: the so-called *unbiased expectations hypothesis*:

Unbiased Expectations Hypothesis: If an investor has available to him or her two investment opportunities involving assets that differ only by maturity (so they are drawn from the risk class), then the expected return on the two investments should be the same, provided: the same amount is invested and with the same time horizon for the investment. For now, assume that the investor does not value liquidity – an assumption that will be relaxed later.

The simplest explanation of this theory is by way of example.

Example: Suppose an investor wished to invest $1000 for two years, and has two investment options available: investment long, labeled L, and investment short, labeled S.

Investment L: Purchase a 2-year pure, risk-free asset, which carries an annualized rate of return, or yield to maturity of R, which is known at the time of the investment to be 10 percent.

At the end of two years, the total return on this investment (including principal) is:

$$\text{Total Return (L)} = \$1000(1+R)^2 = \$1210 \quad (7.10)$$

Investment S: This investment still requires that the investor tie up his or her money for two years. However, the investment is in a one-year, risk-free asset. At the end one year, the investment is "rolled-over," with the principal and interest used to purchase another identical one-year, risk-free asset.

The interest rate that the investor would receive the first year, denoted r_1, with the subscript indicating the first year of the investment, is known and is seen to be 6 percent. However, the investor does not know what that rate will be during the second year, so he or she must form expectations of the rate. Denote that expected value by Er_2, where again the subscript indicates now the second year of the investment. At the end of the two-year investment period, the total expected return on this investment (including principal and interest) is:

$$\text{Total Expected Return (S)} = \$1000(1+r_1)(1+Er_2)$$
$$(7.11)$$

Now apply the unbiased expectations hypothesis to compare these two investments. It states that the investor should expect to receive the same total return from either of these two investments, since they are both available in the marketplace and require the same initial investment and have the some time horizon of two years. Therefore:

$$\text{Total Expected Return (S)} = \text{Total Return (L)}$$
$$(7.12)$$

or,

$$\$1000(1+r)(1+Er) = \$1000(1+R)^2 \qquad (7.13)$$

Since the $1000 cancels on both sides of this equation, the relationship between these interest rates is independent of the total amount invested. Solving for the expected value of the short-term interest rate for the second year, we get a prediction from the unbiased expectations hypothesis:

$$Er_2 = \frac{(1+R)^2}{(1+r)} - 1 = \frac{1.10^2}{1.06} - 1 = 0.1415 \text{ or } 14.15\%$$

(7.14)

The theory suggests that had the investor expected the short rate to be higher than this value in the second period, then he or she would always go short, earning less in the first year, but expecting to be more than compensated by the higher return in the second year. Obviously, if every investor had this same expectation, then everyone would go short and the price of the short asset would rise, thereby lowering the current short rate, r_1, while the price of the long asset would fall, thereby raising the current long rate, R. This process would continue until an equilibrium was restored whereby investors would be indifferent between the two investments.

Conclusion:

$$\text{If } R \begin{pmatrix} > \\ = \\ < \end{pmatrix} r_1$$

$$\Rightarrow \text{ in the future, } r \text{ is expected } \begin{pmatrix} \Uparrow \\ \text{not change} \\ \Downarrow \end{pmatrix}$$

This exercise can be generalized by applying the unbiased expectations hypothesis in comparisons of assets with *any* two maturities. For example, compare a sustained investment in a one-period, risk-free asset with an investment of a similar amount in an N-period asset which is to be held to maturity. Think of one period as a year and N periods could be 5, 10, or 30 years. Equating the total returns on a $1000 investment of the two investment options after N periods in accordance with the unbiased expectations hypothesis gives:

$$\$1000(1 + R)^N = \$1000(1 - r_1)(1 + Er_2)\ldots(1 + Er_N) \tag{7.15}$$

Equation (7.15) indicates that the investor is forming expectations about the entire future path of short-term interest rates. In general, if the current long rate is above the current short rate, the short rates are expect to rise, and if the current long rate equals the current short rate, then the markets are not anticipating changes in future short rates. In the more unusual case where the current long rate is less than the current short rate, the markets anticipate a fall in short rates in the future. Mathematically, these conclusions can be summarized as follows:

$$R > r_1 \Rightarrow r_1 < Er_2 < Er_3 < \cdots < Er_N$$
$$R = r_1 \Rightarrow r_1 = Er_2 = Er_3 = \cdots = Er_N$$
$$R < r_1 \Rightarrow r_1 > Er_2 > Er_3 > \cdots > Er_N$$

Suppose this formula repeatedly applied by varying N from 2 up to, say, 30 years. Then, it would be possible to determine the entire future path of short rates expected by the markets by simply observing the current rates on assets for all maturities, i.e., for N = 1 to 30. These calculations can become very complicated, but they are routinely carried out by traders in the markets. So, what are the implications of this theory?

8.8   The Treasury Yield Curve

Consider the Treasury market, which is comprised of a series of financial assets that are all free of default risk and vary over a wide range of maturities. Information from one of many sources of financial news could establish what the current interest rates are on Treasury securities across all maturities.A plot of these interest rates or yields versus their term to maturity is referred to as the *Treasury yield curve.*

Here is a thought experiment: Suppose you were to obtain this information every day for 20 years and plot the Treasury yield curves, then averaged across all of those graphs. What would you expect this yield curve look like?

According to the unbiased expectations hypothesis the slope of the yield curve reflects the markets expectations of future short rates. When the short rate is expected to rise, the long rate is higher than the short rate and the slope of the yield curve is positive. When the short rate is expected to fall, the long rate is below the short rate and the slope of the yield curve is negative. However, logic would suggest that on average short rates are neither expected to rise nor to fall, i.e., they don't go infinity nor do they generally turn negative. This reasoning would suggest the following patterns for the Treasury yield curve:

The so-called *"normal shape" of the yield curve* is how it would appear on average, and the argument suggests that it would be flat. During those times when the markets are anticipating increases in the short rate, the slope of the yield curve is positive, and when the markets anticipate falling short rates, the yield curve should have a negative slope.

The Liquidity Premium

Unfortunately, these predictions do not totally match one's intuition. If we were to conduct the experiment described above to determine the normal shape of the yield curve, we would likely conclude that on average the yield curve should be upward sloping.

What was missing in the theory is the role played by liquidity in creating a so-called *liquidity premium* that biases long-term interest rates upward relative to short rates. That is, when comparing short and long rates, consideration must be give to the perspectives of both

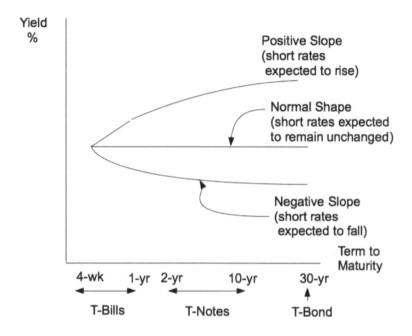

Figure 7.6 Yield Curve according to the Unbiased
Expectations Hypothesis

the investors and the issuers of the assets. Typically, an investor who values liquidity will have to receive a higher rate of return on longer term assets in order to receive compensation for having lost access to those funds for a longer period of time. The suggestion is that investors would prefer to invest short. However, issuers of the securities would prefer to issue longer term assets to avoid the risk of rising rates in the future that could cause their borrowing costs to rise. They prefer to borrow long.

The magnitude of the liquidity premium tends to vary over the business cycle. It reflects *interest rate risk*, or the uncertainty associated with future short-term interest rates and tends to increase when short rates become more volatile.

The general formula identifying the term structure relationship between a one-period and an N-period asset that includes the liquidity premium would appear as follows:

$$(1 + R)^N = (1 + r_1)(1 + Er_2)(1 + Er_3) \ldots (1 + Er_N)$$

$$+ \text{ liquidity premium} \qquad (7.16)$$

As a consequence, the liquidity premium tends to bias upward the slope of the yield curve. That is, the longer the maturity of the asset, the greater is the liquidity premium, which tends to increase the interest rate on the longer term asset on average. As shown in Figure 7.7, the normal shape of the yield curve therefore has a positive slope. A flat yield curve suggests that the short rates are expected to fall by just enough to offset the upward bias of the liquidity premium.

When short rates are expected to rise in the future, the yield curve is even more steeply sloping upward. While a downward sloping yield curve, which is referred

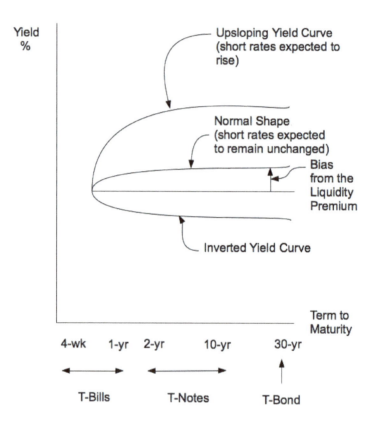

Figure 7.6 Actual Yield Curve when the Liquidity
Premium is Present

to as an *inverted yield curve*, implies that the markets are expecting steep declines in short rates in the future.

Research into the Movements of the Yield Curve

Recent research has delved more deeply into the issue of what kinds of events cause the yield curve's overall shape to change. Statistically, yield curves may change along any of at least three different dimensions: level (or intercept), slope, or curvature.[3] As the upper left panel of Figure 7.7 suggests, a change in the level or intercept of the yield curve means that interest rates all along the curve move roughly in parallel, shifting the whole curve up or down. Macroeconomic forces, such as increased inflation, a weaker economy, or significant technological change, may have their greatest impact on a yield curve's level.

In contrast, the curve's slope or steepness changes when shorter-term interest rates rise or fall by greater amounts than longer-term interest rates. One measure of the slope of a yield curve is the longest-term interest rate, r_l, minus the shortest-term interest rate, r_s, contained in the curve divided by the difference in their terms to maturity. When this interest rate (or yield) spread is positive, the yield curve is generally upward sloping. Statistical evidence from U.S. data suggests

---

[3]See Dai and Singleton (2000) and Wu (2003) and Wheelock and Wohar.(2009).

that shifts in Federal Reserve monetary policy are one of the major influences on the yield curve's slope. This effect is captured in the upper right panel of Figure 7.7, which depicts the central bank tightening money and credit conditions by raising short-term interest rates from r_s to r_s*. If long-term interest rates initially do not change (as shown) or change by a lesser amount than short-term rates (as is usually the case), then the average slope of the curve declines. In this example, the initial slope is seen to be steeper than the final slope.

Finally, as the lower panel of Figure 7.7 depicts, the curvature of a yield curve may change when interest rates in the middle of the maturity spectrum are impacted, such as by a shift in economic conditions of moderate length. This development would tend to give the yield curve a greater or lesser "hump" along its midsection. These various dimensions of a yield curve – its level, slope, and curvature – suggest that these curves are far more complex and more intimately connected with the economy and government policy than was once thought.

Forecasting with the Treasury Yield Curve

The financial markets become very nervous when an inverted yield curve appears.[4] The reason is that ev-

---

[4]See Stojanovic, Dusan, and Mark D. Vaughn (1997).

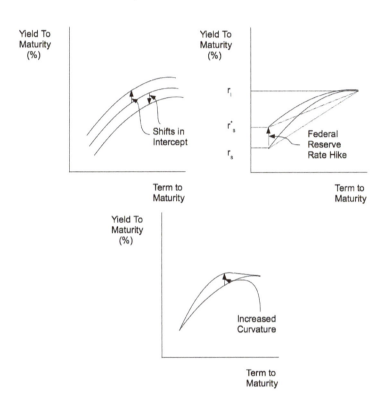

Figure 7.7 Changes in the Shape of the Yield Curve

ery recession since World War II has been preceded by an inversion of the yield curve. Although, it has sometimes been a false signal, with a yield curve becoming inverted and no recession followed. Why is this phenomenon of an inverted yield curve presaging an economic recession observed with such regularity? An answer can be found in the Fisher equation:

Fisher Equation:

$$\text{Nominal Interest Rate (R)} = \text{Real Interest Rate (r)}$$

$$+ \text{Expected Inflation Rate}(E\pi) \qquad (7.17)$$

The nominal interest rate is approximately equal to the sum of the real rate plus the expected rate of inflation. When the economy enters into a recession: the real rate falls ($r \Downarrow$) as the demand for credit declines, and inflation also falls as the demand for goods and services declines, thereby reducing the market's expectation of inflation ($E\pi \Downarrow$). When the markets anticipate a weakness in the economy, both of these factors show up in the projections of future short-term interest rates and trading of Treasury securities ultimately produces an inversion of the yield curve associated with the anticipated sharp decline in short rates.

The yield curve is therefore closely watched by the financial markets as an indicator of future corporate profits and therefore of the value of corporate stocks.

An inversion of the yield curve, when supported by other evidence of an economic slowdown, can send the stock market into a downward spiral.

8.9 Summary

This chapter has explored several aspects of the important market for U.S. government debt. It was pointed out that nearly every large portfolio manager in the world holds some U.S. Treasurys in his or her portfolio because these securities are both free of default risk and are among the most liquid financial markets in the world. These features enable quick portfolio adjustments to risk and to investment opportunities to be made.

Due to this popularity, Treasury yields are among the world's most important interest rates, with many other interest rates, as well as terms on many financial contracts tied directly to them. The 3-month T-bill rate a key short-term interest rate in the economy, while the yield on the 10-year T-note is a key long-term interest rate that influences mortgage rates among others.

The market for U.S. government debt is created by government securities dealers who quote bid and ask rates for T-Bills and bid and asked prices for T-notes and T-bonds. Their trading activity keeps the markets very liquid and very efficient, with any relevant information quickly reflected in their prices.

The Treasury yield curve is therefore watched closely for pricing anomalies that well-positioned traders may be able to exploit. This yield curve is also watched closely by analysts on Wall Street. An inversion of the yield curve is generally taken as a signal that the economy is weakening, thus suggesting a decline in corporate profits, and the stock market usually responds with a selloff. Savvy investors are therefore always well advised to keep a watchful eye on the U.S. Treasury market.

Key Terms

Congressional Budget Office, or CBO
Gross Domestic Product, or GDP
federal expenditures
government revenues
federal deficit
federal debt
government surplus
structural deficit
Affordable Care Act
marketable securities
nonmarketable securities
Social Security Trust Fund
Treasury bills
Treasury notes
Treasury bonds
Treasury Inflation Protection Securities (TIPS)
on-the-run Treasurys
Government Securities Dealers
make a market
bid rate
asked rate
asked yield
maturity date
days to maturity
bid-asked spread
investment rate
yield to maturity
par value

discount rate
purchase price
market price
coupon
coupon rate
coupon payments
CPI inflation rate
Fisher equation
secondary market
primary market
reverse auctions
single-price or Dutch auctions
noncompetitive tenders
stopout price
System Open Market Operations (SOMA)
bid-to-cover ratio
Foreign and International Monetary Authorities (FIMA)
term structure of interest rates
unbiased expectations hypothesis
normal shape of the yield curve
liquidity premium
intercept, slope, and curvature of the yield curve
Treasury yield curve
inverted yield curve

8.10   Review Questions

1. Mark wants a 3 percent real rate of return to invest in stock XYZ, and a 5 percent real rate of return to invest in stock ABC. Heidi believes that both stocks are less risky than Mark does and is willing to accept real rates of return of 2 percent on XYZ and 4 percent on ABC. Mark expects the inflation rate to be 3 percent, and Heidi expects the inflation rate to be 5 percent. If the current yield on both XYZ and ABC is 6 percent, then which of these situations would follow?

   a) Mark would be willing to invest in XYZ, but not in ABC, while Heidi would not want to invest in either.

   b) Mark would invest in both XYZ and ABC, while Heidi would not invest in either.

   c) Both Mark and Heidi would be willing to invest in XYZ, but not in ABC.

   d) Both Mark and Heidi would be willing to invest in both XYZ and ABC.

2. An investor buys a U.S. Treasury bond whose current yield to maturity is 6 percent. The investor is subject to a 33 percent federal income tax rate on any new income received. His real after-tax return from this bond is 2 percent. What is the expected inflation rate in the financial marketplace over the life of the bond?

3. ndicate which applies. The liquidity premium:

   a) is negative only during an economic recession.

   b) is the result of greater price volatility for longer-term assets.

   c) biases the slope of the yield curve downward.

   d) causes long rates to always exceed short rates.

4. Suppose that the actual U.S. Treasury yield curve is approximately flat. This yield curve would suggest that the markets are expecting:

   a) short rates to remain essentially unchanged in the future.

   b) long rates to increase in the future.

   c) long rates to increase in the future.

   d) short rates to fall in the future.

5. Indicate which is true. The unbiased expectations hypothesis of the term structure of interest rates:

   a) applies only to assets that have the same maturity.

   b) applies only to assets that have the same default risk.

   c) ignores maturity of assets.

d) ignores the market risk of assets.

6. An investor wishes to ride the yield curve to higher profits on an investment of $1,000. He observes in the market a zero-coupon T-note with one year left to maturity yielding 5 percent and another zero-coupon T-note yielding 7 percent with two years to maturity. What investment strategy should he pursue? Show how this investment strategy would be superior to a simple buy-and-hold strategy. Under what conditions will this strategy succeed? When will it fail?

7. Repeat Problem 7, but where the market interest rates are: 7 percent for the one-year, zero-coupon bond and 5 percent for the two-year, zero-coupon bond.

8. Synchron Corporation borrowed long-term capital at an interest rate of 8.5 percent under the expectation that the annual inflation rate over the life of this borrowing was likely to be 5 percent. However, shortly after the loan contract was signed, the actual inflation rate climbed to 5.5 percent, where it is expected to remain until Synchrons loan reaches maturity. What is likely to happen to the market value per share of Synchrons common stock? Would its stock price be more affected or less affected than the price of its bonds? Explain your reasoning.

9. Which of the following are TRUE?

   a) There has never been a recession wince World War II that was not preceded by an inverted yield curve.

   b) An inversion of the yield curve can occur if the markets anticipate a strong recession coming up since it raises expected inflation due to a weak consumer economy and also increases real interest rates due to weak loan demand.

10. According to the Expectations Hypothesis of the yield curve that INCLUDES the liquidity premium, a flat yield curve is consistent with market expecting:

    a) long rates to fall.

    b) short rates to fall.

    c) short rates to rise.

    d) short rates to neither rise not fall.

11. An investor, with a 2-year investment horizon for a $1000 investment has the options of: (a) buying a 2-year T-note and holding it until it matures, or (b) purchasing a one-year T-Bill and "rolling-it-over" in a second one-year T-bill when the first T-bill matures. If the current T-note is currently yielding 4 percent and the current T-bill rate is also 4 percent, then:

a) the investor would expect to receive a total return at the end of 2 years of $1081.60 if he purchased the T-note, and this would exceed the expected total return if he adopted the investment strategy (b).

b) the investor would expect to receive a total return at the end of 2 years of $1080.00 if he purchased the T-note, and this would exceed the expected total return if he adopted the investment strategy (b).

c) the investor would expect to receive a total return at the end of 2 years of $1081.60 on his investment regardless of the investment strategy he adopted.

d) the investor would expect to receive a total return at the end of 2 years of $1080.00 on his investment regardless of the investment strategy he adopted.

USE TABLE 1 TO ANSWER QUESTIONS 12 through 15.

Table 1: US Treasury Securities
Trading Day: November 12, 2010

"On-The-Run" Treasury Bills

MATURITY	DAYS TO MAT	BID	ASKED	CHG	ASK YLD
Dec 9 10	87	0.105	0.100	-0.010	0.101
Feb 10 11	180	0.130	0.125	unch.	0.127
Oct 20 11	343	0.248	0.243	0.020	0.246

"On-The-Run" Treasury Bonds & Notes

COUP	MAT MO/YR	BID	ASKED	CHG	ASK YLD
1.000	Oct 12	100.6875	100.7187	-0.03125	0.2732
1.250	Oct 15	99.28125	99.59375	-0.59375	1.3431
2.625	Aug 20	98.21875	98.28125	-0.90625	2.7100
3.875	Feb 40	93.40625	93.46875	-0.46875	4.2650

TIPS Bond

COUP	MAT MO/YR	BID	ASKED	CHG	ASK YLD
2.125	Feb 40	110.59375	110.6250	-2.46875	1.6650

** **Assume that BOTH T-bonds maturing on Feb 40 were initially issued on the same date at par.**

12. The outcome of trading in the "on-the-run" 3-month T-bill and all "on-the-run" U.S. Treasury T-notes and T-bonds on November 12, 2010 that is listed in Table 2 resulted in:

    a) the price of ALL of those Treasury securities

rose.

b) the price of ALL of those Treasury securities fell.

c) a rise in the price of the 3-month T-Bill and a decline in the price of T-Notes & T-bonds.

d) a decline in the price of the 3-month T-Bill and a rise in the price of T-Notes & T-bonds.

13. Based on the information in Table 1, an investor in T-Bills could buy the six-month "on-the-run" T-Bill at a price that ensures him a yield to maturity of:

a) 0.100 percent.

b) 0.130 percent.

c) 0.127 percent.

d) 0.246 percent.

14. The market's expectations of inflation over the next 30 years:

a) was 1.750 percent at the close of trading on November 12, 2010.

b) rose by 2.000 percentage points as a result of trading on November 12, 2010.

c) had risen by 0.85 percentage points from the date of issuance of the TIPS bond until the close of trading on November 12, 2010.

    d) fell by 0.460 percent from the date of issuance of the TIPS bond until the close of trading on November 12, 2010.

15. An investor who purchased the 10-year on-the-run T-note at the close of trading on November 11, 2010 reviews his purchase at the close of trading on November 12, 2010. He concludes that:

    a) his purchase at a price of $99.59375 per $100 in par value was a poor investment, since he could only sell it at a loss to another investor who would be demanding a yield to maturity on the note of 1.3431 percent.

    b) his purchase at a price of $99.1875 per $100 in par value was a poor investment, since he could only sell it at a loss to another investor who would be demanding a yield to maturity on the note of 2.7100 percent.

    c) his purchase at a price of $98.28125 per $100 in par value was a good investment, since he could now sell it for a gain to another investor who would be demanding a yield to maturity on the note of 2.7100 percent.

    d) his purchase at a price of $99.0000 per $100 in par value was a good investment, since he could now sell it at for a gain to another investor who would be demanding a yield to maturity on the note of 1.3431percent.

16. Visit one of today's sources of financial news (such as The Wall Street Journal) where you can find a complete listing of all U.S. Treasury securities along with the trading activity from the previous day. Identify the T-bills with 14, 91, and 182 days to maturity (or as close to these terms as you can find).

    a) Which of these U.S. Treasury securities have the lowest yield to maturity?

    b) Based on the information from part (a) how would you describe the slope of the yield curve over the maturity range covered by T-bills?

    c) Does your answer to part (b) suggest anything about how the slope of the yield curve in the less-than-one-year maturity range changed as a result of the previous days trading activity?

    d) If there was a change reported in part (c) and if this change would have been due exclusively to a changed perception of future inflation by the financial markets, would the markets have raised or lowered their expectations for inflation?

Dai, Q., and K. Singleton. 2000. "Specification Analysis of Affine Term Structure Models," *Journal of Finance* 55 (October): 1943-78.

Sack, Brian, and Robert Elsasser. 2004. "Treasury Inflation-Indexed Debt: A Review of the U.S. Experience," *FRBNY Economic Policy Review,* Federal Reserve Bank of New York, (May): 47-63

Stojanovic, Dusan, and Mark D. Vaughn. 1997. "Yielding Clues about Recessions: The Yield Curve as a Forecasting Tool," *Economic Review,* Federal Reserve Bank of Boston: 10-21.

Wheelock, David C., and Mark E. Wohar. 2009. "Can the Term Spread Predict Output Growth and Recessions? A Survey of the Literature," *Review,* Federal Reserve Bank of St. Louis (September/October): 419-40.

Wu, Tao. "What Makes the Yield Curve Move?" 2003. *FRBSF Economic Letter,* Federal Reserve Bank of San Francisco, no. 2003-15 (June 6)

Part III

Financial Institutions

Chapter 9

The Banking System

This chapter is devoted to an understanding of the structure of the banking system in the United States, the important roles that the *depository institutions*, most notably *commercial banks*, play in the economy, and how and why they are so heavily regulated. In Chapter 3, the total assets in the banking system, which includes *savings and loans* and *credit unions*, was seen to be approximately $16 trillion. This figure is roughly equal to the value of assets under management by mutual funds, and nearly as large as those assets managed by *pension funds*, whose investments are distributed between the stock market, the bond market, and the money markets, that total around $19 trillion. However, the use made of these funds by the banking system differs considerably from those of mutual funds and pension funds. Therefore, a close look at the balance sheets of depository institutions is necessary in order to see how they derive funds, and into what investments those funds are ultimately channeled. To do so, the focus will be on commercial banks, which are the most important of these depository institutions and whose activities are closely related to those of savings and loans and credit unions.

As emphasized in Chapter 7, with the important exception of the mortgage markets, most of the markets in which commercial banks are involved are money markets. Funds are primarily raised from small deposits of households, which are used to leverage the banks' capital and expand their balance sheets. The massive bank failures during the Great Depression of the 1930s, when many funds placed on deposit with banks were lost, made clear the importance of safe and sound practices of banks. The result was the creation of the Federal Deposit Insurance Corporation (FDIC) to ensure the safety of bank deposits and prevent bank runs in the future. This safety net has been remarkably successful, as not $1 of insured deposits has been lost since the FDIC began operation.

Guaranteeing the safety of deposits does have a cost. The loss of incentives for depositors to monitor the activities of banks can lead to excessive risk-taking among banks. Moreover, the banking industry can realize *economies of scale*, such that larger banks can operate at lower costs in many of their financial market activities, thus leading to a natural tendency for continued bank consolidation. Once banks grow very large, with assets over \$1 trillion, the failure of such a large institution could endanger the viability of the entire banking system. To avoid this eventuality, these large banks were generally seen to be "too big to fail," which is another source of "*moral hazard* as described in Chapter 6, whereby bank management is provided with yet another incentive to take on more risk in investments by chasing after the higher expected rates of return that accompany high-risk assets. For these reasons, the banking sector in virtually every western economy is one of the most heavily regulated industries in the country.

9.1 Bank Structure

The structure of the banking system in the United States is somewhat unusual in that it has by far the largest number of banks per capita of any country in the world. As of August 17, 2017, there were 4,982 domestically chartered commercial banks operating in the United States.[1] In contrast, Japan, whose economy and population is roughly half that of the United States, has approximately 120 banks.[2] Canada, whose economy is approximately 1/10th the size of the United States, has 32 domestically chartered commercial banks.

---

[1]Data compiled by the Federal Financial Institutions Examining Council. and available via the Federal Reserve Bank of St Louis's FRED database.

[2]Japanese bankers Association.

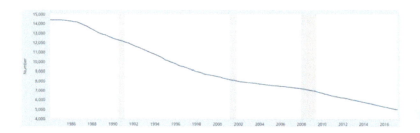

Figure 9.1 Number of Commercial Banks in the
United States
Source: Federal Reserve Bank of St Louis

There is an historical reason for the large number of
banks operating in the United States, stemming from
very restrictive state regulations that prohibited banks
from opening branches across state lines, and in many
cases allowing individual banks to possess only one
physical building. Beginning in the 1980s, these re-
strictions were gradually eliminated and, as shown in
Figure 9.1, there has been a steady decline in the number of banks from its peak in 1984 of 14,400 banks.
While there have been a number of outright bank clo-
sures, this decline has been overwhelming driven by
bank consolidation.

Today, the large number of banks masks the true
nature of concentration in the banking industry. Of
the $16.2 trillion in assets in U.S. banking system, the
largest five banks in the United States account for approximately 48 percent of the total assets, including

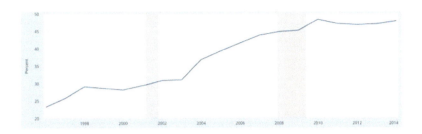

Figure 9.2 Bank Concentration: Percentage of Total
Assets Held by the Largest 5 Commercial Banks in
the United States
Source: Federal Reserve Bank of St Louis

four banks (JPMorganChase, Bank of America, Wells
Fargo, and Citgroup) that each possess over $1 trillion
in assets.

As described in Chapter 4, concern over a failure
of one of these mega-banks has driven legislators to
enact provisions contained in the post-Great Recession
Dodd-Frank Wall Street Reform and Consumer Protection Act of 2010 mandating greater oversight, stricter
regulations, and the so-called "funeral plans" requiring
these institutions to devise acceptable plans for liquidation in the event they were to become insolvent. These
regulations are broadly in line with international banking standards that have been adopted since the financial crisis of 2007-8. By virtually all accounts, they
have clearly strengthened the banking system both domestically and internationally, but remain controver-

sial due to the significant increase in the regulatory
burden that they have imposed on the affected banks.
These issues will be discussed toward the end of this
chapter.

9.2   Bank Liabilities

The Federal Reserve reports that all commercial banks
operating in the United States as of March, 2016 have
assets totaling approximately $15.7 trillion. Where do
banks obtain the funds to make these investments?

As shown in Table 9.1, the lion's share of funds
– that is, $11.7 trillion or 72% of total assets, – is de-
rived from *deposit accounts*. These deposits are divided
into two broad categories: (a) *core deposits*, which are
comprised of *transactions deposit accounts (or checking
accounts), savings and MMDAs*, and *small certificates
of deposit, or CDs*. Collectively, they account for $10
trillion, or 63% of total assets. The second category
is *large time deposits (or large, negotiable CDs)*, which
make up the remaining $1.6 trillion, or 10% of total
assets.

The other major source of funds is *borrowings*, which
comprise $2 trillion, with the source of those funds rep-
resented by borrowings from other banks in the important *federal funds market, repurchase agreements*, and
borrowings from the Federal Reserve at the so-called
discount window.

These numbers suggest that core deposits are the

Liabilities	trillions of $	Percentage of Total Assets
Deposits	**11.7**	**72.2**
CORE DEPOSITS	10.2	63.0
(Checkable Deposits & Savings Accounts and Small CDs)		
LARGE NEGOTIABLE CDs	1.6	9.9
Borrowings	**2.0**	**12.3**
(Federal Funds, RPs & Discount Window)		
Other Liabilities	**0.8**	**4.9**
Total Liabilities	**14.5**	**89.5**

Table 9.1: Liabilities of Banks Operating in the U.S. (May, 2017)

bread-and-butter of bank financing. They enable banks to expand their lending in a secular way over time as the deposit base grows. However, banks' needs for funds can emerge quickly. For example, a large bank may have IBM as a major corporate client that it values highly and to whom it has extended a line of credit at some cost to IBM. If IBM came to the bank to draw down that line of credit, the bank would have to honor its request, and would need to find a source of ready funds. It could not rely on core deposits, since they have no way to increase them on short notice. They can raise deposit rates, but must wait for customers to respond. For this reason, the other sources of short-term funds are extremely important to the daily management of the bank.

The bank has essentially four principal options from which to choose when raising funds quickly. These options include large negotiable CDs, federal funds, repurchase agreements, and discount window borrowings from the Federal Reserve. Let's examine these in turn.

Large Negotiable CDs

As discussed in Chapter 7, *large negotiable CDs* have denominations typically in excess of $100,000 and have the attractive feature that a buyer can sell them to a third party if need be, thus enhancing their liquidity. The bank can advertise these CDs at an attractive rate, and large institutional investors, particularly MMMFs, which have assets that are maturing every day and need to be reinvested, will gladly purchase the CD. Note that the cost to the bank is a *marginal cost*, that is, the interest rate paid on these CDs does not affect any other deposits that it has on the books. In contrast, if it were to raise rates on any of the Core Deposits (other than small CDs) it is essentially raising an *average cost* that would have to be paid on all existing deposits as well as any newly attracted funds. This higher cost of these funds is a second reason for not relying on them as a source of short-term funding.

Federal Funds

The second source of short-term funds to a commercial bank is to borrow in the *federal funds market*. This market has undergone dramatic changes since the onset of the Great Recession.[3] Prior to 2008, a federal funds market transaction consisted of an *interbank overnight loan*, where a bank that was short of cash reserves that it needed to meet its reserve requirements with the Federal Reserve, would borrow from a bank with excess reserves, that is, reserves it held over and above those needed to meet their reserve requirements.[4] As described in the next section, banks are required to hold a certain amount of *legal bank reserves* as determined by their volume of deposits. The two cash assets that qualify as legal bank reserves are *vault cash* and *deposits at the Federal Reserve* that are maintained by the banks who are members of the Federal Reserve system. Prior to 2008, deposits held by banks in their Federal Reserve accounts were prohibited by Congress from receiving interest. Given that legal bank reserves were the only non-interest bearing financial assets that the banks possessed, they managed them closely, attempting to keep excess reserves to a minimum.

When banks agree on a contract for a loan in the

---

[3]See "Federal Funds and Interest on Reserves," 2013. Federal Reserve Bank of New York (March).

[4]There is also a much smaller market for *term* lending in the federal funds market with maturities stretching out to two-weeks.

federal funds market, the contract would include an interest rate that is referred to as the *overnight federal funds rate*. This interest rate was largely determined by the monetary policy decisions of the Federal Reserve which sets a *target* for the interest rate at which they would like to see most federal funds transactions clear. This target rate has a very strong influence on all other short-term interest rates in the economy. The process by which the Federal Reserve achieves this target will be described in detail in the next chapter.

In 2008, there were two major changes that affected the operation of the federal funds market.[5] The Federal Reserve was authorized to pay interest on the reserves of depository institutions held in accounts with the Federal Reserve. The purpose was to remove what had been referred to as a "reserve tax" on those deposits that banks generally had to pass along to depositors by lowering the deposit interest rates they would pay. The Federal Reserve has since fixed this *interest rate on excess reserves, or IOER*, at a level above the federal funds target. This decision has had the effect of discouraging banks from lending in the federal funds market, since they can earn a higher interest rate on a risk-free deposit account at the Federal Reserve.

However, not all participants in the federal funds market are eligible to receive interest on their Fed-

---

[5]See Craig and Millington (2017) for a discussion of the changes that have taken place in the federal funds market since 2008.

eral Reserve deposits. In particular, those participants who are not eligible to receive interest on the Federal Reserve deposit accounts are (primarily) *Government-Sponsored Enterprises, or GSEs)*, that is, Fannie Mae and Freddie Mac, the two mortgage giants that were described in Chapter 4, along with the Federal Home Loan Banks, that supply funds to financial institutions exclusively to support lending in the mortgage markets. These GSEs have a need to invest overnight funds and are active lenders in the federal funds market. As a consequence of the interest rate structure established by the Federal Reserve with IOER greater than the overnight federal funds rate. The GSEs have become the net lenders in the federal funds market, while the commercial banks with deposits at the Federal Reserve that qualify for IOER have become the net borrowers. Essentially, the commercial banks are arbitraging the spread on the two rates by borrowing at the federal funds rate from the GSEs and lending to the Federal Reserve at the higher IOER.

This regulatory change that authorized the Federal Reserve to pay interest on deposit accounts maintained by the member banks coincided with the financial crisis of 2008-2009 that was described in detail in Chapter 4. One response to this crisis was a massive increase of reserves injected into the banking system by the Federal Reserve in an effort to ease conditions in those largely "frozen" credit markets. How these two events – the advent of interest on reserves and the financial crisis

– have fundamentally altered how short-term interest rates are determined in the economy is a very important topic that will be taken up in the next chapter.

Arbitraging Bank Sources of Funds

In addition to large negotiable CDs and federal funds, banks in need of a quick source of funds may also turn to the repurchase agreement market that was described in detail in Chapter 7. Banks will therefore want to choose the least cost source of funds, which would tend to cause the interest rates on these three types of assets to move closely together. This process is facilitated by the fact that many banks can participate on both sides of these markets, i.e., as either a lender or a borrower.

Take an example of a large bank that was not in need of any quick funds, but nonetheless monitored these markets and observed that the federal funds rate had dropped considerably below the RP rate. This rate spread would present a nearly pure arbitrage opportunity for the bank. It could borrow in the federal funds market at the lower interest rate and lend in the RP market at the higher interest rate, thus enabling the bank to make a profit with a net investment of zero, while incurring essentially no risk.[6]

---

[6]A *pure arbitrage* occurs when there is a zero net investment that yields a profit without incurring any risk. Since costs associated with identifying short-lived inefficiencies in the market and performing the necessary transactions to exploit them are always present in theses cases, pure arbitrage opportunities can

It would not take very many banks acting in this way to drive up the interest rate in the federal funds market, as the demand increased, while driving down rates in the RP market, which would be experiencing an increase in supply. This process would continue until an equilibrium was restored between the two market interest rates. This important market mechanism is how the Federal Reserve is able to effectively exercise a lot of control over short-term interest rates by essentially targeting only the federal funds rate. The next chapter will cover this process in detail.

Borrowing at the Federal Reserve's Discount Window

The final short-term funding source for banks in which funds can be raised quickly is to borrow from the Federal Reserve at the so-called *discount window.* The interest rates paid on these borrowings are administered rates set by the Federal Reserve as part of its decisions on monetary policy and in support of its regulatory responsibilities.[7]

The discount window actually has three separate functions. Traditionally, banks in agricultural areas experience significant seasonal swings in demand for

---

only be approximated. However, when these costs a minimal, trading on these market inefficiencies can be very profitable.

[7]See a description of the discount window facility operated by the Federal Reserve on its website at: https://www. federal-reserve.gov/monetarypolicy/discountrate.htm

loans associated with harvesting and planting seasons. However, many of the commercial banks servicing rural areas have a limited deposit base and are not large enough to have ready access to the money markets as would a so-called "money center bank" in New York City. To meet this seasonal loan demand, the Federal Reserve regularly makes this credit available to the rural banks in need. The interest rate charged on this *seasonal credit* is generally kept close to the federal funds rate target, reflecting the borrowing costs to banks in the broader market.

However, the Federal Reserve also stands ready to meet its traditional obligation as *lender of last resort* to banks suffering a short-term liquidity shortfall. In normal times, the interest rate paid on these borrowings, referred to as the *discount or primary credit rate* is set above the federal funds rate, thus discouraging reliance on the Federal Reserve as a source of funds to the banks. The administration of the discount window borrowing with respect to these loans was significantly altered in the aftermath of 9/11, when the demand for liquidity spiked sharply in response to the perception of the riskier world that seemed to have suddenly taken hold of the markets. The Federal Reserve supplied this liquidity, but did not have a gauge to determine how much was enough. This episode will also be discussed in the next chapter.

Finally, "troubled banks" may be granted loans in order to assist in approved restructuring of their balance sheets that would enable them to come back into compliance with the Federal Reserve's guidelines for safe and sound banking practices.[8] These less creditworthy institutions are charged an interest rate on their *secondary credit* that is above the primary credit or discount rate, reflecting the lower quality of these loans.

9.3 Bank Assets

On the asset side of the bank's balance sheet, several groupings of assets as shown in Table 9.2 that are useful when considering both the operations of the bank and what role the banking system plays in the financial markets.

Cash Assets

Cash assets are highly liquid and generally used to facilitate daily operations. They have a secondary benefit of reducing the risk assessment of the bank's portfolio holdings, and thereby help the bank meet its capital requirements, as discussed more fully below. These assets do not yield significant interest income to the bank

---

[8]The Federal Reserve and FDIC maintain lists of troubled or problem banks, but these lists are not made public for fear of encouraging unwarranted withdrawals on already weakened institutions. For a discussion of how a bank shows up on the FDIC's problem bank list, see "Problem Bank List,'" at: http://problembanklist.com/problem-bank-list/

Assets	trillions of $	Percentage of Total Assets
Cash Assets	**2.3**	**14.2**
Bank Credit	**12.6**	**77.7**
Investments	3.4	21.0
Loans and Leases	9.2	56.8
Interbank Lending	**0.1**	**0.1**
Other Assets	**1.3**	**8.0**
Total Assets	**16.2**	**100.0**

Table 9.2: Assets of Commercial Banks Operating in the U.S. (May, 2017)

and are therefore typically kept to a minimum. However, still in the aftermath of the *credit crisis*, banks have continued to hold unusually high levels of cash assets, which is an important topic that will need to be discussed in more detail in the next chapter.

Banks maintain a stock of *cash assets* that includes *vault cash* or the *currency* it has in its vaults and ATM machines, *deposits in accounts with the Federal Reserve*, *deposits that it maintains with other banks*, and a category referred to as *cash items in process of collection*, or checks drawn on other depository institutions that the bank has yet to clear.

Banks must hold a minimum amount of the *legal reserves* of vault cash plus deposits at the Federal Reserve in relation to certain liabilities. The Federal Reserve sets these so-called *reserve requirements*. Currently, banks are required to maintain legal bank reserves in the amount equal to 10 percent of their volume of *transactions accounts* (or checking accounts) outstanding.

However, banks may hold these reserves in the form of deposits at the Federal Reserve for a number of reasons.[9] These deposits enable the banks to engage in transactions that can be accomplished with simple accounting entries to the these accounts, and can be managed with electronic transmissions over Fedwire, described below. These transactions include federal funds market transactions, transactions in the RP market, checking clearing between banks, and payments or receipts from the Federal Reserve. They also help the bank satisfy *reserve requirements*, and they earn interest on excess reserves as determined by the Federal Reserve in conjunction with its monetary policy decisions.

Banks will maintain deposits with each other in order to help them with the clearing of checks drawn mostly on banks in their local geographical area. They also assist in transactions involving so-called *correspondent banking*, whereby a small bank may wish to offer services, such as a *trust department*, to its clients, but doesn't have sufficient business on its own to war-

---

[9]The interest rate paid on deposits held to meet reserve requirements differs from the interest rate paid on excess reserves. Currently the interest rate paid on required reserves is zero.

rant maintaining its own trust department in house. It can therefore offer those services provided by the larger bank.

As of May 2017, banks held \$2.3 trillion in various cash assets, representing 14% of their total assets. The vast majority of these assets were in deposits at the Federal Reserve.

Bank Credit

A key term in identifying the role of commercial banks in the economy is *bank credit*. It represents the total amount of credit that is created by the banking system. It has several components including the most important income-generating assets owned by the bank.

There are two major categories of bank credit: *investments* in various types of *debt securities*, which comprise 21% of total assets, and *loans and leases*, that account for 57% of total assets. *Interbank lending* represents funds that move between banks and are not part of bank credit. While they only account for less than one-tenth of one percent of total assets, they are important for the daily operations that support the various activities of the banks.

Investments are typically made up of *fixed income securities* and include: *Treasury securities, municipal bonds*, and the recently burgeoning group of *mortgage-backed securities, or MBSs* that played such a critical role in the credit crisis of 2007-2008. Banks have been reducing their holdings of MBSs, but as of May 2017, they still held $1.7 trillion in MBSs, representing approximately 10% of total assets in the banking system. Investments are generally used by banks to balance the risk and liquidity of their overall asset portfolio. They are generally highly liquid and carry a low level of risk, both of which reduce their potential for interest income for the banks.

The bread and butter assets of commercial banks are in their loan portfolios. An important category of these loans is referred to as *commercial and Industrial (or C&I) loans*, which at $1.7 trillion accounts for about 18% of banks' loan portfolios. These are business loans, most of which have relatively short maturities of a year or less. They represent one of the primary sources of credit for small businesses that are not able to access the capital markets by issuing stocks or bonds. Large corporations also rely on commercial banks for what is referred to as *working capital* loans, i.e., borrowings used to meet ongoing expenses, such as the firm's wage bill or payments made to its suppliers, when sales revenues fall short of those needs. Interest rates on these loans are generally higher than the principal alternative of commercial paper that large corporations with high credit ratings are able to access. Nonetheless, large firms will usually maintain open lines of credit with commercial banks for a fee, since this line of credit is a requirement for these firms to be able to sell their commercial paper in the open market.

Real estate loans remain the most important interest-earning asset of commercial banks, with $4.1 trillion on their books as of May 2017, representing nearly one-half of their total loan portfolio and nearly one-fourth of their total assets. While the banks own only $1.8 trillion in *home mortgages* outright, they actually have a much larger share of the market, when their indirect financing through *home equity loans* and MBSs are included. The total then increases to $3.5 trillion, which is nearly 25 percent of the total mortgage market of $14 trillion. Banks are also heavily involved in lending for *commercial real estate* ventures, which is as important to their bottom line as traditional C&I loans, with $1.9 trillion currently on the books.

One of the largest liabilities of households is *credit card debt*. Banks are the principal issuers of credit cards with some $700 billion in assets. Other *consumer loans* – including *auto loans*, *student loans*, etc. – comprise another $600 billion in assets. While not shown here, credit unions are strong competitors with commercial banks in these markets, and have gained significant market share during the past 20 years with some favorable court rulings that allowed them to expand their membership base.

A relatively small category of the *loan portfolio* in bank credit is *non-bank reverse repurchase agreements*. These are essentially assets to the bank, where they have entered into an RP with non-bank borrowers as a lender, and is said to be "reversing-in securities."

Interbank loans do not belong to bank credit, since these transactions reflect monies moving from one bank to another and never getting outside the banking system. The two important categories when banks are on the lending side of the transactions are referred to as *federal funds sold* and *bank reverse repurchase agreements*. While the total is relatively small at about $112 billion, these assets play a critical role in the daily operations of commercial banks.

The remaining assets of the bank are primarily comprised of their buildings, office equipment, etc.

9.4 Bank Equity Capital

Bank equity capital is the difference between the value of the bank's assets and its liabilities. It represents the value of the banking firm or the *net worth* of the firm against which claims are held by the bank's stockholders. It totals $1.8 trillion for all domestically chartered U.S. commercial banks.

Bank Equity Capital	trillions of $	Percentage of Total Assets
Total	1.79	11.0

Table 9.3: Capital Account of Banks Operating in the U.S. (May, 2017)

There are two broad components to bank equity

capital. *Capital paid in*, which equals the amount of funds raised by the banks at the time of issuance of new shares of common and preferred stock, and the *surplus & undivided profits*, which represents the cumulative bank's net income either held as *retained earnings (the surplus)*, or yet-to-be-declared as dividends or reinvestment in the bank's business (the, so-called, *undivided profits*).

As was discussed early in Chapter 4, bank capital is seen by regulators as a buffer to insulate depositors' funds from write-offs of bad assets by the bank. As a consequence, regulations designed to ensure safe and sound management practices at the bank focus on whether a bank has sufficient capital in proportion to the size and in relation to the risk of its asset portfolio. These are referred to as *capital requirements* and are enforced in banks in virtually every nation in the world.

9.5   The Basel Accords

In the modern banking era, funds are able to move around the globe quickly and at low cost. As a consequence, banks have had the opportunity to seek out countries where capital requirements are low. This enables them to increase the risk they take in selecting the assets in which to invest or increase the leverage they employ in funding those assets.

To address this problem, nations from the major

industrialized countries have attempted to coordinate their regulations by adopting standards for assessing a bank's so-called *capital adequacy*, i.e., whether the bank has sufficient capital relative to its size and the risk represented by its asset holdings.

These international meetings have taken place in Basel, Switzerland and have come to be called the *Basel Accords*. The first such meeting was in 1988 and produced the so-called *Basel I Accords*. Since then, significant modifications to the agreements have been undertaken, first in 1992, producing the *Basel II Accords*, and most recently in 2010-11 in response to the worldwide financial crisis, when substantial changes were put into place in the new *Basel III Accords* designed to strengthen the capital requirements on banks operating in all of the signatory countries.

Basel I and Basel II

Under the Basel I Accords, the basic structure of *capital requirements* is first to assess the risk associated with each individual asset owned by the bank, and attach a risk-weight from 0 for no risk to 1 for a maximum risk. The dollar volume of the assets are then multiplied by their *risk weights* and summed across all assets to create the *risk-adjusted asset base*.

Banks are then required to maintain a minimum amount of bank capital as a percentage of the risk-adjusted asset base. This requirement stresses the burden of risk that must be borne by stockholders, although some additional liabilities of the banks are also counted toward meeting capital requirements.

The Basel II Accords were essentially a refinement of the Basel I Accords to take into account many of the risk-management tools employed by the world's largest banks. It allowed those banks to perform their own risk assessment to recognize their unique risk-management practices, although the risk assessment had to be made transparent to regulators.

Basel III

The logic of capital requirements is that the owners of the bank should incur the greatest share of the risk associated with defaulted assets. However, the financial crisis revealed a number of other aspects to banking activities that needed to be addressed. Basel III was the outcome of negotiations to address those problems.

The first step was to tighten up on the risk assessment of the assets. Problems with reliance on the ratings agencies, as discussed in a Chapter 4, caused many high-risk CDOs and MBSs to receive AA ratings and a low risk assessment by regulators. Banks are now required to run *stress tests* of their portfolios to see how they would respond under various possible future scenarios reflecting differing economic and financial market conditions as specified by the regulators. These stress tests are then used to assess the overall level of risk inherent in the bank's asset portfolio, and whether the bank has sufficient reserves to absorb any losses it would incur under those severely adverse economic conditions.

The resulting risk-adjusted asset base is used to define the capital requirements as before. However, capital requirement ratios were significantly increased, with an even greater emphasis on equity capital, as some minor components of bank capital are no longer eligible to help meet these requirements..

In addition to strengthening capital requirements, the Basel committee recognized that one of the problems during the financial crisis of 2007-2008 was the lack of liquidity in the banks that would enable them to meet unexpected withdrawals from their funding sources or unplanned payment demands of creditors. To address this problem, banks were required to increase the liquidity of their asset portfolios and enhance the maturity match of their medium-term assets and liabilities. The latter requirement was to ensure that banks don't rely excessively on short-term debt to fund long-term illiquid assets (which, as described in Chapter 4, had led to the collapse of Lehman Brothers and Bear Stearns).

Individual countries were free to set their own regulatory requirements, but the provisions of Basel III were intended to be the minimum requirements for all signatory countries. In the United States, the Basel III accords were adopted and are being implemented, with some provisions ultimately strengthened. Particular emphasis has been given to the stress tests on financial institutions deemed to be "too-big-to-fail" as required by the Dodd-Frank Act. To date, these provisions have substantially improved the ability of the banks to whether the strain on their balance sheets resulting from severe economic conditions that may present themselves.

9.6   Summary

Commercial banks were major causalities of the financial crisis. They had extended their reach both globally and into markets that proved to be at the center of the crisis. As a consequence, regulations proved to be inadequate to handle the ever-widening scope of their activities.

Today, the banking system remains under stress in many parts of Europe, although it has stabilized in the United States, with banks more well-capitalized, involved in less risky endeavors, and under stricter regulations designed to prevent a recurrence of the kind of financial debacle that drug the world economy into its worst economic downturn since the Great Depression of the 1930s.

The new regulations emanating from the Dodd-Frank Act and the latest round of Basel Accords on the international stage are yet to be fully implemented and tested, and revisions to these new regulations are likely. They have clearly attempted to deal with the major disruptions that occurred in the late 2000s, but how well those reforms will deal with the future changes that we will surely see in the financial markets is a story yet to be told.

Key Terms

money market mutual funds (MMMFs)
disintermediation
retail money market mutual funds
Institution-only (IO) money market mutual funds
commercial paper
direct paper
dealer paper
covenants
credit enhancements
bridge financing
playing the yield curve
commercial banks
deposit accounts
core deposits
transactions deposit accounts
savings accounts
money market deposit accounts (MMDAs
small certificates of deposits (CDs)
large time deposits
large negotiable CDs
federal funds market
repurchase agreements, or Repos, or RPs
bank borrowings
borrowings from the Federal Reserve
Federal Reserve's discount window
marginal cost
average cost
federal funds

overnight federal funds rate
deposit accounts at the Federal Reserve
electronic funds transfer (EFT) system
Fedwire
funds wire
securities wire
collateral in a repurchase agreement
government securities dealer
RP or Repo rate
repurchase price
delivery-versus-payment (DVP) transaction
haircut on in an RP contract
interest rate risk
par or face value of collateral for an RP
interest income on an RP
demand loan
continuing contracts
discount rate
bank assets
cash assets
credit crisis
vault cash
banks' deposits with other banks
cash items in process of collection
legal bank reserves
reserve requirements
correspondent banking
trust department
bank credit

banks' investment
debt securities
loans and leases
interbank loans
fixed income securities
Treasury securities
municipal bonds
mortgage-backed securities (MBSs)
commercial and industrial (C&I) loans
real estate loans
home mortgages
home equity loans
commercial real estate loans
credit card debt
consumer loans
auto loans
student loans
loan portfolio
non-bank reverse repurchase agreements
federal funds sold
bank reverse repurchase agreements
bank equity capital
net worth of the bank
capital paid in
surplus & undivided profit
retained earnings
capital requirements
capital adequacy
Basel Accords

Basel I Accords
Basel II Accords
Basel III Accords
risk weights
risk-adjusted asset base

9.7   Review Questions

1. What is unique about the structure of the U.S. banking system and how did this structure evolve?

2. How do the measures of bank concentration in the United States based on the number of banks per capita versus the total assets of the banking system held by the largest few banks tell a different story?

3. How are the "too-big-to-fail" banks regulated differently than other commercial banks?

4. What are core deposits in banks and how important are they for long-term sources of funding? How important are they for short-term sources of funding?

5. Who are the principal lenders and who are the principal borrowers in the federal funds market? Explain why the markets are segmented in this way.

6. Wha is the difference between an average cost and a marginal cost of deposit funds to commercial banks, and how does it play a role in choices that must be made for raising funds?

7. How do arbitrage opportunities in the markets for short-term funding sources cause interest rates in

those markets to move together? Explain by way of example.

8. What are the principal objectives of the Federal Reserve's discount window? Answer this question in terms of the institutions that are borrowing the funds and the interest rates they must pay the Federal Reserve to have access to those funds.

9. What are the primary reasons banks hold cash assets? What special features among cash assets do deposits at the Federal Reserve have?

10. What is meant by bank credit, and what is its composition?

11. What are the principal attributes to the bank of its investment portfolio versus its loan portfolio?

12. How important is the banking system in providing credit to the housing market?

13. In what way to firms rely on commercial banks? Does if vary between large versus small firms? Explain.

14. What is Fedwire and how is it used in federal funds transactions and RP transactions?

15. How would characterize the significance of commercial banks in the housing (residential real estate) market?

16. Describe in your own words the purpose of imposing capital requirements on banks, how they relate to the bank's balance sheet, and why there may be a need for an international standard such as those set be the Basel Accords.

9.8 References

Craig, Ben and Sara Millington. 2017. "The Federal Funds Market since the Financial Crisis," *Economic Commentary,* Federal Reserve Bank of Cleveland, Number 2017-07: (April 5).

"Federal Funds and Interest on Reserves," 2013. Federal Reserve Bank of New York (March). Available at: https://www.newyorkfed.org/aboutthefed/fedpoint/fed15.html

Japanese Bankers Association provides data on its member banks at: https://www.zenginkyo.or.jp/en/outline/list-of-members/

Office of the Superintendent of Financial Institutions provides data on domestically chartered banks at: http://www.osfi-bsif.gc.ca/Eng/wt-ow/Pages/wwr-er.aspx?sc=1&gc=1&ic=1#WWRLink111

Description of the Federal Reserve's discount window operations can be found al: https://www.federalreserve.gov/monetarypolicy/discountrate.htm

Description of the FDIC's criteria for placing a bank on the problem bank list is: "Problem Bank List" available at: http://problembanklist.com/problem-bank-list/

Chapter 10

The Federal Reserve

This chapter focuses on the organization and operation of the *Federal Reserve*. It is the *U.S. central bank*, and was created after a series of banking crises and severe recessions in the late 19th century. It was intended to be the *lender of last resort* to financial institutions to ensure their ability to withstand a run on the bank, in the event that the bank's assets were of sufficient merit to warrant support. It was also intended to provide a so-called *elastic money supply*. In so doing, the Federal Reserve supplies liquidity to the banking system at times when the economy begins to enter a significant slowdown and bank lending would otherwise have to contract as deposit funds began to dry up. This contraction of bank credit would thus occur at the very time that more credit is needed for businesses and consumers to weather the poor economic conditions and would thereby exacerbate the severity of an economic downturn.

While these objectives have remained central to the activities of the Federal Reserve, its role in the economy has expanded over time. First, after the Great Depression of the 1930s, the Federal Reserve undertook a more active role in the nation's economic policy, when its decision-making authority was centralized at the Board of Governors in Washington, D.C. Most recently, following the financial crisis that accompanied the Great Recession of 2007-2009, the regulatory responsibilities of the Federal Reserve was once again expanded.

Despite the crucial role played by the Federal Reserve in the U.S. economy, its operations are not well understood by the general public. In the past, the Federal Reserve itself was somewhat responsible for this lack of understanding, when its policy deliberations were held in private meetings and the decisions of those meetings were not publicly revealed until long after the policy makers had met again and perhaps changed its policy. Today, the Federal Reserve seeks maximum *transparency* in the conduct of its decision-making and actions.[1] Nonetheless, it remains under intense scrutiny by Congress and is watched very closely by participants in the financial markets, since its ac-

---

[1]See "What Steps Has The Federal Reserve Taken To Improve Transparency?" at the Federal Reserve Bank of San Francisco website: http://www.frbsf.org/education/publications/doctor-econ/2006/september/transparency/.

tivities can have profound implications for the value of financial assets. However, the details of the Federal Reserve's operations are complicated and remain a mystery to a large segment of the population.

The goal of this chapter is to describe the organization of the Federal Reserve, the policy mandate given to it by Congress, and how its policy decisions are made and implemented in support of that mandate. This knowledge should make the reader not only a more informed citizen, but a more savvy investor.

10.1 The Origin of the Federal Reserve and its Mandate

The Federal Reserve was created by Congress with passage of the *Federal Reserve Act of 1913*. Since that time, the responsibilities of the Federal Reserve and its authority to act as both a principal regulator of the financial system and a chief architect of the nation's macroeconomic policy have increased significantly.

Its current mandate encompasses the following:

1. It designs and implements monetary policy in accordance with the "so-called" *dual policy mandate* of *price stability*, generally implying low and stable inflation, and *maximum sustainable employment* that fosters long-run economic growth.

2. As the lender of last resort, it is empowered to supply funds to financial institutions that are un-

der short-term economic stress, but are otherwise sound.

3. Along with the *Federal Deposit Insurance Corporation (FDIC)* and the *Comptroller of the Currency*, the Federal Reserve is one of the principal regulators of the banking system.

4. With the passage of the *Dodd-Frank Act*, described in Chapter 4, it became the chief regulator of *"too big to fail" firms* that could represent a *systemic threat* to the financial system as a whole.

5. Finally, the Federal Reserve is responsible for maintaining an efficient payments system in the United States. This includes the important role of *Fedwire* in facilitating huge volumes of large transactions on a daily basis.

10.2   The Structure and Organization of the Federal Reserve

The *Board of Governors of the Federal Reserve System* serves as the Federal Reserve's upper management and is located in Washington D.C. It includes seven Governors: the Chair (currently Janet Yellen), a Vice Chair (currently Stanley Fischer), a second Vice Chair for Supervision, that was newly created under Dodd-Frank, and whose primary focus is on bank regulation, along with four other Governors, all of whom are appointed for a single, non-renewable 14-year term. From among the seven Governors, the Chair and Vice Chair are appointed for 4-year terms, but can be reappointed up to the maximum of 14 years, when their term as Governor expires. In addition, there are over 200 PhD staff economists at the Board who closely monitor economic conditions, make recommendations for the design and implementation of both macroeconomic policy and financial regulations, and conduct basic economic research.

Along with the Federal Reserve Board, there are 12 *District Federal Reserve Banks*, one of which is located in each of the 12 districts into which the U.S. economy was partitioned 1913 (with Alaska and Hawaii added later to the 12th District on the west coast). These District Federal Reserve Banks give regional representation to the policy decisions and regulatory oversight of the banking system. At each of those banks, other than the Federal Reserve Bank of New York, there is a President, who is nominated by the Board of Governors and confirmed by the *District Bank's Directors*, who are typically prominent business and labor leaders, along with consumer advocates. Each district bank has a staff of 12-30 PhD research economists. The staff at the Board of Governors produce many of the economy's important economic statistics, such as measures of the nation's money supply, industrial production, and various financial statistics, and maintain important data bases, including bank data and the *Financial Accounts of the United States.*

The *Federal Reserve Bank of New York* has special roles to perform within the Federal Reserve System and, as such, is to receive greater oversight from Congress under Dodd-Frank through the appointment of its President, who now (after Dodd-Frank) must be nominated by the President of the United States, rather than the Federal Reserve Board, and must also now be confirmed by the Senate.

The New York Fed's special roles include:

1. conducting *open market operations*, which will be examined in detail later,

2. maintaining suveillance of the financial markets, by closely monitoring activities of the major financial institutions,

3. implementing the Treasury Department's decisions on intervention in the currency markets, and

4. conducting Treasury auctions, as discussed in a Chapter 8.

Each of the twelve District Federal Reserve Banks provides services to the commercial banks that are *members of the Federal System* and are headquartered in its District. These services include: (i) check-clearing, (ii)

access to short-term borrowings from the Federal Re-
sere at the *discount window*, and (iii) the provision of
currency for the bank's daily operations. The District
Banks also perform the function of regulatory oversight
over the banks within their District.

10.3 Policy-Making Committees

There are essentially two policy committees at the Federal Reserve, with overlapping responsibilities. One is
the *Federal Open Market Committee (FOMC)*, which
consists of twelve members. Its Chair is the *Chair
of the Board of Governors* and its Vice Chair is the
President of the Federal Reserve Bank of New York,
reflecting the special role of the New York Fed in implementing the Fed's monetary policy decisions. The
remaining six Governors of the Board of Governors are
also members. The final four seats are held by Presidents of the remaining eleven Federal Reserve District
Banks, who serve rotating terms as voting members.

The FOMC is charged with establishing the nation's monetary policy. This consists of setting a target for the overnight federal funds rate and establishing
any balance sheet adjustments through asset purchases
or sales in the open market.

The second policy making group is the seven-member
Board of Governors. They approve recommendations

from the District Banks on the discount rate, set reserve requirements for depository institutions, fix the interest rate paid on bank reserves, and approve federal charters for, and interpret regulations governing, commercial banks.

10.4   The Dual Policy Mandate: Price Stability

To direct the Federal Reserve's macroeconomic policy decisions, Congress has given it a dual mandate. One set of objectives is *price stability.* This objective has been given substance with an informal target of an underlying average inflation rate over what might be thought of as the medium run of 6 to 12 months of two percent.

The rationale for this target is that inflation in excess of two percent would induce too much volatility into prices, thereby creating *inflation uncertainty* that would lead to significant economic inefficiencies. Inflation below two percent would run the risk of plunging the economy into a state of *deflation* (or falling prices) as occurred in Japan's so-called lost decade of the 1990s, when it experienced essentially zero economic growth throughout that period.

So what is the appropriate inflation measure? There are many possible choices. One option could be the *consumer price index (or CPI)* or the *implicit price de-*

flator for *personal consumption expenditures (or PCE)*, given that they represent broad measures of inflation that affect consumers. However, they include food and energy prices that are extremely volatile and tend to give false readings of the underlying trends in inflation.

Since it is these trends with which the Fed is primarily concerned, it focuses instead on the so-called *core inflation* measures, or the CPI or PCE that have had the food and energy components removed. These core inflation measures have essentially the same trend as the CPI or PCE, but without the large swings that appear in those latter measures of inflation from one month to the next.

Since changes in monetary policy affect the economy with a lag, the Federal Reserve is concerned about the future. To gauge how inflation is likely to manifest itself in the future, the FOMC monitors measures of private-sector expectations of future inflation. In addition to market surveys, one important measure, is the yield spread on the 30-year coupon T-Bond versus the 30-year TIPS, as was discussed in Chapter 7. When the market's expectations of future inflation is low, the *inflation premium* in interest rates will also be low, as suggested by the Fisher equation.

10.5   The Dual Policy Mandate: Maximum Sustainable Employment

The second goal given to the Federal Reserve as part of its dual mandate is to try to keep the economy as close as possible to its *maximum sustainable level of employment*, which would coincide with *maximum sustainable economic growth.*

This objective is defined by attempting to maintain what is referred to as the *natural rate of unemployment.* This objective differs from, say, minimizing unemployment, since there will always be some *frictional unemployment* in the economy due to new entrants to the workforce and to individuals transitioning between jobs.

The *workforce* is defined as those either employed or actively looking for work. Of course, over time, the workforce grows with population, but it can also experience secular changes due, not only to demographic shifts (such as the baby-boomers coming of age), but also to changing attitudes toward work (with changing views of retirement or, as was the case in the 1970s, when women entered the workforce in large numbers). Economic conditions also result in changes in the number of *discouraged workers*, who have simply stopped looking for work.

It is not easy to measure the *natural rate of un-*

employment at any point in time. An alternative is what is referred to as *potential GDP,* which is the level of output consistent with the economy's resources being fully employed, and which thus coincides with the natural rate of unemployment.

The Federal Reserve and Congressional Budget Office have devised statistical measures that approximate potential GDP and use these measures to project how far the economy is from operating at its full potential. Using this statistic, the important measure the Federal Reserve focuses on in deciding whether the current state of the economy warrants a change in the stance of monetary policy is the *GDP Gap*, which is defined as the percentage deviation of actual GDP from potential.

$$\text{GDP Gap} \equiv \frac{\text{Actual GDP - Potential GDP}}{\text{Potential GDP}} \times 100\%$$
(10.1)

A *negative GDP Gap* implies that the economy is underperforming and the Fed would attempt to stimulate the economy by lowering interest rates. A *positive GDP Gap* indicates that demand in the economy is outstripping the ability of the economy to produce goods and services, and leads to higher inflation. In this instance, the appropriate policy response of the Fed is to raise interest rates in order to reduce demand.

As shown in Figure 10.1, when the economy is booming, the GDP Gap tends to be positive, as it was for an extended period in the 1960s and the 1980s, and

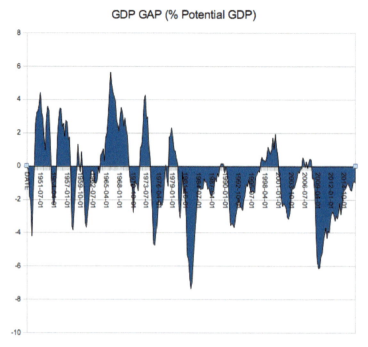

Figure 10.1: The GDP Gap
Source: Congressional Budget Office

when the economy is in recession, the GDP Gap is negative, as occurred during the deep recessions of the mid-1970s, the early 1980s, and the recent Great Recession, from which it is still recovering.

10.6 The Federal Reserve's Balance Sheet

Monetary policy actions are primarily reflected in adjustments in the Federal Reserve's balance sheet. Typically, these adjustments involve both sides of the balance sheet, i.e., to its assets and its liabilities.

Assets of the Federal Reserve

Table 10.1 lists the principal categories of assets held by the Federal Reserve. They include: *Gold Certificates*, *Special Drawing Rights* (which represent its account with the *International Monetary Fund, or IMF*), *Foreign Currency*, and *Domestic Coin*, each in relatively small amounts. Taken together these items represent a little over one percent of the Fed's total assets. Its primary asset has always been *Securities*, which total over $4 trillion. Of these securities, the larger portion is comprised of *U.S. Treasurys*, totaling $2.5 trillion, which represents 55 percent of the Fed's total assets and nearly 13 percent of the federal debt.

Traditionally, Treasurys have represented more than 90 percent of the Federal Reserve's total assets. However, in an effort to deal with the financial crisis, the Fed supported the housing market by purchasing over one and one-half trillion dollars in *Mortgage-Backed Securities, or MBSs*. Over time, as the Federal Reserve "normalizes" its policy stance following the ex-

ASSETS	TOTAL (Billions of $)
Gold Certificate	11
Special Drawing Rights	5
Foreign Currency	21
Coin	49
Reserve Bank Credit	4,435
- US Treasurys	2,465
- Federal Agency	8
- MBSs	1,781
- Loans	<1
- Other Net Assets	180
Total Assets	4,521

Table 10.1: Consolidated Balance Sheet of the Federal Reserve System (June 21, 2017)

traordinary steps it took to combat the Great Recession (which is described toward the end of this chapter), it is expected that the Fed will remove these MBSs from its portfolio holdings and return to its more traditional portfolio composition consisting primarily of U.S. Treasurys.

The Liability Side of the Federal Reserve's Balance Sheet

The *liabilities of the Federal Reserve* represent its principal sources of funds. They consist of three major contributors: *Federal Reserve Notes*, or paper currency, *Reverse Repurchase Agreements*, and *Deposits of Depository Institutions*. The latter play a central role in the Fed's policy activities.

LIABILITIES & CAPITAL	(Billions of $)
Federal Reserve Notes (currency)	1,556
Reverse Repurchase Agreements	446
Deposits	2,471
– Depository Institutions (Reserves + Term)	2,165
– US Treasury	225
– Foreign Official	5
– Other	76
Other Net Liabilities & Capital	48
Total Liabilities and Total Capital	4,521

Table 9.2: Consolidated Balance Sheet of the Federal Reserve System (June 21, 2017)

Prior to the Great Recession, banks kept their deposit balances with the Federal Reserve relatively low, since they were non-interest bearing assets. However, in recent years, banks have maintained unusually large reserve balances. As discussed in the previous chapter, banks must maintain a minimum of legal bank reserves to meet the Federal Reserve's reserve requirements, which are currently 10 percent of the bank's transactions deposits or checking accounts. Deposits at the Federal Reserve represent one of the principal means by which many banks meet these requirements. Historically, it was typical of banks to hold just enough legal bank reserves to meet required levels. That is, the *excess reserves* in the banking system, or those reserves over and above *required reserves* were typically close to zero.

As of June 21, 2017, with banks holding nearly $2.2 trillion in deposits at the Federal Reserve, excess reserves total approximately $2 trillion. As described in the previous chapter, the primary reason for these large deposit balances is that since 2006, the Federal Reserve has been authorized to pay interest on reserves held by depository institutions in their deposit accounts at the Federal Reserve. Commercial banks were then able to borrow federal funds from GSEs at the market-determined federal funds rate that was typically below the IOER at which the commercial banks invest those funds with the Federal Reserve.

This regulatory change coincided with the rapid expansion of the Fed's balance sheet (as shown below) during the Great Recession. The Federal Reserve's asset purchases were principally funded by injecting reserves into the banking system. More recently, the Federal Reserve has sold securities in the Overnight Repurchase Agreement market, which does not affect the size of the Fed's balance sheet. On the asset side, there is decline in the Fed's holdings of Treasurys with an offsetting increase in RP loans. However, there is a decline in reserves in the banking system, as reflected on the Fed's balance sheet. Reserve deposits used to finance the purchase, would be exchanged for the RRP liabilities that the Fed must honor when the Repo contract matures.. These RRP transactions have been used to enhance the Federal Reserve's ability to hit its federal funds interest rate target, as described in the upcoming sections.

10.7 Implementing Monetary Policy

The Federal Open Market Committee (FOMC) meets eight times each year at regularly scheduled meetings and sets monetary policy for the upcoming inter-meeting period, i.e., until they meet again. These decisions are implemented in large measure by the Federal Reserve Bank of New York. Six *policy tools* are available to the Fed[2]:

1. *open market operations*, or the purchase and sale of securities in the open market,

2. the *discount or prime credit rate*, or interest charged member banks in good standing for borrowing from the Federal Reserve at the discount window,

---

[2]For details see 'Policy Tools" available at the website of the Board of Governors of the Federal Reserve System: https://www.federalreserve.gov/monetarypolicy/policytools.htm

3. reserve requirements,

4. *interest on reserves (IOR)* and *interest on excess reserves (IOER)*,

5. *overnight reverse repurchase agreements*, or the temporary sale of securities from the Federal Reserve System's securities portfolio, and

6. *term deposit facility*, through which banks may place some of their Federal Reserve deposits in a separate account earning a higher interest rate than the IOER, effectively removing those reserves from the banking system for the duration of the contract which, for example, may be two to four weeks.

Of these tools, the large excess reserve balances in the banking system have rendered reserve requirements non-binding and therefore currently unavailable as an effective policy tool.[3] The term deposit facility is the only temporary lending facility that was established during the Great Recession that has not been discontinued. It is not being actively used, but is held back as an additional tool if needed to manage the quantity of reserves in the banking system as the Fed shrinks

---

[3]Although the interest rate differential between IOER and IOR could alter the willingness of banks to hold reserves. Currently, IOR is set at zero.

its balance sheet during the "normalization" of monetary policy, which is currently underway, and will be discussed in more detail later.[4]

The FOMC Meetings

At the FOMC meetings, the committee members are armed with a large volume of information that has been prepared by the staff economists of the Board of Governors and the research economists at the various Federal Reserve District Banks. This information is discussed and ultimately distilled into a set of decisions that establish: (i) the Fed's current monetary policy and (ii) provisions for public guidance with respect to future policy options. This information, along with the Fed's assessment of the current state of the economy, is released immediately at the conclusion of each FOMC meeting.

A critically important decision is the selection of a target for the so-called *effective federal funds rate*. This interest rate represents an average of all overnight federal funds loans made each day. How the Fed attempts to hit its target and how well it manages to achieve its target will be discussed below. Recall from the last chapter that when the Fed brings about a change in the federal funds rate, all other short-term interest

---

[4]See Ihrig, Meade, and Weinbach (2015) for a thorough discussion of how the Federal Reserve implements its monetary policy decisions in today's envrionment.

rates will tend to move in the same direction. There-fore, the Fed is approximately fixing short-term inter-est rates for the entire economy. Moreover, we know that the term structure of interest rates implies that longer-term interest rates are a (geometric) weighted average of current and future short-term interest rates, with adjustments for the liquidity premium. There-fore, longer term interest rates can also be significantly influenced by anticipated future Fed policy decisions.

Consistent with its decision on the the federal funds target, the FOMC affirms the decisions of the Board of Governors on the discount rate and interest rate paid on bank reserves. Finally, the FOMC must de-cide on adjustments that are to be made to its balance sheet through so-called *open market operations*, i.e., purchases and sales of financial assets in the open mar-ket. We'll discuss these latter decisions is some detail, as they have changed considerably since the onset of the Great Recession and the policy response that fol-lowed.

At the conclusion of its meeting, the FOMC pro-duces a *"policy directive"* that is sent to the *Desk Man-ager of the New York Fed.* It essentially provides him with guidance on how the policy decisions of the FOMC are to be implemented. The Desk Manager has some discretion in carrying out the policy directive. He must decide:

1. how many securities to purchase or sell,

2. what the maturity of the purchases or sales should be,

3. when to make the purchases or sales, and

4. with whom the transactions are to be made.

10.8   Setting the Interest Rate

Here are the details of how the Desk Manager went about conducting open market operations prior to the Great Recession in order to meet the federal funds target that was decided by the FOMC.

Every morning, the Federal Reserve in Washington received balance sheet information from the banks. Largely based on this information, a projection was made of the demand by banks for reserves, which is dependent upon the overnight federal funds rate. It would then conduct open market operations by, say, buying Treasurys and paying for them with deposits that the member banks have in their accounts at the Federal Reserve. These deposit accounts are bank reserves that are available to be lent in the federal funds market. Through its open market operations, the Fed was able to closely control the overall volume of reserves in the banking system, and therefore determine the aggregate supply of bank reserves available for lending in the overnight federal funds market.

This decision can be characterized on a supply and demand graph for federal funds as shown in Figure 10.2.

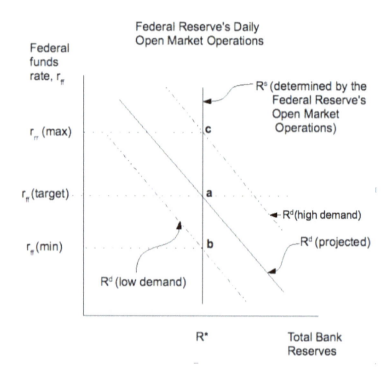

Figure 10.2: Open Market Operations Prior to the Great Recession

The Fed's best assessment of what will be the *demand for total bank reserves*, R^d(projected), is depicted as downward sloping, given that the borrowing bank will reduce its demand as for federal funds as the over-night federal funds rate rises. We've drawn the *supply schedule for total bank reserves*, labeled R^s, to be perfectly inelastic, reflecting the Fed's ability to very closely control the supply of bank reserves through its open market operations. It chooses to supply the amount of bank reserves such that the federal funds market is expected to clear, as shown in Figure 10.2 at point "a" on the graph, with supply equal to the antic-ipated demand at the federal funds rate target chosen by the FOMC, labeled r_{ff}(target).

Of course, the market will clear at the target rate only if the projected demand for bank reserves is cor-rect, assuming the Fed is able to control the supply, such that $R^s = R^*$. If the demand for reserves is higher than projected, say as indicated by the demand sched-ule labeled R^d(high demand), then the federal funds rate will be greater than the FOMC's target. In this case, it would clear at r_{ff}(max). Conversely, if the de-mand for bank reserves is relatively low, as indicated by the demand schedule labeled R^d(low demand), then the market would clear at point "b" on the graph, with the federal funds rate below the target.

Since the Fed cannot perfectly predict what the ag-gregate demand for funds is likely to be, problems can arise when there are unusual conditions in the market that cause large unexpected changes in liquidity de-mand. These conditions could produce a wide range of values for the federal funds rate. This volatility in the federal funds rate introduces risk and uncertainty into the cost of funds for banks, and could lead them to become more cautious in lending, resulting in higher loan rates and a lower volume of loans.

Of particular concern are periods of high liquidity demand when the Fed would like to prevent, if possible, the "spikes" in the federal funds rate that could result. It could potentially achieve this objective by supplying additional liquidity in the form of bank reserves to meet the heightened demand that banks are experiencing for short-term credit.

It was normally only very unusual circumstances that induced large unanticipated increases in the demand for liquidity, given that banks at that time held very little excess reserves (that were non-interest bearing), which rendered the demand schedule relatively stable and predictable. However, one such unanticipated shock to reserves demand occurred on 9/11. The event caused investors suddenly to perceive the world as a riskier place. They sought to shift their investments into risk-free assets, such as U.S. and Japanese government debt, and toward greater liquidity. The problem the Fed had to confront was to determine how much additional liquidity to supply. There was obviously no precedent to guide them.

The Fed's response to was to inform the banks that they could borrow whatever funds were needed at the discount window. In addition, banks did not want to be perceived as taking advantage of the tragic circumstances and reached a "gentlemen's agreement" that any overnight federal funds loans would be made at the Federal Reserve's announced target rate.

Of course, the Fed cannot always count on good corporate citizenship to quell adverse financial shocks that could induce large destabilizing spikes in the federal funds rate. Subsequent to the events of 9/11, a change in the Fed's discount window policy allowed for a market solution to this problem.

Prior to 9/11 the Fed generally set the discount rate below their target for the federal funds rate. However, this provided an incentive for banks to borrow from the Fed, since that was its cheapest alternative. To discourage this borrowing, the Fed required the banks to make a case for why they needed the funds. Essentially, the banks had to exhaust other possibilities before turning to the Fed. In periods of high liquidity demand, the Fed had to guess how much additional liquidity to supply in the form of bank reserves to keep the federal funds rate from spiking.

After 9/11, the Federal Reserve began to set the discount rate above their target for the federal funds rate, thus removing the incentive for the banks to borrow from the Fed as a cheap source of funds. Essentially, any bank in good standing could borrow at the discount window as much as they wished and for any purpose. Apart from reducing the costs to the Federal Reserve of monitoring discount window borrowings so closely, there was another advantage gained by this procedure.

The discount rate effectively sets a cap on the federal funds rate, thus eliminating the spikes that occur during times of high liquidity demand.

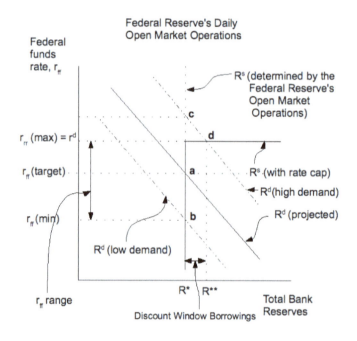

Figure 10.3: Open Market Operations After 9/11

For example, suppose the reserves demand shifted to the right as shown in the Figure 10.3 to a demand curve labeled R^d(high demand). Without recourse to borrow at the discount window, the market would clear at the point labeled "c". However, once the federal funds rate rose up to the discount rate, the banks would

turn to the Federal Reserve to borrow, essentially causing the reserves supply curve to become perfectly elastic. All additional borrowing would take place at the
discount rate, since no lender in the federal funds market could charge a bank anything higher than what
the Federal Reserve charged at the discount window.
In the example, the market would clear at point "d"
with the maximum federal funds rate limited by the
discount rate, despite the increased demand for liquidity that would otherwise have caused the federal funds
rate to spike.

Example of a Typical Open Market Operation

The previous examples assumed that the Federal Reserve can control the total amount of reserves in the
banking system fairly closely by buying and selling
Treasurys. Treasurys are paperless securities whose
ownership is registered with the Federal Reserve by
banks that are members of the Federal Reserve System. Purchases of Treasurys by the Federal Reserve
are from *primary government securities dealers*, whom
we'll abbreviate *GSDs*, (numbering approximately 20)
who are authorized to conduct transactions with the
Federal Reserve.

The Fed acquires Treasurys through one of two means:
outright purchases, which comprise its "permanent holdings" and *repurchase agreements*, which comprise its

"temporary holdings." Here is an example a typical open market operation.

Example: The Federal Reserve purchases \$1B in Treasurys from a GSD. There are 3 parties to the transaction: the Federal Reserve, the GSD, and a bank. Figure 10.3 depicts the T-accounts associated with the transactions.

Government Security Dealer

Assets	Liabilities
- \$1B (Treasury Bond)	
+ \$1B (Bank Deposit)	

Commercial Bank

Assets	Liabilities
+\$1B (Deposits at Fed Res)	+\$1B (Deposits of GSD)

As a result of the transaction, the government securities dealer sees its portfolio holdings of Treasurys (an asset) fall by \$1B. The commercial bank acting as the dealer's agent, notifies the Federal Reserve that it can take ownership of the Treasury in exchange for an increase in the commercial bank's deposit account at

Federal Reserve

Assets	Liabilities
+ $1B (Treasury Bond)	+$1B Deposits of Bank

Figure 10.3: Outright Open Market Purchase of $1B
in Treasury Bonds

the Federal Reserve by the same amount. The commercial bank then credits the deposit account of the GSD by $1B. The net effect is that the dealer has exchanged one financial asset (the Treasury) for another (the bank deposit), while both the commercial bank and the Federal Reserve have seen their balance sheets expand.

RESULT: The amount of reserves in the banking system has risen by exactly $1B, which is how much the commercial bank's deposits at the Federal Reserve have increased.

A repo works exactly the same way, except that after 24 hours, the RP contract expires, and the Fed sells the Treasury back to the original seller, as shown in Figure 10.4. The resale would cause the volume of bank reserves to shrink, unless the Federal Reserve acts to replenish these reserves with either outright purchases or temporary acquisitions of Treasurys under repo.

INITIAL TRANSACTION

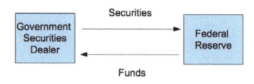

FINAL TRANSACTION
24 HOURS LATER

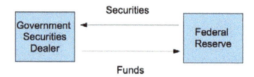

Electronic Transfer of Securities Over Securities Wire
Triggers a Flow of Funds Over the Funds Wire in the
Opposite Direction

Figure 9.4: Repurchase Agreement (RP or Repo) by
the Federal Reserve

Open Market Operations and the System Portfolio

Over time, the economy grows and the demand for liquidity rises, but not at a constant rate. That is, there are swings up and down in the demand for liquidity on a daily basis. To accommodate this increase, the Fed must expand its portfolio holdings of Treasurys through open market operations.

The secular increase in demand for liquidity is met with outright purchases of Treasurys that are added to the permanent holdings of the Fed. However, in normal times, the Federal Reserve only conducts outright purchases 4 or 5 times per year. In contrast, the Fed's RP transactions with temporary purchases or sales of Treasurys are conducted 3 to 4 times per week. Why has the Fed relied so heavily on RPs? The reason, as we stated, is that on a day-to-day basis the demand for liquidity fluctuates for many reasons. If the Fed does not accommodate those changes with increases or decreases in the supply of reserves, the federal funds rate will have to adjust to clear the market, and it would therefore deviate from the Fed's target.

Figure 10.5 illustrates how the Fed attempts to conduct open market operations to keep short-term interest rates from swinging widely around its target.

As shown, the permanent holdings of Treasurys follow a kind of step function, with large periodic outright purchases. However, the daily swings in demand are met with temporary holdings of RPs. Note that

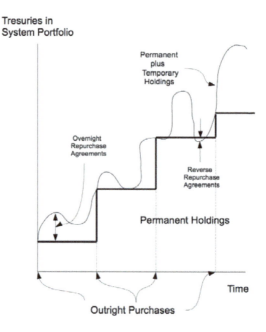

Figure 9.5: Open Market Operations and the Federal Reserve System's Treasury Portfolio

over time, between successive outright purchases, the average size of the Fed's RPs must increase as the secular demand grows. At some point, they become large enough that the Fed chooses to make another outright purchase.

On occasion, the demand for liquidity falls to the point where the permanent holdings result in a supply of liquidity that exceeds demand and the federal funds rate would have to fall below the Fed's target. To avoid this decline in the federal funds rate, the Fed would have to remove liquidity from the system. In that case, the Fed could engage in a *reverse RP*, thus reducing the quantity of reserves in the banking system. More will said of the current use of the reverse repurchase agreement by the Fed as a tool to aid in its control of the federal funds rate.

The Federal Funds Rate and the Federal Reserve Target

How well does the market interest rate follow the Fed's target? Figure 10.6 shows the evolution of the Federal Reserve's target for the overnight federal funds funds rate.

Note that the Fed generally moves the target in series of small steps, usually in 1/4 percentage point increments. In combatting the Great Recession, the target was reduced to close to zero, when the Federal Reserve switched from a single-valued target to a target range that was initially 0-25 basis points (1 basis point equals 1/100 of a percentage point). How they maintain this target range will be taken up subsequently. Beginning in December, 2015, the Federal Reserve has begun to raise the target, but has maintained the 1/4 percentage point target range.

Figure 10.7 shows the actual *effective federal funds rate*, which is representative of the daily average of all

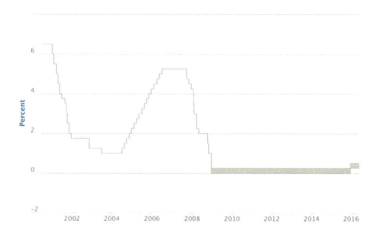

Figure 10.6: The Federal Reserve's Target for the
Federal Funds Rate

overnight federal funds transactions conducted throughout the day, superimposed (in blue) over the FOMC's
target. Obviously, the Fed does a remarkably good job
of controlling the interest rate in this market on average throughout the day. However, there are individual
trades that deviate considerably from this average.

What happened to the federal funds rate during
the financial crisis? A closer look during this period
in Figure 10.8 shows how the Fed ratcheted down the
interest rate with successive cuts in its target from 5-
1/4% to near zero. Notice that during the last steep
cuts, which came on the heals of Lehman Day, the
markets were anticipating the rate cuts and the bulk of

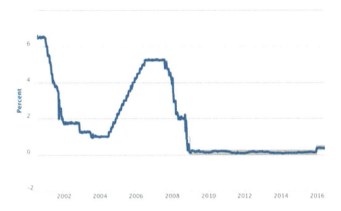

Figure 10.7: The Effective Federal Funds Rate and the Fed's Target during the Great Recession

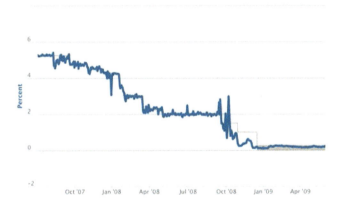

Figure 10.8: The Effective Federal Funds Rate and the Fed's Target during the Great Recession

federal funds traded below the Federal Reserve's target.

By the time the Federal Reserve had cut its target to as low as it felt it could possibly could go when it was facing the *"zero lower bound,"* reserves held in the deposit accounts of commercial banks with the Federal Reserve had ballooned due to the massive open market operations conducted by the Federal Reserve, along with the fact that banks were then receiving interest on their excess reserve holdings. These two factors had complicated the Fed's ability to exercise close control over the federal funds rate, forcing it to shift from a single interest rate target to a target range, originally set 0 to 25 basis points (1/4%).

Since adopting the target range, the Federal Reserve now sets two interest rates to assert control over the federal funds rate, and hence maintain its overall influence on short-term interest rates throughout the economy. Remembering that most federal funds transactions are loans from GSEs, who do not receive interest on their accounts at the Federal Reserve, to commercial banks, that do receive interest on their excess reserves. The commercial banks therefore borrow from the GSEs in the federal funds market and then place these funds on deposit with the Federal Reserve. By setting the interest rate paid on excess reserves, IOER, at the upper limit of its target range, the Federal Reserve is assured that banks would be unwilling to borrow from the GSEs at higher rate. Barring unusual circumstance, such as another 9/11, IOER should

be the maximum rate that the effective federal funds
rate would ever reach.

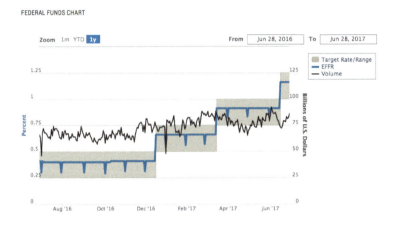

Figure 10.9: The Effective Federal Funds Rate and
the Fed's Target during the Recovery

To set the lower end of the target range, the Federal
Reserve has adopted a new policy tool. While it had
previously engaged in reverse repurchase agreements
to drain reserves form the banking system, the interest
rate on those contracts was market determined. Under the new policy, the Federal Reserve sets an interest
rate on reverse repurchase agreements (RRP) that it
stands ready to pay to any counterparty, subject to a
limit place on the volume of RRPs that it is willing
to undertake. If the Fed's limit is not reached, market participants, including GSEs, government securi-

ties dealers, money market mutual funds, and commercial banks, would never sell securities under RP at a rate below what they could receive from the Federal Reserve. This facility is being used in a limited fashion at this time in the current extraordinary period of low interest rates, and may be discontinued in the future once the federal funds rate returns to a more sustainable long-term level.

As shown in Figure 10.9, the Federal Reserve maintained the 0-25 basis point target range for 7 years before the FOMC chose to raise it by 1/4 percentage point to 25-50 basis points in December 2015. Since then, as shown in Figure 9.9, it has raised the target range three more times to 1-1.25%, with more rate increases in the offing.

10.9   The Federal Reserve's Response to the Financial Crisis

When the financial markets were functioning normally, the Federal Reserve could conduct policy by buying and selling bonds (either with its outright purchases or temporary acquisitions in the RP market) and in doing so control the volume of reserves in the banking system as we have seen. It could then rely on the financial markets to allocate those funds efficiently to where they were most highly in demand.

However, after Lehman Day, the financial markets froze up. Credit dried up. Even the interbank loan market was not functioning properly. The Federal Reserve had to find other means of ensuring adequate liquidity was available to support those entities in the economy with critical demands for credit.

The Federal Reserve responded by:

1. reassuring the public that the banking system was sound;

2. drastically cutting short-term interest rates, as we've seen;

3. acquiring a large volume of MBSs to support that market; and

4. opening up a wide range of direct lending facilities that included, but reached beyond commercial banks and savings and loans, with a particular focus on those institutions that were most in need of funding in the money markets. Support was directed in particular to: (i) the commercial paper market, (ii) the money market mutual funds, and (iii) government securities dealers, who are principal players in the RP market.

One indication of how tight the market for credit became during the financial crisis is the spike that is observed in Figure 10.10 in the so-called *TED-Spread*. This interest rate spread is the difference between the

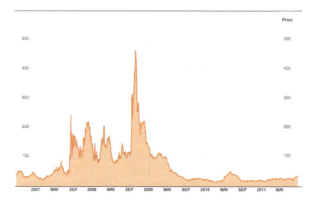

Figure 10.10: The Ted Spread

overnight, interbank lending rate in Europe, similar to the overnight federal funds rate, known as the LIBOR (London Interbank Offered Rate) that was very influential in setting short-term interest rates internationally, and the interest rate on the on-the-run 3-month Treasury Bill.[5] This interest rate spread was normally

---

[5]The LIBOR is an interest rate that was set daily as an average of interest rates that are intended to reflect borrowing costs from a number of British banks. However, in the early 2000s, collusion was discovered among several of the parties involved who were found to be manipulating the interest rate to enhance financial positions that they had taken. The outcome is of the investigation that followed, was one trader received a lengthy jail sentence, and despite efforts to reform the mechanism used to determine the interest rate, LIBOR has been scheduled to be discontinued as a major benchmark interest rate. Its replacement has yet to surface. See McBride (2016) for a thorough discussion

very narrow, at about 50 basis points or less, reflecting the fact that interbank loans are typically very low risk and absent a significant liquidity premium due to their extremely short maturity.

As Figure 10.10 illustrates, the TED-Spread widened to an unprecedented level during the financial crisis of more than 4.5 percent. These wide spreads lasted for more than a year, until normal lending was restored in late 2009, thanks in large measure to the efforts of the Federal Reserve in providing liquidity through its unconventional direct lending facilities.

The Great Recession and the Great Balance Sheet Expansion

As the Fed expanded its new lending facilities, and continued to expand its bank reserves through asset purchases to support the economy during the Great Recession and throughout the sluggish recovery that followed, its balance sheet ballooned. As shown in Figure 10.11, prior to the onset of the financial crisis, the Federal Reserve's assets totaled approximately $870 billion, almost all of which were Treasury securities. Today, that number is over $4.5 trillion. Its balance sheet has more than quintupled.

If we look at the composition of those assets, we see that what the Federal Reserve was doing initially was selling some of its Treasury securities, which were

---

of the scandal.

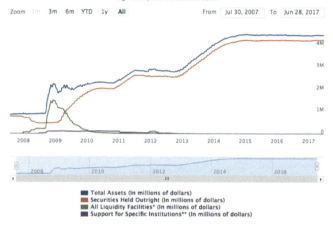

Figure 10.11: Selected Assets of the Federal Reserve

in high demand in the markets, and acquiring claims on many other financial firms by extending credit to them. As the crisis eased, these loans were repaid and the lending facilities closed. However, the economy was still seen to be weak, with the housing market, in particular, in poor shape. So, as the Federal Reserve saw these assets leave its books, it replaced them with Treasurys and it began to aggressively purchase MBSs.

With short-term interest rates already near zero, these *large-scale asset purchases* came to be know as *quantitative easing*. There were three separate periods of quantitative easing that can be identified in Figure 10.11 where the amber line's slope turns sharply positive.

1. Quantitative Easing I (QEI): December,2008 to March 2010): The The Federal Reserve purchased Treasurys and MBSs to replace the temporary emergency lending facilities (in green) that were being systematically closed, thus leaving their total assets (in blue) largely unaffected.

2. Quantitative Easing II (QEII): November, 2010 to June, 2011): The Federal Reserve systematically expanded its Treasury portfolio with monthly, pre-announced outright purchases in the open market.

3. Quantitative Easing III (QEIII): January, 2013 to October, 2014: The Federal Reserve systematically expanded its portfolio holdings of both Treasury securities and MBSs

Of course, balance sheets must balance, which implies that these assets must be supported by an increase on the liability side of the Federal Reserve's balance sheet. Again, Figure 10.12 displays some very unusual changes.

Note that prior to the financial crisis, the lion's share of the Federal Reserve's liabilities was currency. After the aggressive expansion of their balance sheet began, currency – in blue – continued to grow at a very

moderate pace. What ballooned were deposits at the
Federal Reserve of commercial banks. This expansion
of bank's deposits with the Federal Reserve coincided
with the decision by the Fed to begin paying interest
on reserves as has been described.

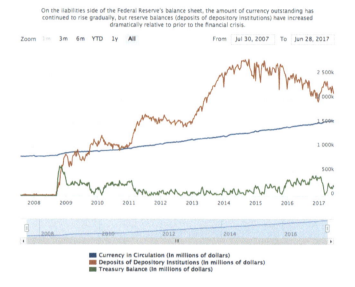

Figure 10.12: Selected Liabilities of the Federal
Reserve

10.10 The Federal Reserve Today

These balance sheet trends reflect the policy decisions that were taken to combat the financial crisis under the leadership of Chairman Ben Bernanke. He effectively steered monetary policy through these difficult and extraordinary times with almost no historical precedent to guide his decisions, for which he has generally received very high marks. When he resigned, the financial markets were functioning well, the banking system was sound, and the economic recovery was well under way. However, short-term interest rates were artificially low, hovering as they were around zero and the Federal Reserve was sitting uncomfortably on a massively bloated balance sheet.

Ben Bernanke's successor, Janet Yellen, was tasked with designing and implementing what some have referred to aa an *exit strategy* or what the Fed terms its *policy normalization.* [6] The key provisions include:

1. raising short-term interest rates to long-term sustainable levels.

2. dramatically shrinking the size of its balance sheet

---

[6]See "Policy Normalization," on the website of the Board of Governors of the Federal Reserve System at: https://www.federalreserve.gov/monetarypolicy/policy-normalization.htm

3. purging MBSs from its asset portfolio holdings

The task is complicated by the need to continue to meet its dual mandate of price stability and maximum sustainable growth and employment. While large changes to its balance sheet and to interest rates are required, they must be be phased in with maximum transparency to avoid disrupting the financial markets, plunging the economy into another recession, or igniting inflation. It is a formidable task, and the road to its fulfillment is one on which the Federal Reserve has only just begun to embark.

10.11   Summary

The Federal Reserve was created by an act of Congress in 1913 to serve as the nation's central bank. As lender of last resort, it was intended to provide a backstop for the banking system in times of economic stress. Its ability to create fiat (paper) money enabled it to provide an elastic money supply, thus expanding credit creation in the economy during economic recessions through its provision of liquidity to the banking system.

Since its creation, the responsibilities of the Federal Reserve have grown. Today, it is charged with achieving a dual macroeconomic policy mandate of price stability and maximum sustainable employment and economic growth. It is one of the chief regulators of the banking system, responsible for monitoring compliance with established safe and sound banking practices and taking a proactive role in ensuring stability in the financial system. The Federal Reserve also plays a central role in providing for an efficient payments system in the economy that enables financial transactions to be efficiently consummated.

The principal policy tools with which the Fed can implement policy decisions are open market operations, the discount rate, the interest rate that it pays on bank reserves, the interest rate on overnight overnight reverse repurchase agreements, and reserve requirements, although the last of these tools is unavailable today due to the large excess reserve balances that banks are currently carrying. These balances came about as a result of the rapid expansion of the Federal Reserve's balance sheet, beginning with the financial crisis leading up to the Great Recession, coupled with the new policy adopted by the Federal Reserve in which bank reserves are paid interest by the Fed.

The extraordinary measures taken by the Federal Reserve in response to the financial crisis and the deep recession that followed, while successful, have left the Federal Reserve with a policy stance that is not sustainable in the long run. Short-term interest rates were near zero, and the Fed's balance sheet had quintupled, including large holdings of MBSs.

Beginning in December 2016, the FOMC undertook its first steps toward policy normalization, which is to include gradually raising short-term interest rates to sustainable levels, while shrinking its balance sheet and purging MBSs from its asset portfolio. It must achieve these objectives with maximum transparency to avoid disruptions in the financial markets, but with deliberate actions that are carefully crafted to neither plunge the economy back into a recession nor ignite the flames of inflation. It is a daunting and very important task that will take years to complete, and in the end, it will help define the "new normal" and what will be the expanded role that the Federal Reserve will play in the economy.

Key Terms

Board of Governors of the Federal Reserve System

Chair of the Board of Governors of the Federal
Reserve System

Comptroller of the Currency

consumer price index (CPI)

deflation

demand for total bank reserves

deposits of depository institutions

Desk manager of the New York Federal Reserve
Bank

discount rate

discount window

discouraged workers

District Bank Presidents

Dodd-Frank Wall Street Reform and Consumer
Protection Act of 2010 (Dodd-Frank)

domestic coin

dual policy mandate

effective federal funds rate

elastic money supply

excess bank reserve

exit strategy

Federal Deposit Insurance Corporation (FDIC)

Federal Open Market Committee (FOMC)

Federal Reserve

Federal Reserve Act of 1913

Federal Reserve Bank of New York

Federal Reserve District Banks

Federal Reserve notes
Federal Reserve's capital account
Federal Reserve's liabilities
Federal Reserve's assets
Fedwire
foreign currency
GDP Gap
gold certificates
frictional unemployment
implicit price deflator for personal consumption
    expenditures (PCE)
inflation premium
inflation uncertainty
interest on reserves (IOR) and interest on excess
    reserves (IOER)
International Monetary Fund (IMF)
large-scale asset purchases
maximum sustainable employment and growth
member banks of the Federal Reserve
monetary policy tools
mortgage-backed securities (MBSs)
natural rate of unemployment
normalization of monetary policy
open market operations
outfight purchases
overnight reverse repurchase agreement
policy directive
potential GDP
price stability

primary government securities dealers
quantitative easing
repurchase agreements
required reserves
special drawing rights
supply schedule for total bank reserves
target for the federal funds rate
TED-Spread
term deposit facility
too big to fail firms
transparency in monetary policy
U.S. Central Bank
U.S. Treasurys
workforce
zero lower bound

10.12   Review Questions

1. How does the Federal Open Market Committee differ from the Board of Governors in terms of their composition and responsibilities for policy decisions?

2. How does the Federal Reserve define *price stability*? Explain the logic behind this definition.

3. What is meant by the *GDP Gap* and how does it relate to the *Natural Rate of Unemployment*?

4. Describe how the Federal Reserve was able to control the federal funds rate fairly closely prior to the Great Recession, and why this enables the Federal Reserve to have such good control over ALL short-term money market interest rates. Refer to changes in the Federal Reserve's balance sheet and how those changes are reflected on balance sheets of commercial banks.

5. How and why did the manner in which the Federal Reserve's administration of the *Discount Window* change after 9/11? State the advantages of the changes.

6. How did and why the Federal Reserve make changes in the way it "controlled" the federal funds rate?

7. What did the Federal Reserve do to combat the financial crisis that accompanied the Great Re-

cession of 2007-2009? What problems have these actions of the Federal Reserve created for its current activities?

8. What is meant by the Fed's "Exit Strategy," and has it made any progress toward achieving its objectives of "policy normalization"?

10.13   References

Ihrig, Jane E., Ellen F. Meade, and Gretchen C. Weinbach. 2015. "Monetary Policy 101: A Primer on the Fed's Changing Approach to Policy Implementation,' *FEDS Discussion Paper Number 2015-17*," Board of Governors of the Federal Reserve System (June 30).

McBride, James.   2016.   "Understanding the Libor Scandal,: Council on Foreign Relations. Available at: https://www.cfr.org/backgrounder/understanding-libor-scandal

On greater transparency in monetary policy, see "What Steps Has The Federal Reserve Taken To Improve Transparency?" at the Federal Reserve Bank of San Francisco website: http://www.frbsf.org/education/publications/doctor-econ/2006/september/transparency/.

"Policy Tools" Available at the website of the Board of Governors of the Federal Reserve System: https://www.federalreserve.gov/monetarypolicy/policytools.htm

See "Policy Normalization," on the website of the Board of Governors of the Federal Reserve System at: https://www.federalreserve.gov/monetarypolicy/policy-normalization.htm

Chapter 11

Subject Index

Chapter 12

Author Index

Chapter 13

Bibliography

Akerlov, George A. 2001. "Writing the "The Market for Lemons": A Personal and Interpretative Essay," Nobel Lecture available at: http://www.nobelprize.org/nobel_prizes/economic-sciences/laureates/2001/aker-lof-article.html

Akerlov, George A. 1970. "The Market for Lemons: Quality Uncertainty and the Market Mechanism," *Quarterly Journal of Economics*, 84(3): 488-500.

Cochrane, John H. 2014. "Eugene F. Fama, Efficient Markets, and the Nobel Prize" (May 20). Available at: http://review.chicagobooth.edu/magazine/winter-2013/eugene-fama-efficient-markets-and-the-nobel-prize

Craig, Ben and Sara Millington. 2017. "The Federal Funds Market since the Financial Crisis," *Eco-*

nomic Commentary, Federal Reserve Bank of Cleveland, Number 2017-07: (April 5).

Dai, Q., and K. Singleton. 2000. "Specification Analysis of Affine Term Structure Models," *Journal of Finance* 55 (October): 1943-78.

Fama, Eugene F. "Efficient Capital Markets: A Review of Theory and Empirical Work." 1970. *The Journal of Finance* Vol. 25, No. 2, Papers and Proceedings of the Twenty-Eighth Annual Meeting of the American Finance Association New York, N.Y. December, 28-30, 1969 (May): 383-417

Geisst, Charles R. 2004. Wall Street: A History ? From its Beginnings to the Fall of Enron. Oxford University Press.

Hicks, John R. 1962. "Liquidity," *The Economic Journal,* vol. 72, no. 288. December: 787-802.

Ihrig, Jane E., Ellen F. Meade, and Gretchen C. Weinbach. 2015. "Monetary Policy 101: A Primer on the Fed's Changing Approach to Policy Implementation,' *FEDS Discussion Paper Number 2015-17,"* Board of Governors of the Federal Reserve System (June 30).

Kelley, Eric, K. and Paul C. Tetlock. 2017. "Retail Short Selling and Stock Prices." *Review of Financial Studies,* Vol 30(3), 801-834.

Keynes, John Maynard. 1930. *A Trestise on Money.* Harcourt Brace and Company: New York.

Kodres, Laura E. 2013. "What Is Shadow Banking?" *Finance and Development*, IMF: June.

McBride, James. 2016. "Understanding the Libor Scandal,: Council on Foreign Relations. Available at: https://www.cfr.org/backgrounder/understanding-libor-scandal

Morrison, Alan D. and William J. Wilhelm, Jr. "Investment Banking: Past, Present, and Future," 2007. *Journal of Applied Corporate Finance.* 19(1): 8-20.

Radford, Richard A. 1945. "The Economic Organization of a P.O.W. Camp," *Economica*, vol. 12, no. 48, November: 189-201.

Sack, Brian, and Robert Elsasser. 2004. "Treasury Inflation-Indexed Debt: A Review of the U.S. Experience," *FRBNY Economic Policy Review*, Federal Reserve Bank of New York, (May): 47-63

Stigum, Marcia and Anthony Crescenzi.. 2007 *Stigum's Money Market*, 4th ed. McGraw-Hill Education: New York. Available as a free download at: https://archive .org/stream/MarciaStigum/Marcia%20Stigum%2C%20 Anthony%20Crescenzi-Stigum%27s%20Money%20Market-McGraw-Hill%20%282007%29#page/n1/mode/2up

Stigum, Marcia. 1998. *The Repo and Reverse Markets,* McGraw-Hill Companies: New York.

Stojanovic, Dusan, and Mark D. Vaughn. 1997. "Yielding Clues about Recessions: The Yield Curve as a Forecasting Tool," *Economic Review,* Federal Reserve Bank of Boston: 10-21.

Summers, Bruce. "Negotiable Certificates of Deposit," 1980. *Economic Review,* Federal Reserve Bank of Richmond (July/August).

Wheelock, David C., and Mark E. Wohar. 2009. "Can the Term Spread Predict Output Growth and Recessions? A Survey of the Literature," *Review,* Federal Reserve Bank of St. Louis (September/October): 419-40.

Wu, Tao. "What Makes the Yield Curve Move?" 2003. *FRBSF Economic Letter,* Federal Reserve Bank of San Francisco, no. 2003-15 (June 6)

General Websites

Organization for Economic Cooperation and Development (OECD) "OECD Data: Insurance Spending" can be found at: https://data.oecd.org/insurance/insurance-spending.htm

Trends in Family Wealth, 1989 to 2013 (Congressional Budget Office, August 2016), www.cbo.gov/publication

/51846.

http://www.nobelprize.org/nobel_prizes/economic-sciences/laureates/2001/popular.html

https://www.federalreserve.gov/faqs/money_12845.htm

"Financial Accounts Guide" to the *Financial Accounts of the United States: Flow of Funds, Balance Sheets, and Integrated Macroeconomic Accounts (Z.1 data release)*. 2017. Board of Governors of the Federal Reserve System. Available at: https://www.federalreserve.gov/apps/fof/ Describes these extensive financial accounts for the U.S. economy that are compiled quarterly by the Federal Reserve.

Data for Economic Flows reported in Table 3.7: *Financial Accounts of the United States: Flow of Funds, Balance Sheets, and Integrated Macroeconomic Accounts (Z.1 data release)*. 2017. Tables: F.101, F.103, F.106, F.107, F.111, F.133. Board of Governors of the Federal Reserve System. Available at: https://www.federalreserve.gov/releases/z1/current/z1.pdf

Data for Economic Stocks reported in Table 3.8: *Financial Account of the United States: Flow of Funds, Balance Sheets, and Integrated Macroeconomic Accounts (Z.1 data release)*. 2017. Tables: L.111, L.114, L.116, L.116, L.118, L.119, L.120, L.121, L.122, L.128, L.130. Board of Governors of the Federal Reserve System. Available at: https://www.federalreserve.gov/releases/

z1/current/z1.pdf
"The Great Depression." The History Channel. Available at: http://www.history.com/topics/great-depression

"Mortgage Debt Outstanding," Board of Governors of the Federal Reserve System, Data Release June, 2017. Available at: https://www.federalreserve.gov/econres-data/releases/mortoutstand/current.htm

"Failed Bank List," 2017. Federal Deposit Insurance Corporation. Available at: https://www.fdic.gov/bank/individual/failed/banklist.html

"Buffet Warns on Investment 1time bomb'," BBC News, March 4, 2003. Available at: http://news.bbc.co.uk/2/hi/2817995.stm

"Report on the Troubled Asset Relief Program – June 2017." Congressional Budget Office. Available online at: https://www.cbo.gov/system/files/115th-congress-2017-2018/reports/52840-tarp.pdf

"Executive Summary: Dodd-Frank Wall Street Reform and Consumer Protection Act." American Bankers Association. July 14, 2010. Available at: https://www.congress.gov/bill/111th-congress/house-bill/04173

"Summary of Dodd-Frank Financial Regulation Legislation," Harvard Law School Forum on Corporate Governance and Financial Regulation, July 7, 2010. Available at: https://corpgov.law.harvard.edu/2010/07/07/summary-of-dodd-frank-financial-regulation-legislation/

"H.R.4173 - Dodd-Frank Wall Street Reform and Consumer Protection Act," 111th Congress,(2008-2011). Available at: http://www.aba.com/Issues /Reg Reform /Pages/RR_ExecSummary.aspx

http://www.consumerfinance.gov/regulations/ability-to-repay-and-qualified-mortgage-standards-under-the-truth-in-lending-act-regulation-z/ with a particularly useful summary on this website: "Detailed summary of the rule"

A description of the "debt-to-income" calculation that is part of the rules can be found at: http://www.fha.com /fha_requirements_debt.cfm

"Putting Compound Interest to Work: With Zero Coupon Bonds," 2005-1013. The Securities Industry and Financial Markets Association. Available at: http:// www.investinginbonds.com/learnmore.asp?catid=6&id =46

"The ABC of Credit Ratings," Office of Investor Education and Advocacy of the Securities and Exchange Commission. Available at: https://www.sec.gov/investor/alerts/ib_creditratings.pdf

"Bond Basics Tutorial." 2010. from Investopedia.com. Available at: http://www.investopedia.com /university/bonds/.

For a brief history of the New York Stock Exchange, go to: https://en.wikipedia.org/wiki/New_York_Stock_Exchange

"Money Market Fund Statistics." 2017. Securities and Exchange Commission. (June 30). Available at: https://www.sec.gov/divisions/investment/mmf-statistics/mmf-statistics-2017-6.pdf

"Commercial Paper Rates and Outstanding Summary" 2017. Board of Governors of the Federal Reserve System. Available at: https://www.federalreserve.gov/releases/cp/

"Federal Funds and Interest on Reserves," 2013. Federal Reserve Bank of New York (March). Available at: https://www.newyorkfed.org/aboutthefed/fedpoint/fed15.html

Japanese Bankers Association provides data on its member banks at: https://www.zenginkyo.or.jp/en/outline/list-of-members/

Office of the Superintendent of Financial Institutions provides data on domestically chartered banks at: http://www.osfi-bsif.gc.ca/Eng/wt-ow/Pages/wwr-er.aspx?sc=1&gc=1&ic=1#WWRLink111

Description of the Federal Reserve's discount window operations can be found al: https://www.federalreserve.gov/monetarypolicy/discountrate.htm

Description of the FDIC's criteria for placing a bank on the problem bank list is: "Problem Bank List" available at: http://problembanklist.com/problem-bank-list/

On greater transparency in monetary policy, see "What Steps Has The Federal Reserve Taken To Improve Transparency?" at the Federal Reserve Bank of San Francisco website: http://www.frbsf.org/education/publications/doctor-econ/2006/september/transparency/.

"Policy Tools" Available at the website of the Board of Governors of the Federal Reserve System: https://www.federalreserve.gov/monetarypolicy/policytools.htm

See "Policy Normalization," on the website of the Board of Governors of the Federal Reserve System at: https://www.federalreserve.gov/monetarypolicy/policy-normalization.htm